THE END OF ASPIRATION?

"A fresh and original look at social mobility using powerful personal narratives that vividly bring to life the human scale of social mobility."

Diane Reay, University of Cambridge

"An accessible and illuminating book that shines a light on the processes which lock many hard-working people out of prosperity in Britain."

James Bloodworth, author of Hired *and* The Myth of Meritocracy

"A passionate and pertinent contribution to a growing literature on social mobility in an age of inequality."

Lynsey Hanley

"A detailed, often painful anatomy of a crisis. Exley's blend of exhaustive research and empathetic human narrative creates a devastating composite picture of how, at every stage of our lives, through every institution we encounter, wealth and privilege all too often shape experience and opportunity. A book that should not only be read, but urgently acted upon."

Sam Byers, author of Perfidious Albion

"Exley has managed in this book to take a subject that is all too often given to dry, earnest analysis and more than a little hand-wringing and made it entirely accessible. It is anchored in robust research, but its the humanity, storytelling, and acute observations he brings to the subject of social mobility that makes this a stand-out read."

Mary O'Hara, The Guardian *and author of* The Shame Game

THE END OF ASPIRATION?

Social mobility and our children's fading prospects

Duncan Exley

First published in Great Britain in 2019 by

Policy Press
University of Bristol
1-9 Old Park Hill
Bristol
BS2 8BB
UK
t: +44 (0)117 954 5940
pp-info@bristol.ac.uk
www.policypress.co.uk

North America office:
Policy Press
c/o The University of Chicago Press
1427 East 60th Street
Chicago, IL 60637, USA
t: +1 773 702 7700
f: +1 773 702 9756
sales@press.uchicago.edu
www.press.uchicago.edu

British Library Cataloguing in Publication Data
A catalogue record for this book is available from the British Library.

Library of Congress Cataloging-in-Publication Data
A catalog record for this book has been requested.

ISBN 978-1-4473-4832-0 paperback
ISBN 978-1-4473-4834-4 ePub
ISBN 978-1-4473-4835-1 Mobi
ISBN 978-1-4473-4833-7 ePdf

Cover design by Liron Gilenberg
Printed and bound in Great Britain by TJ International,
Padstow
Policy Press uses environmentally responsible print
partners

MIX
Paper from
responsible sources
FSC
www.fsc.org
FSC® C013056

Contents

Acknowledgements

Many thanks to the people who agreed to be interviewed for this book. Special thanks also go to Jean Exley, Peter Exley, Robin Henry, Archie Shocolinsky-Dwyer, Tim Stacey and especially Emma Taggart.

Others to whom I am grateful for their help, time, advice and/or insights include: Jake Anders, Louise Ashley, Trevor Baynham, Craig Beaumont, Lauren Bellaera, Andrew Berwick, Sally Broughton-Micova, Prateek Buch, Sarah Dauncey, Jim Dickinson, Helen Donohoe, Jan Ellis, Sonia Exley (no relation), Sam Freedman, Sam Friedman, Andy Fugard, Lynsey Hanley, Nick Hillman, John Hills, Ruth Holdaway, Avril Hollings, John Hood, Sophie Hostick-Boakye, Imran Hussain, Jo Hutchinson, Lewis Iwu, David Johnston, Bill Kerry, Ruth Lupton, Michael Mercieca, Alan Milburn, Nik Miller, Hashi Mohamed, Kiran Nihalani, Michael Orton, Josh Oware, Andrew Pattison, Natalie Perera, Nick Plumb, Tom Powdrill, Rikki Price, Mike Savage, Jim Shepherd, Keir Starmer, Johnny Rich, Craig Rimmer, Claire Robinson, Darren Rodwell, Michael Slavinsky, Stefan Stern, Fiona Stone, Cameron Tait, Katy Theobold, Selina Todd, Helen Walbey, Julie Walsh, Ben Watson, Ben Whittaker and Max Wind-Cowie.

Thanks also to all at Policy Press, especially Ali, Kathryn and Rebecca, and to Dawn Rushen, for production editing and forbearance.

ONE

The world's great meritocracy

What the hell am I doing here?

When I was a teenager I took a photograph of my dad – a middle-aged man, posing in his underpants and a tie. He was making a joke at his own expense, following years of mockery from his wife and kids about his habit of *always* wearing a tie. He was the only person I've ever met to have a 'gardening tie', a frayed old tweedy thing.

If you're guessing that I'm using the 'frayed old tweedy thing' as a metaphor for Dad's overall persona – eccentric faded gentry or something – you'd be wrong. Dad was the son of a labourer who got what used to be called 'ideas above his station'. He gained qualifications, bought a house, had a collection of classical music and, rather than drop his aitches, would err towards putting aitches where no aitches belonged. And he wore a tie.

Dad's story isn't rags to riches; it's not even blue collar to white collar. The house he lived in when he died was on the same street he had lived in as a child. Dad was an electrical engineer; not the sort of engineer who sits at a desk and designs things, but the sort who goes into coalmines and grapples with the machinery (a 'pit electrician'). Still, in the Yorkshire coalmining town where we lived, Dad's aspirations were enough to make him known as someone who 'thinks he's posh'.

It's easy to dismiss my dad as a Hyacinth Bucket (pronounced 'Bouquet'), with aspirations that weren't matched by his background, education or occupation, especially if you're snobbish enough to think that classical music and neckwear are

1

no business of the working classes. But Dad's aspirations *were* matched by the careers of his children. My sister, Jane, was the only girl from her school year to go to university, and (according to the Institute of Economic Affairs) the organisation I used to run, The Equality Trust, is part of the 'establishment'.[1]

As part of my research for this book I spoke to a boy I had sat next to in school. He was cleverer and more diligent than me. He did not go to university, and lives in the same mining village (now ex-mining village) where he was brought up. One of the reasons I began writing the book you're now reading is that, for a long time, I've been wondering why some people get to achieve aspirations that were unattainable for their parents while others don't seem to get the opportunities they deserve.

I'm not the only one interested in this. In recent decades, opportunity and aspiration have become bigger and bigger themes in the rhetoric of each succeeding prime minister. Margaret Thatcher defined her mission as unleashing 'the real driving force in society ... the desire for the individual to do the best for himself and his family.'[2] John Major, in his first party conference speech as Prime Minister, said 'we are the Party of opportunity ... there will be no barriers in the Britain we are building.'[3] Tony Blair (who ascribed Labour's failure to win the 1992 General Election to its failure to appeal to voters' aspirational values[4]) pledged to build 'an opportunity society where all have an equal chance to succeed.'[5] Gordon Brown spoke of creating an 'age of aspiration.'[6] David Cameron made 'lack of social mobility' the central theme of his first party conference speech after winning a majority.[7] And within hours of becoming Prime Minister, Theresa May promised that her government would 'do everything we can to help anybody, whatever your background, to go as far as your talents will take you.'[8] Ratcheting up that rhetoric a few weeks later, May declared an intention to make Britain 'the world's great meritocracy.'[9]

It isn't always clear exactly what politicians mean when they talk about 'opportunity', 'aspiration', 'social mobility' and 'meritocracy'. Different people use the same terms to mean different things. So, to try to be clear about terminology from the start, 'social mobility' usually means migration between one social class and another (from working class to middle class, for example) and 'meritocracy' usually means rewarding people for their talent and effort rather than their privilege. These terms, and the concepts underlying them, are more controversial than they first appear. Social mobility may give individuals the chance to climb out of poverty, but it doesn't necessarily reduce the total number of people in poverty if those who 'climb up' do so at the expense of others falling down. Others have said that to extol social mobility is effectively to suggest that anyone who doesn't have a middle-class job and lifestyle has somehow failed at life, and the term 'meritocracy' was originally meant as a warning, against a belief system that regards anyone who fails to meet the dominant definition of 'talented' as being undeserving and ultimately disposable.[10] On the other hand, the idea that we should all have unconditional rewards isn't popular either. The proportion of the public who think 'fairness is about getting what you deserve' outnumber those who think 'fairness is about equality' by well over two-to-one.[11]

Despite – or perhaps because of – the strong support from powerful and influential people for either 'getting what you deserve' or 'equality', the powerful and influential people have delivered neither.

Although the terms 'social mobility' and 'meritocracy' are used in this book, its main themes are opportunity and aspiration, and specifically, the opportunity to realise the aspirations that are held by the majority of us as we start our adult lives: for 'a job I love', a home to call our own, and for a rewarding relationship and/or family.[12] The book is also about whether we are given the opportunity to live a life determined by our own choices rather than the norms of the social or economic class we were born into (usually this means the freedom to pursue opportunities normally only available to those from 'higher' social classes, but we will also encounter people who have struggled to pursue aspirations regarded as 'below' them). Unlike social mobility and meritocracy, the opportunities to attain those aspirations are – in my experience – frequently discussed in 'ordinary families' and are the basis of deeply held and widely shared personal and political values; which suggests they have the potential to be the basis of a popular and unifying political narrative and programme.

The purpose of this book is to ask to what extent the UK offers us or our children the opportunity to attain those widely held aspirations, what barriers are standing in the way, and whether our government and other decision-makers (including ourselves as individuals) are willing and able to take sufficient meaningful action to create an 'opportunity society'. It draws on the work of experts – of academics working in economics, sociology, psychology and history – and of people and organisations working to create fairer opportunities. But this is not an academic book; it is structured around the lives of a group of people who have 'gone up in the world' in a wide range of careers, including acting, business, law, medicine and politics. It follows them through each stage of their lives and asks what it is about these individuals and their circumstances that lifted them up, or knocked them down, and what we can learn from their experiences.

Writing books isn't something lads from mining villages typically get to do, so I've been proudly mentioning it to various friends, family members and anyone else who'll listen. Most of them have assumed I'm writing about people who started their lives in a particular (low-status) section of society and who then 'rose up the social scale'. The words and phrases I've most commonly heard used to describe the group they assumed I'm writing about are 'poor', 'deprived' and 'working class'. But although this book is about the opportunities available to the poor and the working class, it isn't just about them. All of the people in this book are living lives significantly different to those of their parents, in terms of their careers, social circles, lifestyle or finances. Some could be described as rags-to-riches stories, but not all. Some were brought up in working-class families and are now in 'middle-class' jobs. Others began in middle-income families and became part of the 'elite'. This is deliberate. While most of the political rhetoric around social mobility focuses on whether it is possible 'to rise from the bottom to the top', there has, until recently, been little discussion about what is happening to the life chances of 'ordinary' families, neither deprived nor privileged. What are the odds that children from those families will have a fair chance to get the 'top jobs', or, for that matter, their odds of sliding down the social and economic scale into occupational and financial insecurity?

This book focuses in the barriers and opportunities associated with 'class': our social and economic background. People also encounter opportunities or barriers associated with their age, (dis)ability, gender, ethnicity, religion, sex or sexuality. Although this book's primary focus isn't on those characteristics – the world doesn't need another middle-aged, non-disabled white man pontificating about things he's never experienced – we will encounter numerous instances of those barriers or opportunities being faced by the people whose stories are told in the following chapters.

In the next two sections (the most data-heavy sections, after which we move on to more human-friendly material) I tackle the first of the questions posed above, how far the UK is from being an opportunity society.

Old school: backgrounds of the 'establishment'

Friday 15 July 2016, day three of Theresa May's premiership. According to the *Daily Mail*, her quest to build 'the great meritocracy' is going well. 'March of the meritocrats' is the front-page headline, above a story about the Prime Minister's new Cabinet, which has the lowest proportion of privately educated ministers since the days of Clement Attlee in the 1940s,[13] and in which Boris Johnson is the only remaining Etonian.

Despite the headlines, the alumni of private schools were still more heavily represented in Cabinet than they were in society as a whole. Thirty per cent of May's top ministers were privately educated compared to 7% of the overall population. But credit where credit's due: this was a big step forward compared to the coalition government (more than twice as many of whom – 62% – were privately educated), and a big improvement since Margaret Thatcher's days (a whopping 91%).[14, 15]

Of course, a more meritocratic Cabinet doesn't mean a meritocratic country overall. We have to look beyond the individuals at the top, to ask who makes up the wider 'establishment' of people who make and interpret the laws that govern us, who make the economic and business decisions that affect our lives, and whose opinions we read and hear.

Two months after Theresa May took power, David Lammy gave me an example of how far the top layer of UK society was from being 'a great meritocracy'. Lammy was a kid from Tottenham who went on to become its MP and a government minister. 'Last week', he said, 'six new judges were appointed to the Court of Appeal. Five Oxbridge, five men, no coverage.'[16] Aside from the monarchy, the judiciary is the least meritocratic part of the establishment, with 74% of senior judges coming from private schools,[17] making the privately educated 33 times more likely to become a senior judge than are the rest of us.[18] Of course, just because someone is privately educated doesn't *necessarily* mean they are privileged. Some people who went to private schools didn't get there because their parents were wealthy, but rather because they were awarded scholarships. The veteran Conservative MP Ken Clarke is an example of this,[19] but he's a rare example. Data on families who send their children to private schools shows they are, unsurprisingly, 'concentrated at the very top of the family income distribution'.[20]

The remaining branch of UK government, the legislature, is also dominated by the privately educated. Approximately half the members of the House of Lords are privately educated (unsurprisingly, for a group that still includes 92 aristocratic 'hereditary' peers[21]), but the Commons isn't very 'common' either. Like the Cabinet, the Commons' privately schooled contingent is shrinking, but is still over five times overrepresented[22] (as they are in the Scottish Parliament, but not to the same degree in the Welsh Assembly[23]), and the growing numbers of state-schooled MPs aren't exactly 'working-class kids made good'. In fact, the proportion of MPs from manual working-class backgrounds in 2010 was just a quarter of what it had been in 1964, a decline far outpacing the fall in working-class occupations in the country as a whole.[24]

The disproportionately privileged politicians are advised by other, even more disproportionately privileged individuals. Over half of senior civil servants and diplomats were educated in the 'independent sector',[25] as were eight out of ten government advisers[26] (as one Conservative MP complained ahead of the

2015 General Election, 'There are six people writing the manifesto and five of them went to Eton; the other went to St Paul's'[27]). Other people with an influence over policy-makers follow a similar pattern. Forty-three per cent of newspaper columnists were privately schooled,[28] and the think tanks that influence government policy are overwhelmingly led by Oxbridge graduates: two-thirds of the directors of organisations shortlisted for *Prospect* magazine's 2018 Think Tank Awards went to Oxford or Cambridge.[29] (Oxbridge graduates – like the privately educated – aren't always from privileged backgrounds, but as we'll see in Chapter 5 later, they mostly are.)

Outside the 'Westminster village', the private sector performs little better. Research carried out in 2014 by the Social Mobility Commission revealed that independent schools supply 60% of senior bankers, 42% of partners in leading law firms and 44% of the *Sunday Times* Rich List.[30]

The situation is similar at Sandhurst, the British Army's officer training school, where the privately educated made up 43% of 2016/17's cadets.[31]

Even in sport and entertainment, areas that have traditionally been seen as routes to riches for the talented working classes, the privately educated are at an advantage – for example, they were four times more likely to be selected for Team GB at the 2016 Olympics. In pop music, almost one in five Brit Award winners were privately schooled,[32] but that is a small proportion compared to the 42% of actors who won Baftas. (When I mentioned the Bafta winners statistic to the actor Tom Stocks, he looks wearily exasperated, and tells me 'that's the tip of the iceberg', referring to a bigger study that found people with working-class backgrounds comprise only one in ten members of the acting profession, and can expect to be paid £10,000 a year less than their middle-class colleagues.[33]) The overrepresentation of privileged people in the media may be a consequence of their overrepresentation among media decision-makers. Sociological studies suggest commissioning is 'by far the most exclusive' profession in the media industry.[34] Unsurprisingly, a 2018 study of creative industries found that aside from crafts, 'no creative occupation comes close' to being representative of the wider population.[35]

The simple comparison of state- versus privately-educated individuals in the last few paragraphs gives us an inkling into the uneven distribution of opportunity in the UK, but it doesn't give the full picture. First, there is a steep hierarchy *between* private schools. A recent analysis of entries in *Who's Who* suggests that the odds of becoming a member of the 'establishment' are heavily weighted towards the 'old boys' of just nine private schools. People (usually male) who went to these schools do not dominate the 'establishment' to the extent they did when *Who's Who* was first published in 1897, but they remain '94 times more likely to reach the British elite than are those who attended any other school.'[36] Second, not all state schools are the same. Approximately one in 100 English A-level candidates get into Oxford or Cambridge, but at Lady Margaret School, a comprehensive in Fulham, West London, the figure is one in twelve, and one in five at Queen Elizabeth's, a selective state school in Barnet, North West London.[37] *Tatler* (a magazine that boasts of having 'the very richest readers in the country'[38]) now produces an annual guide to which state schools are suitable for 'people like us', including those that still offer A-levels in Classics, Greek or Astronomy, or have 'a musician in residence'.[39]

Geographically, opportunities to enter the elite universities (a good predictor of entry into elite careers) are concentrated in affluent areas of London and the South of England, with smaller concentrations in parts of Greater Manchester, East Renfrewshire and Cardiff.[40]

Things *are* changing – the establishment is much less dominated by people who went to the 'right schools' than it was in the late 19th century, but things are not changing fast enough to keep pace with the values and economic requirements of the 21st century. Nor are they always changing in the right direction. Some professions appear to have recently become *more* elitist (the proportion of privately educated individuals in top echelon media roles rose from 47 to 54% between 1986 and 2014, for example[41]). The 'top layer' of modern Britain remains, in many ways, stubbornly old school.

The past and another country: how we compare

In the introductory chapter to *Slaughterhouse-Five*, Kurt Vonnegut is told 'that there would always be wars, that they were as easy to stop as glaciers', and that writing an anti-war book is therefore as pointless as writing an anti-glacier book.[42] Maybe writing about the barriers to opportunity is the same. Privilege is a fact of life. People whose parents are rich or high status tend to become rich and high status themselves, 'in every society for which we have data'.[43]

Although the complete abolition of class privilege is very probably impossible, if there is fairer access to opportunity in other countries, or in other periods of our own recent history, then there are good grounds for believing that the barriers can at least be significantly reduced. Recent research on social mobility rates can shed some light on this.

It is generally agreed that the chances of social mobility a century ago were much worse, and that they did improve throughout most of the 20th century.[44] But what has happened to social mobility in the late 20th and early 21st centuries is open to interpretation, and is more controversial. It taps into individuals' deep-seated political beliefs about whether our country is fair or unfair, getting better or 'going to the dogs'. And each side can produce evidence to support their own beliefs.

In a particularly influential study, a group of economists used unprecedentedly large surveys, which collected information on thousands of people born in 1958 and a similarly sized group born in 1970, and continued to collect information as the participants aged. Using that data, they found that the 'economic status of the 1970 cohort is much more strongly connected to parental economic status than the 1958 cohort'.[45] In other words, social mobility, having risen throughout most of the 20th century, had gone into reverse. Other researchers made international comparisons and found individuals' incomes to be more strongly determined by their parents' incomes in the UK than in many other developed economies.[46] Later data, comparing educational mobility – the chances that children of low-educated parents will become highly educated adults or vice versa – also show the UK lagging well behind the normal standards for a developed country.[47]

This research provided the government with a dragon to slay: an opportunity to portray themselves as the champions of justice, fighting unfair advantage. The then Prime Minister, Tony Blair, said 'until Britain is a land of opportunity for all, we cannot rest.'[48] Selected findings from the research were included in government briefings and speeches, and were subjected to the usual journalistic treatment of 'first simplify, then exaggerate'.[49] The simplified, exaggerated version became an article of faith in some circles, so much so that in 2016 a *Guardian* columnist was writing that 'social mobility doesn't exist'.[50]

Jo Blanden, the economist who had led the research that compared the 1958 and 1970 studies, felt that her work had been used to justify conclusions way beyond the evidence, pointing out that 'It is certainly not true that mobility has "ground to a halt" or "fallen to its lowest level"'.[51] Blanden and others hadn't said UK social mobility doesn't exist, but their data did suggest that social mobility in the UK is bad (compared to most other developed nations) and had got worse (for people born in the early 1970s compared to the late 1950s).

But other research showed a very different picture. Whereas the economists had measured an individual's chances of moving up or down the income 'league table' relative to their parents, a sociologist, John Goldthorpe, measured the chance of moving up or down the *occupational* scale (for example, whether the offspring of 'unskilled' workers get 'skilled' jobs, or vice versa). Goldthorpe showed that the chances of people rising up the occupational scale increased in the post-war decades, as the number of white-collar jobs increased, following the expansion of the public sector and changes in industry. Goldthorpe was describing a rise in *absolute* social mobility, but very little change in *relative* social mobility (that is, larger numbers of the offspring of manual workers getting white-collar jobs, but not at the expense of the offspring of professionals: there was simply more 'room at the top'). The rate of relative social mobility was not declining, said Goldthorpe, and it was high (over three-quarters of workers born since 1946 had moved up or down the occupational scale).[52] Other studies using sociological data found similar results.[53]

Just as the economists' findings had been used to justify assertions beyond the scope of the research, so were the sociologists' data. James Bartholomew, a banker-turned-journalist, whose usual subject is financial trading but who also writes political pieces advocating, for example, the abolition of the NHS,[54] is a case in point. In an article arguing that 'Britons are on the move upwards', Bartholomew used sociological measures rather than economic ones. Unfortunately for Bartholomew, his eagerness to demonstrate that the UK *doesn't* have a social mobility problem led him to misunderstand an important piece of data underpinning his argument: he argued that Britain's record in breaking the link between parental background and children's performance in school was one of the best in the developed world, but he'd got the figures the wrong way round, and the data actually showed Britain to be one of the *worst* countries in this regard.[55]

Later, Jo Blanden returned to the question of how the UK compares with other countries, reviewing a wide range of – both economic and sociological – studies covering 65 countries. The results again depended on whether an occupational or income measure was used. In occupational terms, Britain as a whole was middle-ranking (although one study, which broke the UK data down to show results in its constituent nations, showed Scotland and Northern Ireland performing worse than average). But in income terms, the UK was among the worst of the countries studied, a point reinforced by later research with new data, suggesting that if anything, the economists' figures had 'understated the true extent of the UK mobility problem'.[56]

In my view, the economists' data is the more reliable. I'm not convinced the occupational measures are truly comparing like with like. In the 1960s and 1970s, white-collar jobs were associated with good levels of pay, respect and security, which often isn't the case now. In my home town, men whose fathers worked 'down the pit' may now be working in a call centre. According to the occupational scale, those men have 'gone up in the world', but that isn't how it feels to them. In some cases, occupation is a good measure of class, but in other cases, it isn't.

Is a waiter in a hipster cafe the same class as one in a greasy spoon, or an accountant in Canary Wharf the same as one in the back office of a Wrexham builder's merchant? Is Adele the same class as a club singer in Dundee?

However, even the economists' data doesn't support the contention that 'the country is going to the dogs'. Recent figures showing trends in the 1990s and 2010s reveal that a shift took place: Brits whose incomes were in the bottom fifth had a better chance of moving up the income league table than their counterparts in any other developed country. These most-recent figures refer to differences within generations, so they can't be easily compared to the inter-generation data discussed above, but they do show, as the economic policy commentator Gavin Kelly has pointed out, that policy can make a difference (the new data covers a period when the creation of the National Minimum Wage and tax credits improved the incomes of millions of low-paid people). But while the new data showed rising odds of moving between the bottom and middle of the income spectrum, they *didn't* show that the chances of moving into the highest income strata had risen. In fact, quite the opposite: 'the upper echelons of society are ever more hermetically sealed'.[57]

The inaccessibility of 'the upper echelons of society' is one feature of the UK's social (im)mobility that consistently shows up across a range of measures. It has been found by researchers looking at income and wealth[58] and at 'social and cultural' capital.[59] Examples of the dominance of people from privileged backgrounds in the 'establishment' are one illustration of this phenomenon, but a more colourful example comes from research that uses records spanning eight centuries. Economic historians used the surnames of students at Oxford and Cambridge as a way of determining to what extent families were able to move in or out of the educational 'elite'. They found that the families who had gone to Oxbridge in the 13th century tended to be the same families who went in the 21st century, and concluded that 'Social mobility in England in 2012 is little greater than in pre-industrial times'.[60] In the eight centuries since 1230, we may have moved on from worrying about the Mongol Horde to worrying about Brexit, but the elite has remained remarkably constant.

The elite aren't just well insulated from the risk of sliding down the class scale; they are also, in financial terms, climbing even further above the rest of us. Although overall income inequality has been relatively stable in recent decades (partly due to policies that reduced child and pensioner poverty), the difference in incomes between the top 1% and the remaining 99% has been growing (the top 1%'s share of post-tax incomes, having declined since the 1920s, almost *quintupled* between 1978 and 2013, to levels last seen in the 1940s,[61] leaving the rest with a shrinking slice of the pie).

The problem for those of us in the bottom 99% isn't just that our children are being kept out of the best jobs by the children of the top 1%. Living standards over the coming years are predicted to stagnate for middle-income households and to fall for those with low incomes,[62] and in occupational terms, people born in the early 1980s are the first group since comparable records began (in 1946) to be in lower-status jobs than their parents were at the same age. Our children are now more likely to slide down the scale than to climb up.[63]

Who's who

The data discussed in the previous two sections are measures of social mobility. The rest of this book is about a different but closely related subject: the chances of successfully pursuing aspirations usually denied to people of a certain social or economic class, and the opportunities and barriers encountered by those who attempt to do so.

I interviewed the following individuals, whose experiences are used as illustrations of these opportunities and barriers.

Stuart Alford is a barrister and a Queen's Counsel (QC), now working as a Partner at the global law firm Latham & Watkins. He was formerly Head of Division at the Serious Fraud Office, where he led the team that investigated and prosecuted banks involved in the major rate-fixing fraud now known as the Libor scandal. Stuart describes his Kenilworth upbringing as 'solidly middle class'.

Rozina Ali is an aesthetic and microvascular reconstruction surgeon with a practice in London's Harley Street and Chelsea. The author of numerous articles in medical journals and textbooks, she has also appeared as a TV presenter on BBC Horizon's 'The truth about looking young' and Channel 4's 'How not to get old'. Rozina was raised in Liverpool, as the daughter of first-generation British-Pakistani parents who worked as 'a factory worker and a housewife'.

Alvin Carpio is on one of *Forbes* magazine's '30 under 30' list of 'the brightest young entrepreneurs, innovators and game changers'. Having previously worked for the anti-poverty charity, the Joseph Rowntree Foundation, Alvin is now Chief Executive at The Fourth Group, an organisation he founded to 'address the challenges and opportunities brought by the fourth industrial revolution'. Alvin was raised in Plaistow, East London, by his mother, a Filipina ex-pat, who worked as a cleaner.

Mark Dixon is the founder and Chief Executive of the International Workplace Group, best known for the Regus chain of serviced offices, a business now valued at over £2 billion. He is also the owner of the Château de Berne estate in Provence. In 2018, Mark's net worth was calculated at US$1.2 billion.[64] Essex-born Mark is the son of a Ford motor engineer.

Jackie Doyle-Price was elected as the Conservative MP for Thurrock in May 2010 and now holds a ministerial position in the Department of Health and Social Care. She previously worked for the City of London Corporation and South Yorkshire Police. Brought up on Sheffield's Wisewood housing estate, Jackie is the daughter of a builder.

Charlotte Dring is a civil servant, currently working as Private Secretary and Head of Office to the Director-General for EU Exit Delivery at the Department for Environment, Food and Rural Affairs. Formerly at the Ministry of Housing, Communities and Local Government, Charlotte entered the Civil Service as part of the 'accelerated career path to leadership' known as the 'Fast Stream'.[65] Charlotte is from Cleethorpes, the daughter of a marine electrician who worked at the Docks in nearby Grimsby.

Dean Hanley is a digital service designer who has worked in government departments, the NHS and the private sector. He has also worked in publishing. Dean was brought up on the Stoke Aldermoor estate in Coventry, where his father worked in a car factory before being made redundant when Dean was a child.

David Lammy was brought up in Tottenham and has been the area's (Labour) MP since 2000. For much of his childhood, David was raised by his mother, who was born in Guyana and juggled multiple jobs – including as a home help, care worker and 'Avon lady' – to support David and his siblings. A barrister and former government minister, David has recently been a leading parliamentary campaigner for the rights of people caught up in the 'Windrush scandal', those affected by the Grenfell Tower tragedy, and for fair access to 'elite' universities.

Joanne Martin is a medical student at the University of Aberdeen. Joanne, whose mother works as a part-time cleaner and whose father worked at a Royal Mail sorting office, was brought up in Possilpark in Glasgow. Having initially been rejected by all four medical schools to which she'd applied (despite having the right grades), she has since been a speaker at university conferences on participation in higher education.

Paul Monekosso Cleal is now a Strategy and Leadership Adviser, and non-executive board member or adviser to a variety of bodies including the Premier League, having previously been a Partner at the international accountancy company PwC. Paul was also a member of the government's Social Mobility and Child Poverty Commission (now the Social Mobility Commission). He was raised in Croydon, South London, by his mother, who worked as a typist and occasional seamstress.

Stuart Sime is Professor of Law at the City Law School (part of City, University of London). A qualified barrister, he is also editor of a practitioner textbook of civil procedures and a manual on company law. The son of a shipwright, Stuart was brought up in Portsmouth.

Maria Solomon is a solicitor now working as a welfare benefits adviser and trainer. Maria grew up in Salford, where her mother worked as a hospital cleaner. Maria's father, originally from Cyprus, worked in a cafe before later running his own fish and chip shop.

'**Stephen**' (not his real name) grew up as a middle-class boy in a northern industrial town, and rose to become the chief executive of a large international company. He is now close to retirement.

Barbara Stocking is President of Murray Edwards College at the University of Cambridge. She was previously Chief Executive of Oxfam, and has also worked in the NHS, the King's Fund and the (American) National Academy of Sciences. The daughter of a postman, Barbara is from Rugby, in Warwickshire.

Tom Stocks is a young actor from Bolton, recently appearing in the film *Giantland*. Tom is also founder of Actor Awareness, 'a campaign fighting for more equality, diversity and working-class talent in the arts'. Tom worked alongside Inside Film to create the documentary film *The acting class*, about barriers facing working-class actors, in which he appears alongside Christopher Eccleston, Maxine Peake and Samuel West.

Jane Upton spent three decades as a social worker, before leaving the profession and moving to the seaside. Formerly known as Jane Exley, she is the author's big sister.

TWO

Early years

Dutch lessons

Giving children the best 'life chances', it is often assumed, has to start right away, on day one: 'the road to a better life starts at birth'.[1] But there are reasons to believe that this assumption isn't true.

In the 1960s, the Dutch military started to notice something odd about their new recruits. There were noticeably more underweight candidates than usual. A few months later, the numbers of underweight boys had dropped back, only to be replaced by a new cohort with an unusually high incidence of obesity. A few months later still, everything returned to normal.

What this cohort have in common is that they were born in the Western Netherlands in 1945-46, but the reason for their ill health goes back earlier than that. It starts in 1944, when Nazi forces were occupying part of the country. The allied armies were closing in, and Dutch railway workers downed tools, to avoid helping their occupiers. In response, the German commanders restricted food supplies, just before winter began. Within a month, daily rations had been halved. Within six months they were halved again. The weather was brutally cold, and people resorted to eating grass and flower bulbs dug from the frozen earth. The famine lasted until the allies arrived in May, leaving thousands dead.

The military service recruits of the 1960s were the offspring of women who were pregnant during the famine. While the mothers of the underweight cohort were in the later stages of pregnancy during the famine, the obese recruits were born to women who were in the early stages of pregnancy at the time. The early-stage embryos were experiencing their mothers' undernutrition and malnutrition, and permanently adapted to counteract the problem: their obesity as adults is a response to prenatal hunger.

A surprising effect of the famine is that not only were the sons and daughters of women caught in the famine more likely to be obese, but so were their grandchildren. The 'Dutch Hunger Winter' is perhaps the best-known example of *epigenetics*, a branch of science that has shown that although our DNA is inherited from our mother and father, it has 'wiggle room': it can be amended in the early, embryonic stage of pregnancy in response to the environment, and certain functions can be turned on or off, and may remain turned on or off for generations. So no, the road to a better life does not start at birth; it may have even started before your mother's birth, in the experiences of your grandmother.[2]

The Dutch experience raises questions. Are there other aspects of our children's mental and physical development that can be affected by events that took place before they were born, and that reduce their 'life chances', putting some people at a disadvantage from birth?

Across the Atlantic, researchers have been attempting to determine why poor black Americans have poorer test scores and lower high school graduation rates than poor white Americans. Various explanations have been offered, including that schools in predominantly black areas attract less-skilled teachers. But Patrick Sharkey, Sociology Professor at New York University, looked at another possible explanation: the effect of neighbourhood on children's test scores. As expected, Sharkey found that children who grew up in a 'middle-class' neighbourhood did better than those who grew up in a 'poor neighbourhood', but he found something else, something more surprising. Those children whose mothers had moved from a 'middle-class' to a 'poor' neighbourhood did better than those whose mothers had moved the other way: looking at where the children's mothers were brought up was a better predictor of children's test scores than looking at where the children themselves were brought up.[3]

A likely explanation for Sharkey's findings is stress. Medical records from Sweden have shown that if a woman experiences a death in the family while pregnant, the child's mental health is likely to be worse. The Swedish data showed these children to have a 25% higher rate of attention deficit hyperactivity disorder (ADHD) than the rest of the population, and a higher rate of anxiety and depression.[4] The mothers in Sharkey's example, who were brought up in 'poor' neighbourhoods, might not have had such an acute shock as a bereavement during pregnancy, but they had the chronic experience of living in neighbourhoods with high levels of crime and anti-social behaviour, and constant, nagging money worries.

Of course, some of the neighbourhoods involved in Professor Sharkey's experiments were unusually stressful places, but in today's UK, stress and shortage is something that, to a greater or lesser degree, affects mums-to-be in both low-income and middle-income families, with financial vulnerability now widespread. According to YouGov sampling in 2016, almost one in three 'middle-class' people (managers, professionals and white-collar workers) were so financially 'close to the edge' that they couldn't afford an emergency expense of £500.[5] Two years later, analysis by the RSA concluded that 'economic insecurity is "the new normal"'.[6]

The long-term effect of maternal stress is one way in which having low-income parents can set children back before they are even born, and in which the richest families can give their offspring a head start over those in the middle of the income scale. Indirectly, the most privileged parents have 'bought' better life chances for their offspring. But is it possible to do that more directly, to buy goods or services for an as-yet-unborn child that will enhance their performance later, in their education and career?

The price of a good start

The website of Pregnant CityGirl – who describes herself as 'Ex-City trader turned blogger, trendspotter and now mummy' – recommends BabyPlus, 'A pre-natal education system which effectively straps around your growing waist for 2x one hour

19

"lessons" per day".[7] An article in *Spears* magazine – 'a must-read for the ultra-high-net-worth (UHNW) community' – quotes the manufacturer's claims that 'its alumni have "enhanced intellectual abilities later on in life"' (but also mentions 'gullible, pushy parents who pour money into faddish educational programmes for their pint-sized progeny'[8]).

Faddish educational programmes are of debatable effectiveness, but a more reliable way of prenatally purchasing decent 'life chances' is to make sure pregnant women are able to buy nutritious food. This gives policy-makers a conundrum: on the one hand, people like Alison Garnham, of the Child Poverty Action Group (CPAG), advocate a 'pregnancy premium' (a top-up to the social security payments given to low-paid families) so mums-to-be can afford to eat properly;[9] on the other hand, there is widespread worry that low-income families would spend the extra money unwisely (in 2012, the Conservative MP Alec Shelbrooke proposed legislation to prevent social security payments from being spent on 'goods such as cigarettes, alcohol, Sky television and gambling'[10]). This raises a question, of how policy-makers could ensure expectant mothers can afford to eat healthily without inadvertently funding the purchase of items that may damage children's life chances.

Paul Gregg, Professor of Economics and Social Policy, can help answer this question. Together with colleagues, Gregg studied the effects of a series of reforms in the late 1990s and early 2000s – such as the introduction of Child Tax Credit – that increased the incomes of large numbers of low-income families. As expected, the families increased their spending on food, buying more nutritious items. But also, more money *did* have an effect on how much families spent on alcohol and tobacco: spending on these items actually went down.[11] The likely explanation for this is that people are more likely to drink and smoke when they are stressed, and families whose incomes were increased by tax credits were less financially stressed. (When similar payments – Earned Income Tax Credits – were introduced in some US states, babies born to mothers in those states had higher birth weights, which gave them an advantage in later life because higher birth weights are associated with better health and child development.[12]) Unfortunately, recent cuts to social security rates in the UK are likely to reverse these gains.[13]

Children growing up in families suffering financial stress is a problem that now extends far beyond the groups we typically regard as 'poor', to include large numbers of ordinary middle-income people. The Minimum Income Standard is a calculation of the costs of maintaining 'a minimum, socially acceptable quality of life', covering the costs of healthy food, clothes, utility bills and so on.[14] In 2015/16, 44% of the UK's children were living in households that did not meet the Minimum Income Standard, including the majority of children in London.[15] A large proportion of the population are having to make impossible, stressful decisions between essentials. This is now being exacerbated by inflationary pressures arising from weakening effect of the Brexit vote on the value of the pound, with the effects of Brexit itself still to become clear. The cold tide of disadvantage, which can pull down children's life chances from before day one, is lapping at the feet of middle Britain.

The impossible girl

I mentioned in Chapter 1 that my sister, Jane, was the only girl in her school year to go to university. But when Jane was a toddler, her chances of educational success didn't look good. Parents' occupations and education are both very strong predictors of their children's progress, and Jane was the daughter of a manual worker who'd failed the '11-plus' exam.

Also, something unusual happened to Jane shortly after she was born: Dad's first marriage ended in divorce, and he was granted custody of Jane. It doesn't sound so unusual today, but in a Yorkshire mining town in the early 1960s, single parents were remarkable, and single fathers almost unheard of.

Parental divorce isn't usually regarded as a desirable factor in children's early years. Dad, as a single parent, faced a common problem: if he worked enough hours to provide for his daughter, how would he have enough time to care for her? Combined with Dad's social class and level of education, the odds of Jane doing well at school looked poor. The odds of her starting school, as she did, as the most educationally advanced child in the class, looked impossible. But in Jane's case, Dad's divorce wasn't a disaster, because something else unusual happened to her. A heroine entered the story. A heroine named Auntie Mavis.

Dad's big sister wasn't a stereotypical heroine. She was a teacher, and a lay preacher in the chapel I went to as a child. Auntie Mavis didn't put up with any nonsense, and 'nonsense', as far as I could tell, included most modern conveniences. Her house contained no telephone, her black-and-white TV was rarely used, and she did the weekly washing in an old twin-tub, squeezing the sodden clothes through the rollers. Even in the 1980s, Mavis' house looked like a museum exhibit about the 1950s.

Auntie Mavis's no-nonsense Methodist zeal included a put-your-money-where-your-mouth-is commitment to social justice, both at a global level (much of the money she wasn't spending on modern conveniences was being donated to overseas aid work) and at a personal level. When her brother's marriage ended, she put her career on pause to care for Jane.

Auntie Mavis was a sort of Methodist Mary Poppins – no nonsense didn't mean no fun. As Jane says, 'Mavis' ethos was that you have to be positive, to take joy and pleasure out of every day.' Usually, that meant the joy of discovery and the pleasure of learning: 'at every opportunity there was education. We'd go for walks and she'd be "reading" me *The Jungle Book* – from memory! She was interested in things, in people, social duty, religion, drama and poetry. There was a thing in Germany called Oberammergau;[16] she talked about that a lot. It was taken as read that learning was a source of happiness ... it wasn't enforced, wasn't "you must"....'

Educationalists talk about the importance of 'school readiness' as a predictor of children's later performance in school and their careers as adults, and being brought up by an enthusiastic, able educator who made learning enjoyable meant that Jane had bucket-loads of school readiness. She remembers starting school able to read at a level the other children could not, waiting for them to catch up: 'I was sat there, impatient. You can imagine: a right little madam.'

In the 16th century, when the Jesuits were setting up schools across Europe, they did so under the motto 'Give me a child until he is seven and I will give you the man.' Jane lived with Mavis until Dad married my mum – from the age of 18 months to the age of seven.

School readiness and parenting

The high level of 'school readiness' that gave my sister an early boost is an attribute most commonly found among children from higher-income families. If you are a middle-income family, your children will start school an average of 5.2 months behind children from the richest fifth of households (but 11 months ahead of children from families in the bottom fifth[17]). Whether it is possible to even up the odds, so that children from all income groups are well prepared for school, depends on whether families with low or middle incomes can replicate the effect Auntie Mavis had on Jane *without* 24-hour access to an educated aunt. Another of my interviewees, Maria, provides an example that suggests it *is* possible.

Maria Solomon's mum didn't have much enthusiasm for education when she was a girl; she told Maria that in her last two years at school she 'went to lessons she liked, she went for a "walk about" for those lessons she didn't like, and when she didn't feel like going to school at all then she "just didn't turn up, just wagged it".'

But like Jane – and unlike her own mum – Maria went to school already able to read, having been taught *by* her mum. Maria thinks her mum's late-onset respect for education might have been a result of regret over her own limited qualifications, but it may also have been the influence of her partner, who acted as Maria's pre-school maths tutor. Maria's dad doesn't sound like the most likely champion of education either, as a man who lived in a Salford council flat and worked in a cafe, but Maria talks about an ethos of valuing education: 'It's a Cypriot thing. In my family anyway.' Maria's dad's family might not have been rich, but education was seen as a source of potential opportunity: 'people from my family grew up on farms in Cyprus that had no running water, but they still went to university.' There was a culture of learning.

Jane and Maria are individual examples of people benefiting from cultural resources unavailable to most. On a national scale, helping parents to help their children become school-ready is a huge challenge, especially if parents themselves struggled in education, or saw little or no career benefit from their education. But it is a challenge that has been taken on by a number of agencies. Good work has been done to create a culture of learning among the UK's parents, from early learning support in Sure Start centres to persuading the writers of *EastEnders* to show characters reading with their children.[18] In recent decades, low-educated parents have responded very positively, more than doubling the time they spend on educational activities, from less than 30 minutes a day in the 1970s to over 70 minutes in 2015.[19]

However, the willingness of parents to overcome their own unsatisfactory experiences of education in order to improve their children's experience of education raises a question: what happens to the children of parents whose parents are not willing or able to make their children school-ready, and who arrive at primary school unable to speak in proper sentences? It is a question that has not yet been adequately answered.

For the parents who are trying to 'raise their game', there are threats to the support they can expect. One of these is the cuts to early learning support services. Funding for children's centres was halved between 2010 and 2018, and 508 centres closed.[20] Imran Hussain, former Director of Policy at CPAG (now Director of Policy and Campaigns at Action for Children), says that even where centres remain, services are being reduced: 'despite all the talk about early intervention, the upshot is that early intervention has been cut.'

Another threat is that although parents with modest educational qualifications have raised their game, the most highly educated parents have been able to raise their game further and faster, so they now spend 40 minutes more per day on educational activities than 'low-educated' parents.[21] The Social Mobility Commission suggests that the anti-social hours common in many jobs may be putting low- and middle-income parents at a disadvantage by restricting the time they can spend with children, but the cost of 'enrichment opportunities' is also a factor. The highest-status groups are far more likely to have attended paid-for parenting classes, to have lots of 'discovery' room in their homes and gardens, and to be able to afford cultural visits and resources.[22]

Professor Alison Gopnik, a specialist in child development, traces this competitive 'arms race' back to the 1970s, when the concept of 'parenting' – the idea of the child as something to be 'shaped' by their parents – became common in the US. Many parents in the US, and increasingly elsewhere, responded to the parenting arms race by anxiously micro-managing their children's development (and in doing so, suppressed children's innate innovative curiosity, making things 'miserable for parents and children').[23] Reports of lesson-weary three-year-olds being chided for their 'sloppy' work in maths certainly don't sound much fun.[24]

The prospect of children being forced through joy-sapping 'enrichment' programmes is part of a bigger issue that I hadn't really registered until someone made me reassess my thinking: at a meeting in Parliament, Ruth Lister, a Social Policy Professor and now a member of the House of Lords, talked about the risk that we all become so obsessed with children's chances of becoming successful adults that we forget to ask whether they are having good childhoods, and treat children not as 'human beings', but as 'human becomings'.[25] After that meeting, I went home and looked through my research notes, and found hundreds of references to what children 'will grow up to be'. I realised that I'd started thinking this way too, thinking of childhood experience as little more than preparation for adulthood.

Turning childhood into a training camp is not good for anybody. Of the socially mobile people I've interviewed, those who appear to be most successful, in their careers and their overall wellbeing, tend to be those who have discovered their own path through life, rather than having been forced. Those who regard life as a series of adventures rather than a series of chores seem to do the best. I'm not the first to notice that: there is now a whole industry dedicated to encouraging a 'positive mindset' in children. So the idea of 'positive mindset' is the next subject to explore.

A positive mindset

You can watch the video on YouTube – it shows a room, empty except for two items of utilitarian furniture – a table and a plastic chair – and a wastepaper bin. There's fluorescent light on a murky green wall. It's the sort of room in which you'd expect to find police officers questioning suspects. We see a woman enter the room with a child of maybe seven years old, a boy with blond hair. The boy is instructed to sit at the table. The woman leaves and shuts the door behind her.[26]

The blond-haired boy is taking part in a now-famous experiment in which children are left alone with a single marshmallow on a Styrofoam plate and given a choice – to eat the marshmallow or to wait 15 minutes. If they wait, they get *two* marshmallows. The video shows a succession of children trying, with varying degrees of success, to control their desire to eat the marshmallow. They look at it, try not to look at it, pick it up, put it down again, drum their fingers and squirm in their seats. Some of the children stuff the sweet into their mouths almost immediately. None look like they're finding it easy.

The 'marshmallow test' was originally carried out by Walter Mischel, a psychologist at Stanford University in the 1960s, testing children aged four to six to assess (among other things) whether family breakdown had an effect on children's capacity for self-control. But the really interesting results came years later, when follow-up studies showed the children who demonstrated strong self-control in confectionery-related challenges also grew up to get better test scores as adolescents.[27]

The implication of Mischel's experiments, that skills such as self-control are predictors of success in later life, caught the attention of people who had an interest in life chances. Other experiments were carried out, assessing which behaviours were associated with success in a variety of situations. In 2004, new cadets at West Point military academy in the US were asked to agree or disagree with a list of statements (such as, 'I finish whatever I begin'), and the results of the test were found to be a good predictor of which recruits would successfully complete the academy's famously gruelling seven-week training.[28] A broader assessment of the evidence can be found in a review published in 2014 which found 'non-cognitive' skills have a positive effect on 'a person's future success, over and above the impact on their education'.[29]

This sort of evidence began to fuel the idea that the children of ordinary families were failing to become successful adults as a result of their own attitudes and expectations. Books on the subject, including Carol Dweck's *Mindset* (2006) and Angela Duckworth's *Grit* (2016), became bestsellers. In the UK, these books were cited in politicians' speeches, and in 2016 the Department for Education adopted 'building character and resilience in every child' as a key policy priority.[30]

Several of the people I spoke with are examples of the power of a positive mindset. Dr Rozina Ali is an especially good example. The daughter of Pakistani parents ('a factory worker and a housewife') from Liverpool, her school in Toxteth 'had to shut early when the riots were on'. Rozina is now a consultant plastic surgeon; the techniques she has developed appear in medical journals, and she has frequently appeared on TV, including as a presenter of the BBC science programme *Horizon*. According to a Pakistani newspaper, she is one of 20 'super women' of Pakistani heritage, alongside astronauts, athletes and captains of industry.[31]

Rozina is unusual even among the people whose stories are told in this book. Other people spoke of feeling like a fish out of water in the middle-class environment of university, but Rozina says studying at St Thomas's Hospital Medical School (like being in 'a boys' public school') 'was fun … there was no hardship to it.' Other people spoke of unaffordable costs that slowed their progress, but Rozina says, 'if you want to do it, what's money?' Other people tell me about the barriers they encountered in their careers, but Rozina says, 'I can't think of a single dream I haven't made come true.'

If you are looking for an example of someone whose mindset has been a major factor in their success, Rozina is about as good an example as you're likely to find. She is positive and persistent in the face of challenges, such as her reaction on returning from a year-long surgical placement in Taiwan: 'I came back to no money, but you survive, y'know … you just get on with it.' She sees setbacks as learning experiences: 'If I go through the day without making at least three mistakes, I've not learned anything.'

She has a committed passion to her goals (she decided to be a surgeon as a young child). She tells me – as do a number of the other upwardly mobile people I interviewed – that she sees life as an 'adventure'. Rozina has not had an easy ride: some of her experiences (as we'll see later) have been wounding, but Rozina's 'ability to self-soothe' helps her get up and carry on.

There is a correlation between people, like Rozina, who display various 'mindset' attributes (social, emotional, enterprise and discipline skills[32]) and those who have achieved careers success.[33] This suggests an opportunity for the policy-makers and organisations that want to encourage more upward mobility: can we teach our country's children to 'be more Rozina'?

Can a positive mindset be taught?

Some experts believe a positive mindset *cannot* be taught. Russ Whitehurst, a former Director of the Institute of Education Sciences at the US Department of Education, says the research shows that such patterns of behaviour are innate. Attempts to change a person's character, he says, are 'barking up the wrong tree'.[34] Whitehurst can point to a number of instances in which interventions intended to promote a 'growth mindset' had no significant measurable effect.[35]

If Whitehurst is right, then attempts to teach positive mindset are as doomed as the attempts by British schools in the 20th century to force left-handed children to become right-handed. Many 'lefties' remember that as children they had their left hands tied behind them, or were hit with rulers for writing with their left hand. Children who were subjected to these methods later reported psychological side-effects, from bed-wetting to neurosis, but they did not become right-handed.[36]

On the other hand, forcing children to write with their right hands *did* make them better at doing so than they would have been if they had been allowed to write naturally, and some 'character education' interventions appear to have been successful, if not in changing children's underlying propensities, then at least in helping children to make the most of their strengths and to manage their weaknesses.

And there are examples of 'mindset' projects that did produce measurable results. An example cited by Carol Dweck is a school in an American First Nations reservation that adopted Dweck's techniques (and also mentoring programmes and to encourage cultural pride[37]), and went from being one of the worst-performing in the district to one of the best, beating schools that catered for the children of Seattle's Microsoft employees.[38]

Frequently, the interventions that appear to be most effective are those that instil a sense of self-esteem and self-control, a sense of being in control of one's own life.[39] Effectiveness also appears to be greater when interventions are more sustained and holistic, rather than one-off 'jabs'.[40]

The upbringing of some of my interviewees also appears to have instilled a sense of being in control of one's own life in a sustained and holistic way. Rozina remembers her father as being an un-stereotypical factory worker, who read a broadsheet newspaper and spent his weekends taking the family to the Liverpool Planetarium and the Walker Art Gallery. Rozina and her sisters were encouraged to think big, in a way that other girls she knew were not. (In later years she was told that she and her sisters had been used as examples in other Pakistani-heritage families, to warn girls against immodest ambitions that harmed marriage prospects: 'careful you don't end up like the Ali girls!') The Ali girls, says Rozina, had been told that 'you can be anything you want to be', and 'no one around me ever said "you can't".'

Most of the people I interviewed didn't embody the phrase 'yes we can' as fully as Rozina, but they tended to use similar phrases to describe their family mindset. Jane tells me that Auntie Mavis' ethos was 'very much "you can be who you want to be"' and Charlotte says her mum advocated a more specifically feminist version ('women can do whatever they want'). But this ethos wasn't universal: Dean (who initially struggled at school) describes his father as someone who 'didn't like "ideas above your station".'

Some of my interviewees' parents didn't just talk positive, but were themselves an inspiring example. David says that as a child he was 'very aware' that his mother 'made lots of sacrifices for us' and that he wanted to 'support her, after my father left'. A lot of

David's motivation, he says, 'in the end comes down to wanting to fill my mum with pride'. Charlotte says something similar about her mother: 'losing her made me more determined – I have to do well for her. Every success I have is a credit to her.' Again, this wasn't universal to the people I interviewed, but it was common.

If day-to-day family life can function as a 'long-term, holistic intervention' that creates a mindset of being in control of one's own life, it prompts a question: what effect do the family life experiences of the *wider population* have on our children's attitudes and aspirations?

Life lessons

During the Great Depression in the 1920s and 1930s, a boy in Chicago called Dusko Condic was made homeless. His father had died and his mother couldn't afford the mortgage payments. Decades later, a 77-year-old Dusko was interviewed for America's National Public Radio service, telling the interviewer that the experience of living through the Depression made him stronger: 'Tomorrow I could lose everything, but somehow I'm not afraid. I really am not.'[41] These sorts of stories have become part of the mythology of the American Dream: 'when the going gets tough….' But the mythology is largely a myth. The effect of the 1920s and 1930s on most people was not a positive one in terms of mental attributes usually associated with upward social mobility. Economists who studied the financial behaviour of people who lived through the Depression found that the long economic trauma had made them less confident about the future, more risk-averse and less opportunity-seeking.[42] This effect is especially strong on younger people, but the effect persists as they age.[43]

In contrast, it is noticeable that my upwardly mobile interviewees, in their early years at least, overwhelmingly did *not* experience the feeling of being in financial free fall that traumatised people in the Great Depression. Paul is typical, describing his household finances as at the 'bottom end of the financial scale but very, very stable.' Some had fathers working in the sorts of industries that once offered working-class 'jobs for life' (shipbuilding, manufacturing, the Royal Mail). Some owed their financial stability to the sheer hardworking tenacity of mothers who took whatever jobs they could find: typing, sewing or selling Avon cosmetics door-to-door. (In some cases, mothers were acting as human shock-absorbers, protecting their children from poverty, but at a physical and psychological cost that affected their own health in later life.) Charlotte says she grew up with a feeling that 'someone has my back'. When someone has your back, you can have more 'front'.

Some of my interviewees' families experienced periods of unemployment, but the social security system in place at the time limited the financial distress. When the factory in which Rozina's father had worked closed down, the family income was maintained at a good-enough level for long enough to allow him to find another job that offered a steady income.

It is also noticeable that interviewees' childhood housing situations were secure, even if in some cases crowded (Maria's flat housed eight people, but she felt that 'No matter what, there'd be a roof over my head'). Everyone's parents were either homeowners – sometimes jointly with a relative – or council tenants. David Lammy's parents had been able to buy a house in the early 1970s, close to Tottenham's Broadwater Farm estate, where his cousins lived, with a mortgage manageable enough for his mother to pay from her own income after David's father left. David says this makes him very lucky, and gave him a 'solid foundation'.

But what David said next suggests that succeeding generations are less likely to have the 'solid foundation' of security that most of my interviewees had. He talks, sad and angry, about the constituents he meets as Tottenham's MP – people who find themselves 'moving from one bloody private rented accommodation to the next', compounded by living 'from one benefit cheque or pay cheque to the next, or on a zero-hours contract'. David says 'I think that is much more increased today … that kind of poverty is a disaster for social mobility, because you've got no base from which to move. It's a trauma that destroys your ability to focus at school, to construct a relationship.'

Families don't have to be in the sort of situations David describes to feel they are living from one pay cheque to the next.

'You might have a job', as Theresa May said in 2016, 'but you don't always have job security.'[44] Figures from the economist John Philpott show that 22% of the workforce are self-employed or on temporary or 'zero-hours' contracts, up from 18% 10 years ago, although there are indications that the growth in zero-hours contracts is now levelling off.[45]

Nor do you need to be unusually poor to experience insecure housing. As the housing charity Shelter found, one in three working families are 'only one paycheque away from losing their home'.[46] And more than one in four children are now growing up in privately rented homes, in which landlords, after an initial six or twelve months, are typically able to evict tenants at two months' notice, without giving a reason. This proportion is set to rise further, having already trebled in just 13 years.[47]

These effects are compounded for families whose pay is low or unreliable enough to qualify for Universal Credit (or similar payments), and who find that social security is leaving them feeling far from secure but rather threatened and humiliated: Universal Credit requires claimants to wait for over a month from making a claim to actually receiving anything, and it is estimated that a million working families will be exposed to benefit sanctions once Universal Credit is fully implemented.[48]

These increasingly common vulnerabilities have a significant impact on the mental health and outlook of adults and children. Academic studies of housing overwhelmingly 'point to the increased risk of poor health and negative educational, social or psychological outcomes' arising from 'multiple, enforced moves'.[49] Professor Francis Green has described how, 'when people moved from a secure to an insecure job, they suffered a substantial increase in mental distress', with 'knock-on effects on family members'.[50]

If an adult's experience of life is 'all snakes and no ladders', with large risks of income loss but little or no opportunity for promotion, combined with humiliating disrespect from employers, landlords or the benefits system, they're likely to feel too burned out to be an enthusiastic and engaged parent, and likely to pass on to their children a world view characterised by powerlessness and pessimism, rather than aspiration and ambition. When the 'marshmallow test' was re-run in 2018, a new finding came to light: that affluence appeared to be a *determinant* of a 'positive mindset' rather than just a result of it. The children who scoffed the treat immediately tended to be those whose life experience had taught them to grab opportunities immediately, because they may not be here later.[51]

Those who haven't experienced being caught in the feedback loops of insecurity, fear and shame can find it hard to appreciate how hard it is for children to think positively in such circumstances – the worries that won't go away because they're beyond your control, which your parents can't soothe because they are being hounded by the same things; the additional worries as your parents' relationship gets fractious under the pressure; the compounding of all that by the effects on your schoolwork. The likelihood of depression is increased.[52] The effect is familiar to anyone with childhood experience of having been violently 'ganged up on': the first punch you could deal with, sidestep and respond. The second, from half-behind you, not so much, because you were still dealing with the first. Then a shin-kick took your hands away as you instinctively reached down to the pain, leaving you open for the first proper blow in the face that left you floored by red nausea. Before long you're on the ground, curled up, your brain overloaded with the din and the flashing pain; you're way past responding, you're just hoping it'll go away.

Imagine trying to maintain a positive mindset in that situation.

Having attended an academic conference about the potential of 'mindset' interventions to improve life chances,[53] I got the impression – to put it mildly – that there wasn't much enthusiasm for it. Some of the participants made similar points to those I have just made, that it's hard to adopt a positive mindset if you're overwhelmed by negative experiences. Others showed how the evidence had been distorted by simplification, extrapolation and exaggeration on its route from academia to policy-maker (a fairly normal feature of policy-making, in my experience). Some saw character education as new form of missionary work, in which low-income people are declared to be missing something, something that privileged people can teach them: 'you could save yourselves from your poverty if you just started thinking as we do'. Others pointed to the risk of attributes that are part of useful diversity rather than useless defects – like introversion or left-handedness – being discouraged. I've also encountered academic scepticism based on a suspicion that the government prefers to teach people how to cope with adversity rather than to tackle its causes. Dr Angela Donkin, of the Institute of Health Equity, is a former civil servant who worked on early intervention policy, but dispenses with civil service jargon to warn that the focus on resilience (aka 'bouncebackability') provides an excuse for the government to 'make life shit – 'scuse my French – it's OK as long as we've got lots of resilience!'[54]

The scepticism about 'mindset' interventions isn't baseless, and using 'mindset' interventions as an *alternative* to addressing the causes of disadvantage, rather than a supplement to it, is counterproductive. (Children who believe that success or failure is in their own hands, but then encounter insurmountable barriers, tend to develop a sense of personal inadequacy that actually undermines their motivation.[55])

But mindset interventions, if they can be shown to have a sustained positive effect, should not be dismissed as a means of *supplementing* approaches that address structural problems, and helping to counteract the long-term psychological effects of insecurity and disrespect. This book contains numerous examples of situations in which people from non-privileged backgrounds are held back by structural, social and economic barriers, but there are also instances in which the barriers are a lack of confidence or other 'soft skills'. We have to recognise that there is no political structure under which some people do not suffer disadvantage, so we need to both help people cope with disadvantage and address the causes of their disadvantage.

Family structure

Under recent coalition and Conservative governments, the idea that promoting marriage is central to increasing social mobility has been an influential one. Fiona Bruce, a Conservative MP elected in 2010, says that any government that is serious about improving life chances 'must be committed to reversing the endemic level of family breakdown currently experienced in Britain'.[56] As a result, the government has introduced policies such as the Marriage Allowance, a tax benefit for married couples, and there is pressure to go further, to 'take more risks in supporting marriage through public policy', which usually means tax advantages for married couples (that is, relative tax disadvantages for unmarried and single parents) as a way of boosting children's life chances.[57]

The people whose stories are told in this book come from a mixture of single-parent and two-parent families. Along with my sister, finding herself in a single-parent family in early childhood, David's father left when he was 12, and Paul was born to a single mum: Paul's father was a Cameroonian medical student who had returned to Africa. Paul would see his father 'very occasionally', but he and his mother did not see his father's money, leaving them 'pretty poor ... very poor'.

Despite individual examples like Jane, David and Paul, the children of single or separated parents usually lag behind. Single parents frequently put in heroic efforts to raise their children well, but two adults together are more likely to have more time and more money to spend on their children.

Other research, however, casts doubt on the assumption that single parenthood is a major cause of poor life chances, suggesting the causes and effects are at least partly the other way around: that poor life chances cause single-parenthood. In a large American study, researchers noticed that the more skilled jobs were available in a particular area, the more likely it was that people in that area would wait until they were married to have their first child.[58] The professor who led the study says this is a *response* to conditions in the jobs market: that women are less likely to marry the father of their unborn child if he doesn't have a well-paid job.[59]

Lack of money isn't the only thing that puts families under pressure. Relationships also suffer when people are overworked, when they don't have enough time and energy for their partner, their children or other domestic responsibilities (and this doesn't help employers either, as their productivity is reduced[60]). Happily, the figures show that the UK is relatively good at going home on time: we have shorter working hours than our European neighbours, putting in eight minutes a day less than the EU average.[61] Unhappily, however, the figures can be misleading. Large numbers of workers in the UK are part time, which keeps our average hours looking low, but if we only look at full-time workers, hours are longer than the European standard. In 1999 the EU's Working Time Directive put a 48-hour limit on weekly working time, but workers can opt out from this limit (often under pressure from employers), with the result that one in eight UK employees now works 48 or more hours a week.[62] The amount of time we spend getting to and from work is also rising – the average daily commute is just under an hour (57 minutes), with 3.7 million workers travelling for two hours or more each day.[63]

This combination of long hours and long commutes is putting strain on relationships. More than four in ten parents questioned for the Modern Families Index said work pressures 'affected their relationship with their partner "often" or "all the time"'. Even when these pressures don't break relationships, they can harm children's life chances. Forty-four per cent of parents say they spend too little time with their families, and a quarter of parents admit that overwork has led them to have rows with their children.[64] There is a balance to be struck, between the inspirationally hardworking parent and the overworked parent. Having a parent who is distracted, irritable or barely coping can have a significant effect on children's mental health: those children will find it harder to develop self-confidence and other elements of a 'positive mindset'.

The safety net

As part of the research for this book, I found myself in a meeting that never happened: according to reports in the popular press, it had been cancelled.

This all started because of a book that attracted little attention when it was published at the end of 2015. The book is Adam Perkins' *The welfare trait*, which argues that children who grow up in families eligible for means-tested social security payments are at risk of 'welfare-induced personality damage'.[65] (As we'll see in Chapter 9, the idea that the personalities of the 'lower classes' have deficient personalities isn't only applied to poor people; some self-described members of the 'world class' say similar things about the middle classes.)

The book got a lot more attention the following February, when protesters threatened to disrupt a talk by Perkins, scheduled to take place at the London School of Economics and Political Science (LSE). The LSE, fearing violence, postponed the event, – but was reported as having cancelled it – at which point the media got interested. The *Daily Mail* ran a story, written by Perkins himself and headlined 'The ugly truth about benefits CENSORED by a left wing hate mob'.[66] Similar stories appeared elsewhere.

The talk was rearranged, as a ticketed event rather than an open meeting to deter protesters, and took place on 29 June 2016. Perkins made a presentation about his book and Dr Kitty Stewart, an academic expert in social policy, gave a response. Dr Stewart, it's fair to say, wasn't impressed. She pointed out that the book 'fails to meet basic standards of social science research', ignored evidence that contradicted the author's view, and drew conclusions that the evidence didn't support.[67] One of Perkins' weirder innovations was to take data on the breeding behaviour of insects and apply it to humans. Basically, the book is bad research reaching the wrong conclusions. So, an expert assessment of the book put Perkins' ideas firmly back in their box.

Except it didn't, because Dr Stewart's thorough refutation of Perkins' work wasn't reported. (To be fair, I did find one report, in a higher education periodical.[68]) The majority of the newspaper-reading public was left with the impression that there was a plot to suppress proven evidence that people receiving social security payments are innately 'workshy, aggressive and anti-social'.[69]

In reality, people receiving social security payments are ordinary people like you and me. The vast majority of us will receive such payments at some point in our lives. When we pay tax (as VAT or Council Tax or Income Tax or whatever), we are paying back money that has already been spent on us in childhood and 'paying forward' money that will be spent on us as pensioners. The proportion of 'welfare' spending that goes to 'unemployment benefit' is around 1%, and most people who claim it will do so for less than three months.[70] Despite widely believed claims that there are 'thousands' of children 'growing up in families where their parents and grandparents have never worked',[71] professional researchers who set out to study such families couldn't find a single example.[72]

Several of my interviewees mentioned the role of social security in allowing their families to provide them with the early-life security in which they could develop and pursue their aspirations, Rozina being an example already mentioned. Another example is Sir Clive Cowdery, who says being a 'beneficiary of the welfare state' as a boy was crucial to his becoming the successful businessman and philanthropist he is today.[73]

Despite the reality of social security as a safety net that the vast majority of us will use at some point in our lives, perceptions of it are grossly distorted. The average public estimate of the proportion of social security spending that goes to unemployed people is 17 times its true size. These distorted perceptions have allowed the government to cut the incomes of individuals and families who are on low or middle incomes, and increase the stigma and harassment they experience, which, in turn, harms the life chances of their children. If the expected changes to working patterns – and economic shocks such as may be caused by Brexit – result in more people having to find new jobs or having their incomes reduced, even temporarily, we will all become more likely to need social security.

Adam Perkins and his ilk are leading a campaign of misinformation that threatens the financial security, and the life chances, of us all.

Childcare

There is a wide consensus among experts that the pre-school years are a major factor in children's development, and that childcare (including nurseries and pre-school education) is an important element in that development. This consensus has led governments across the political spectrum to invest in free childcare places. Free childcare, initially limited to four-year-olds, started in the early 2000s, so the effect on children's educational development when they reach secondary school age has only recently become apparent, and the experts now know how much effect this investment has had.

The experts' assessment, which appeared in an academic journal in 2016 (by Jo Blanden et al), was that the educational effects on children at the age of five were 'so small as to be economically negligible', and by the time the children get to 11 years old, there are 'no apparent benefits'.[74] There may have been non-educational benefits, such as improved behaviour, but no apparent long-lasting effects on children's school performance from an investment that currently costs around £2 billion a year.

This is surprising as well as shocking, because in other countries free, universal childcare has been 'an engine of social mobility'. In France, children who benefited from free childcare introduced in the 1960s and 1970s were found to be 'more likely to succeed at each step of their schooling career and on the labour market'.[75] In Norway from the late 1970s, a similar policy led to large increases in the number of children getting good grades at school and going to university (and decreases in the number of girls who became teenage mums[76]). In these countries and others, there was a narrowing of the gaps in life chances between privileged and non-privileged children.

So why didn't it work in Britain? Blanden et al offer a number of explanations. First, that there was a 'crowding out' effect: in more than two-thirds of cases children had been in childcare anyway, so the only difference was that parents who had previously been paying for childcare, or having their employers pay for it, were now getting at least some of it for free. But this clearly isn't the only explanation, because significant numbers of children were getting childcare who previously had not, and these tended to be children from more disadvantaged households, who most needed good-quality pre-schooling. But 'good quality' is the nub of the problem: the pre-schooling the disadvantaged children were now getting was *not* good quality.

The problem appears to have arisen because the government, rather than providing new childcare places, instead provided *funding* for new childcare places. Much of the childcare itself is provided by private sector companies, who keep their costs down by employing unqualified staff. Whereas in the public sector almost all the relevant staff are fully qualified, in the private sector the figure is estimated to be somewhere between a fifth and a tenth. The unwillingness of some childcare providers to employ pre-school teachers who are fully qualified (and therefore higher-paid) is reflected in a declining number of graduates entering the profession. Between 2013/14 and 2017/18, the number of Early Years teachers recruited dropped from over 2,300 to 595.[77] The most-privileged parents made sure their children were in the best-quality pre-schools, and other children got what's left.

Where pre-school provision is held to high standards, the results can be remarkable. The most impressive results come from intensive programmes targeted at the children who need it most. Two initiatives that were launched in the US State of North Carolina in the 1970s[78] were *very* intensive, working with children from eight weeks old to five years old, and at some points in the process involved children being present from 7.45am to 5.30pm, five days a week, 50 weeks a year.[79] As you'd imagine, that sort of programme isn't cheap, but it is cheaper than not doing it: economists calculated that the savings to the taxpayer (in terms of reduced crime, greater tax-take because participants went on to better-paid jobs and so on) far outweighed the costs. The estimated rate of return was a very healthy 13.7% a year.

But while there is a strong argument for free, high-quality childcare, especially for the children who need it most, there is such a thing as too much childcare. One of the few disadvantages suffered by children of affluent families is that they are more likely to find themselves in childcare for such long hours that they develop behavioural problems.[80] Pre-school children need good pre-school teachers, but they also need good parents. The long hours, long commutes and short tempers that damage relationships also have an effect on children's school-readiness. When both parents are working full time, there is a significant negative effect on their children's educational attainment.[81] Unfortunately, many are not allowed – by employers or by financial pressures – to cut working hours in children's early years. Nor, for those with middle or low incomes, is it usually possible to rearrange working hours so they are home when their children are awake. The charity Working Families found that although more than two-thirds of parents with salaries over

£70,000 a year worked flexibly, less than half of those with salaries of £40,000 or below did so.[82] So, our childcare system may not be working hard enough for the children of ordinary families, while we – the adults in their lives – may be working too hard.

The die is cast?

As a rule, government reports don't have interesting covers. They have plain typefaces and no pictures. But a report from 2011 broke this rule. It shows, side by side, two CT scans of the brains of three-year-old children. One is labelled 'Normal' and the other 'Extreme Neglect'. The second brain is a lot smaller and has large patches that appear empty.

The report, *Early intervention: The next steps*, was written by an Opposition MP, Graham Allen, by request of the coalition government, in recognition of his longstanding interest in early intervention and as a means of putting the evidence on child development 'above politics'. Allen's report says a 'child's development score at just 22 months can serve as an accurate predictor of educational outcomes when they are 26'.[83] As the CT scan on the report's cover suggested, the circumstances of a child's early years can affect not just what the child has learned, but the size and structure of the brain itself. Allen goes on to say that 55% of brain development happens in the three years immediately after birth (with 25% having happened *in utero*), and that this development is affected by whether parents meet their child's physical, social, emotional and sensory needs.[84, 85]

Iain Duncan Smith, then the Secretary of State for Work and Pensions, was particularly interested in the effects of family environment, on the development of children's brains, which he suggested could be impeded if their mothers had 'different, multiple partners'.[86] Unsurprisingly, this subject gets people upset. It raises horrible questions: are children who perform poorly when they arrive at school a 'lost cause'? Are the children of rich parents doing better at school because, from the age of three, they have better brains than the rest of us? Is family breakdown damaging our children's brains?

Part of the answer can be found in another government-commissioned report, published two months after Graham Allen's. *Social mobility: A literature review*, had the usual plain typefaces and lack of pictures. The review was written by two experts from the Institute for Fiscal Studies and two university professors, and attracted far less attention that Graham Allen's (more specifically, it attracted far less attention than certain *excerpts* from Graham Allen's report). This report found 'growing evidence' that the idea of brains being irrevocably damaged at an early age 'has been somewhat flawed',[87] and referred to increasing evidence of substantial brain development after childhood, including the well-known phenomenon of London's black cab drivers having unusually large hippocampi (part of the brain used in spatial memory) as a result of memorising routes as adults.

More damning – especially for Iain Duncan Smith's suggestions that mothers having multiple partners can damage their children's brains – was the intervention of Bruce Perry, the psychiatrist whose research produced the CT scans that appeared on the front of Graham Allen's report. Perry said that Duncan Smith had 'greatly misrepresented' his work. The neurological damage that Perry had studied had been caused by 'absolute extreme neglect and abuse',[88] including cases of children who had been locked alone in small rooms for years. It had not been caused by the sex lives of single mums.

Nor is it reasonable to think that children's life chances are set in stone by the time they enter school. There is a clear and strong relationship between good child development in under-fives and good life chances in later life,[89] but individuals (including some of the people interviewed in this book – and Albert Einstein, who is said to have been unable to speak until four or five years old[90]) are able to overcome weak starts, and strong starters can falter. Investments in children's early years are necessary but need follow-up investment to be fully effective.[91] As we will see, decisive events that hold our children back or propel them forward can happen at any time in the rest of their lives, starting at school, which is where the next chapter takes us.

THREE

School years

Top at five, bottom at thirteen

In the previous chapter, we met Maria, who defied the stereotypes of a girl from a Salford council estate by starting school with an unusually advanced reading ability. Eight years later, she was again challenging expectations. We might expect that a girl who'd made such a strong start would remain ahead of her classmates, but at the age of 13, she was in a school that separated pupils into 'sets' of differing abilities, and for English lessons Maria was put in the bottom set.[1]

Maria's story isn't unique. Having a good level of 'school readiness' at five years old is an advantage, but there is no guarantee this advantage will be sustained. In fact, for some groups of the UK's children, it normally *won't* be sustained. A child from a deprived background who is ranked as a 'high achiever' at age seven will typically, at sixteen, have been overtaken in their test scores by an 'average achiever' from a privileged family.[2]

The likelihood that our children's potential will be trumped by their privilege (or lack of it) is well known among education experts. In recent decades, efforts have been made to reduce this effect, and in June 2017 a commission of education experts and politicians from across the political spectrum reviewed the progress of these efforts. It found that between the mid-1980s and mid-2000s there had been 'no significant improvement' in narrowing the gap between the educational progress of high-income and low-income children.[3] A month after the

Commission's report, the Education Policy Institute published a report on more recent trends (2007-16). It found that there had been some improvement, but that it had been slow and inconsistent, and for the most disadvantaged children, the adverse effect of their background was actually worsening.[4]

Education should offer all children the chance to attain their aspirations, but Professor Stephen Machin, an expert in the economics of education, says it actually does the opposite: 'Education has not been the great leveller. It's either done nothing for social mobility, or it has reinforced existing inequalities'.[5] This is important, because how well you do in school is a good predictor of how well you do in later life. In the UK, you are 11 times more likely to become severely deprived if you have low levels of educational attainment than if you have a high level of education.[6]

But it is not inevitable that a child's background will so powerfully determine their educational qualifications. There are places in which this effect has been drastically reduced. On average, the educational progress of English children who are classified as 'disadvantaged' is over a year-and-a-half behind that of their 'non-disadvantaged' classmates by the time they finish secondary school. In some areas, however, the gap is less than half as wide: in three London boroughs – Southwark, Wandsworth and Tower Hamlets – disadvantaged pupils at the end of secondary school are seven months behind their classmates and in Rutland eight months. (In the Isle of Wight, by contrast, the most disadvantaged children are almost two-and-a-half years behind.[7])

The rest of this chapter asks why education has 'reinforced existing inequalities', why it has done so more strongly in the UK than is usual for a developed country,[8] and why children's prospects are more constrained by their backgrounds in some areas of the UK than others. It looks at the psychological, social and economic forces that weigh down children from deprived backgrounds while giving the most privileged families' children an advantage.[9]

Faces that fit

Imagine you're about to be shown a passport photograph of a woman you've never met and asked to guess her name from a list of four possibilities: Anne, Caroline, Claire or Emma. What are the odds you will guess the correct name?

Assuming there are about the same number of women with each of the four names in the population as a whole, you might imagine that your odds of a correct guess are one in four, but they are not. When researchers asked volunteers to try putting names to pictures of strangers, their success rate was significantly better than one in four.[10]

There are two reasons why we are good at guessing other people's names (I'll come to the second one later). The first is that certain names are more common among certain groups of people. For example, if we were told that we were about to meet someone called 'Britney', most of us wouldn't expect her to be a pensioner. We would probably also make assumptions about Britney's social class, which, in turn, would lead us to make suppositions about her interests and aptitudes. We typecast each other, and this typecasting starts very early in our lives.

In 2005 a minor scandal erupted when teachers on an online forum were found openly discussing their attitudes to children they hadn't yet met, based on their names. A child called Shane, we learn, is 'a terror' and Chantelle is 'spawn of the devil'. The *Daily Mail* pointed out that most of the names mentioned (one of which was Britney) were not typically given to middle-class children, in an article titled '"Chav" names feared by teachers'.[11]

The teachers caught discussing 'chav names' are not typical of their profession, but the tendency to hold prejudices about behaviour and ability based on indicators of class (and gender and ethnicity and other attributes) *is* typical, not just of teachers, but of all of us. Even if someone's name doesn't give much away, their voice and mannerisms will (even in America, supposedly less class-ridden than the UK, participants in a recent psychological experiment were able to correctly guess strangers' social class after hearing them speak just seven words).[12] These prejudices about behaviour and ability lead to some people being channelled towards opportunities that others are not, to some people being given more encouragement than others, and to some people being 'written off'.

Dean Hanley, now a digital service designer, remembers being on the receiving end of such prejudice, as a child who had chosen to study music in his school in Coventry: 'we had been segregated. In the main room, the kids were being taught about classical music. In the smaller room, we were each given a Casiotone keyboard and told to make up a tune. People in our room were being entered for CSEs. People in the other room were being entered for O-levels ... the kids in the big room were from the posh estates. We were from the council estates, without exception.' Dean finished school with good O-levels: all 'A's and 'B's. Except in music. He got a Grade 2 CSE in Music.

My sister Jane, by contrast, started school with attributes the teachers would likely find reassuring. Not only was she able to read, but her vocabulary and accent had been shaped by one of their fellow teachers. From her first day in class, Jane would have benefited from the subconscious biases that we are all prone to, that lead us to confuse the markers of a 'good' family background (such as name and vocabulary) with being '"naturally" clever'.[13]

The strength of subconscious bias on teachers has been demonstrated in a famous experiment carried out in the 1960s. In a Californian primary school, Professor Robert Rosenthal gave pupils a test, the 'Harvard Test of Inflected Acquisition', and informed teachers that the test had shown some of the children to be 'academic bloomers', with unusually high potential to improve. Rosenthal had lied to the teachers. The Harvard Test was a fiction (the children had, in fact, completed a standard IQ test), and those whom Rosenthal named as 'academic bloomers' had been chosen at random rather than by performance in any test. Once teachers expected certain children to be special, Rosenthal found that they subconsciously treated them differently, giving them more opportunities to answer questions, more encouraging feedback and 'thousands of different ways of treating people in small ways every day'.[14]

Rosenthal's experiment showed that teachers' (groundless) expectations changed their attitudes and behaviour towards the children in their class. But it also changed the children's attitudes to themselves. After two years, when Rosenthal tested the children again, those whom the teachers believed to be 'academic bloomers' had gained more IQ points than the others: they had become what their teachers expected them to become, regardless of any 'innate' ability.

Now, half a century after Rosenthal's experiment, children are still being earmarked for success or failure by their background, and still finding that this process constrains their future academic performance. Mary-Claire Travers, of the UCL Institute of Education, has studied the practice of schools assigning children to different 'sets' and finds that 'ability' setting is influenced by a child's background (as well as gender and other factors). A separate study showed that children in higher streams are rated by teachers as having higher 'ability and attainment' than those in lower streams, even when their performance in tests was identical.[15] Quoting a boy who participated in her research, Travers says those who find themselves in the lower sets see themselves as being in 'the write-off class' and – as Rosenthal might expect – dampen their aspirations accordingly.[16]

This tendency for typecasting each other, and for unwittingly conforming to the type that has been imposed on us, is extremely powerful. It changes us in ways we wouldn't expect. I mentioned above that there were two reasons why we are good at putting names to faces: in addition to the one already mentioned, it is also thought that just as our characters and abilities change to conform to others' expectations of us, so do our *faces* (for example, people whose names are associated with seriousness will be perceived by others as being as serious as their name implies; in response, they will tend to adopt a more serious demeanour, and in time, the muscles and skin of their faces will adapt). As one of the researchers who conducted the name-guessing experiment wrote, 'whatever the first name you give to your child, he or she will end up wearing it'.[17]

Children aren't just typecast by their teachers (and consequently by themselves); they are also typecast by their own parents. Privileged parents will tend to assume their own high social status will be reflected by high academic ability in their children, and find ways to explain away any evidence to the contrary. The sociologist Val Gillies offers an example from her research, of a mother who 'places emphasis on Zoe's "very, very" high IQ in order to contextualize the problem with literacy'.[18] Children are subjected to expectations, about their future careers as well as their ability, well before they have shown any aptitude in exams or tests. Sometimes, what is intended as a statement of our open-mindedness about our children's life choices suggests that subconsciously our expectations are rather narrow, because some options are mentioned and others are not. Catherine and John, a 'middle-class couple' interviewed by the journalist Polly Toynbee for a BBC radio programme on social mobility, said they hoped their eight-week-old son Thomas (whose gurgles can be heard on the recording) will feel able to 'go to university or medical school or whatever it is that he wants'.[19]

Adults don't just sort (their own and others') children into 'types'. They also sort their fellow-parents into types, and decide whether or not to fraternise with each other based on this typology. This, in turn, affects which of their classmates each child will have the opportunity to become friends with and share aspirations with. A study by the Institute of Education found that self-segregation of parents of primary school children strongly affected which children met up out of school and that this, in turn, influenced children's friendship choices. The study involved schools in London, whose pupils came from a mixture of backgrounds, and was 'positive about their diversity', but whereas three-quarters of the children named someone of a different ethnic group as their best friend, 'only a quarter had a best friend of a different social class'.[20]

First impressions count. The first impressions others have of our children can matter for the rest of their lives.

Pride and prejudice

Jane's early upbringing created a favourable first impression that compounded the blessing bestowed by her advanced literacy. But as a 13-year-old, this blessing came to feel like a curse, as she progressed from middle school into a high school that divided pupils into 'streams': 'When I went from Moorthorpe to Minsthorpe, all my friends got put in the middle stream. I got put in the top stream. My friends turned on me. They were saying "tha's posh now". They were saying "don't do it, stay

with us and we'll still be friends". I had a most awful summer.
I didn't tell anybody.... I had nobody.'

Jane's experience of being shamed and excluded for her
'swottiness' is painfully familiar to many individuals who, as
children, were noticeably more engaged or successful in education
than their peers. Andrea Ashworth's memoir of growing up in
Manchester in the 1970s and 1980s refers to girls who 'made
it their business to inflict bruises on brainboxes'.[21] Those of us
who experienced similar treatment are likely to have been told
by adults that it was a product of the jealousy of children who
were unable or unwilling to do well at school, using aggression
to cover the shame of their own shortcomings. But the evidence
suggests that to characterise 'swot bashing' as nothing more
than a manifestation of jealousy and shame is to misunderstand
children's motivations, a common misunderstanding that has
impeded attempts to address a significant barrier by which non-
privileged children are discouraged from engaging in education.
Let me explain:

In the early 2000s a series of focus groups was convened to
assess which factors would encourage non-privileged teenagers
to study at medical school and which would discourage them.
All of the participants were 'academically able and scientifically
oriented', but they included boys 'whose interjections were
directed at subverting the purpose of the focus group through
humour and "bad boy" activities'. These individuals had no
reason to be jealous of the 'clever kids', because they *were* the
clever kids (one had recently won a scholarship to 'a leading
private school'[22]). Clearly, something other than ability envy is
going on.

One explanation is that what appears to be punishment for
swottiness may, in fact, be punishment for contravening the
type-casting that has been imposed on individuals as a result of
their class (or gender or ethnicity). Having picked up on signals
from parents, teachers and each other about which of their
classmates are 'in my group', children begin to define – and
enforce conformity to – the norms and behaviours of their group
(we all have a tendency to do this: even pre-school children have
been observed doing it[23]). The treatment meted out to children
who have a long record of swottiness can be fairly mild, or at

least indistinguishable from the normal everyday brutality of playground interaction. Charlotte, now a young civil servant, says 'you do get stick for wanting to learn, but I didn't care at all, it didn't faze me. I got called a boff, but not in a nasty way.' However, being seen to 'defect', to renounce the codes of behaviour you once appeared to accept, is another matter. Jane was punished, for being seen to defect, by the group she was joining as well as the one she was leaving. Because Jane was the only girl from her middle school year-group to be placed in the top stream at high school, she was isolated and vulnerable: 'The other girls did used to pick on me', she remembers, 'they put pins in my leg under the table.'

Another explanation (not incompatible with the first) began to be suggested by social scientists such as Paul Willis in the 1970s and Christine Griffin in the 1980s, who had undertaken close observation of children's interactions. They suggested that the hostility of some children towards swots (and teachers, and education in general) wasn't rooted in shame about their own poor educational performance, but was actually rooted in a *pride* in their own culture, which caused children to defend it against an education system that seemed to belittle it.[24] Iesha Small, a maths teacher and education researcher, thinks the belittling is still going on: 'The unspoken rule in education', she writes 'is that (white) middle class culture is the only meaningful culture and that we must all aspire to it'.[25]

One of my own memories of school suggests that working-class culture and experience *was* seen as inferior, or at least that I had understood it to be. In an English lesson, the teacher handed out copies of an anthology of poems, and asked each of us to choose one to read out to the class. One of the poems in the book was different to the others, different to any poem I'd ever seen, and it was the only one to be chosen by more than one of my classmates. It was Tony Connor's 'Child's bouncing song' ('... Who're the gentry down our entry – Mrs Smith's got two TVs. What if her coat is a fur coat, all her kids are full of fleas...').[26] I winced in anticipation of the teacher's reaction to something so 'common' being brought into the classroom. In fact, Miss Oliver didn't seem to mind – she was probably pleased to see some rare engagement with poetry – but my assumption that there would be trouble tells you something. The poems I was used to seeing in English lessons weren't about the sorts of people who lived 'down our entry', and some people were alienated by that. Dean (whose qualifications now include a Master's degree in English Literature) tells me about his classmates getting exasperated with Jane Austen: 'we couldn't get it. It was outside of our experience. They say literature is universal. Nonsense.'

An additional explanation for swot-bashing is that the rejection of education (or of the delivery and deliverers of education) can be about pragmatism as well as pride. Willis and Griffin point out that being a 'class clown' can have long-term benefits: if you expect to live and work in the same place as your classmates, it helps to be popular. This makes even more sense as a strategy to the many children whose adult relatives have worked hard and who have seen little reward or respect in return. If your experience is that hard work isn't rewarded, why work hard? Isn't it better to have fun now and a crap job later than to not have fun now and *still* have a crap job later?

But the proud and pragmatic reasons behind swot bashing and disengagement with education appear to be losing some of their power. Incidents of 'norm and rule violation' by children from lower socioeconomic groups appear to be declining.[27] A range of factors may have brought this about, including that the behaviour itself and that the causes of the behaviour are being more effectively addressed (for example, diversifying the range of GCSE set texts to better reflect most pupils' experiences, featuring Shelagh Delaney's *Taste of honey* and Stephen Kelman's *Pigeon English* alongside Austen).[28] But the researchers who recorded the reduced 'norm and rule violation' have proposed another reason: that as manufacturing has declined, so have the chances of getting secure and well-paid jobs for people without educational qualifications, and therefore those children who 'followed rules and respected their teachers, and were consequently despised ... don't look quite so daft as they used to'.[29]

Mis-shapes, mistakes, misfits

Dean had a strong incentive to do well enough at school to go to university: 'I'm a gay man. A man was murdered on that estate because someone thought he was gay. My sister was murdered on that estate ... the main reason I'm socially mobile is I wasn't happy on the council estate, I wanted to get out of the violence. I really hated it, didn't fit in, didn't fit their idea of masculinity.'

Dean's experience is unusually scary, but in one way it isn't completely unusual. Among the socially mobile people I interviewed, childhood memories of feeling not-quite-normal, or even not-at-all-normal, were normal. Paul 'never really quite fitted in' as the only black child in class and the only child of a single mother: 'I was obviously different to everyone else. People saw me as different.' David wasn't the only black child in school, but he was 'a bit of an odd fish, precocious, not good at football, sensitive, not a boysy boy. I've felt like a misfit for a lot of my life.' In Lynsey Hanley's book *Respectable*, which draws on her personal and academic knowledge of social mobility, she says 'I was rubbish at being working class'.[30] (After Hanley's book was published, I asked her what she meant by being 'rubbish at being working class'. She gave me an example, that although she made numerous friends on her first day at her – mainly middle-class – sixth form college, at school she had made none.)

I suspect that misfits are more likely to experience develop and attain aspirations that are 'above their station'. Maybe the ostracism suffered by the 'swots' is less effective against people who are ostracised anyway. Some of my interviewees saw their lack of cultural belonging as a form of freedom (to invert a phrase from Theresa May, if you feel like a citizen of nowhere, you can go anywhere). Rozina sums this up when she says that she 'didn't have community, didn't have anyone else's expectations', and that she was therefore free to set her own expectations.

Not all of my interviewees saw their lack of affiliation as a positive, freeing experience. Jane certainly didn't feel that way about the ostracism she suffered for being put in the 'top stream'. Lynsey Hanley is another example who, despite being ill at ease in her native community, suffered from being distanced from it. The 'dirty secret of social mobility', says Hanley 'is that it hurts'.[31] Hanley is right. As this book continues, we will see that people who climb 'above their station' are often rewarded with isolation, self-doubt and humiliation. And it hurts.

The hurt that Lynsey Hanley and others have is consistently underestimated by policy-makers and others who tend to see the financial poverty in non-privileged communities but fail to see any social and cultural richness, and therefore assume that anyone who doesn't want to 'escape' lacks ambition or sense.

Some people who have experienced social mobility do see their journey as an 'escape'. In some cases they describe their childhoods in terms reminiscent of the testimonies of those who have experienced gender dysmorphia: wanting to live their life in a way that is 'inappropriate' for someone like them. My interviewees' lives include stories of individual determination rewriting futures that may have seemed pre-determined. But mostly, they didn't want to *become* something different: they recognise that their past experience as well as their future aspirations is part of who they are; they just wanted to become something less *constrained* by their background. This is something encountered again and again as this book progresses: a lack of appreciation on the part of the privileged that the price of opportunity can be unacceptably high if it involves the need to 'leave to achieve' or have parts of oneself removed.

Writing about evolution, the poet W.H. Auden wrote that, 'As a rule, it was ... misfits, Forced by failure to migrate to unsettled niches, who altered their structure and prospered'.[32] If we want the pursuit of ambitious aspirations to become normal, rather than being restricted to those who have been 'forced to migrate' because they were a misfit in their native environment, we must allow individuals to pursue their aspirations without feeling that they have to denounce something of themselves.

The power of a good teacher

Although some of my interviewees had the head start of a good level of literacy as primary school pupils, others did not. Dean is an example, whose first school 'just didn't give us reading books. I didn't even know what one was.' Dean's family moved house, and he was transferred to another, better primary school, but the previous one had left him unprepared: 'the teacher called my mum in, said "Dean isn't ready yet".'

Dean's parents' ability to help him was restrained by their own limited education, so Dean's future appeared bleak: at a disadvantage at school and lacking the resources at home that could help him catch up, he was likely to fall further behind, becoming demoralised and disengaged from education. But Dean actually went on to do very well in education, becoming one of the very few from his school to go to university. So how did a boy with negligible literacy go on to get his Master's degree in English Literature?

Just as Jane had a 'fairy godmother' in her pre-school years, Dean had one when he was five. The teacher who'd warned Dean's parents about his inadequate literacy also stepped in to fix it: 'she had much higher expectations of us than most teachers I've come across', says Dean, 'she took me aside, gave me some private time, taught me to read.'

'Everybody remembers a good teacher' was the slogan of a late 1990s teacher recruitment campaign, and the testimonies of my interviewees suggest the slogan is true. Most of them mention at least one teacher who was 'really, really good' or 'amazing'. For Jane, this was Mr Clark (whom we'll meet later): 'I was like a meerkat in his lessons' (as she tells me this, she mimes sitting bolt upright, wide-eyed), 'like I was on fire.' I heard numerous tales of individual teachers who put extraordinary effort into giving a good education to children from 'challenging' schools. Charlotte says, 'coming from a school that was really not very good, if you want to learn you get an awful lot of attention and focus. The teachers were delighted to have someone they can point to, they can show they can get good marks.' Joanne talks about 'really keen' teachers who laid on extra classes; these, she says, tended to have been raised nearby: 'ones who'd experienced social mobility themselves were most encouraging.'

Maria's experiences, on the other hand, illustrate the effect of bad teaching, and how children who have had inadequate teaching are later assumed to have inadequate ability. Her description of junior school as 'poor' is an example of the great British understatement. One teacher 'taught by slaps on girls' legs and boys' bums, psychological warfare'; another told her that 'people who read too much' – like Maria herself – 'have no personality'. She remembers the cruelty as mixed with incompetence: 'I felt like towards the end they panicked and started teaching us random facts. "Cardiff is the capital of Wales", "this is a retina".… Ninety per cent of them shouldn't have been teachers.' (In other schools in the same period Maria is recalling, many pupils found their ability to learn reduced by certain teachers' inability to keep order. In a recent conversation with some of my own former classmates, we discussed the experience of watching a series of incrementally larger items – including furniture – falling past the window, having been defenestrated from the classroom upstairs.)

At the beginning of this chapter, I mentioned that Maria was put in the bottom set for English at secondary school despite having had a highly advanced level of literacy at age five. She attributes this to her secondary school teachers not appreciating how poor her preparation at primary school had been (none of her classmates had attended the same primary, because the success of Maria's dad's chip shop led to the family moving house to a more affluent area, Hazel Grove, when Maria was transitioning into secondary). Prior to being assigned to the bottom set, she had been asked to talk about a poem: 'I'd come from a school in Salford. I hadn't *seen* a poem except at infants' school, something about rhyming the end of sentences? Something about leaves? I didn't know what to do with this thing. On top of that, I still had the Salford accent.'

My interviewees' assessments of the importance of good (or bad) teachers to their progress in school are backed up by 'big data' studies that have only recently become possible. Data from the US show that when an individual high-performing teacher joined a school, their pupils' test scores typically rose by around 5 percentage points. More recent analysis, which is the result of following cohorts of children for several decades into adulthood, found teacher performance also had a significant effect on the numbers who get into college and on other outcomes, including the number of teenage pregnancies. Compared to an average class of children, one that had been taught by a low-performing teacher could expect their collective lifetime incomes to be lower by a quarter of a million dollars.[33]

As my interviewees can testify, there appears to be a substantial benefit for children who are taught by teachers who are encouraging as well as competent. A British study by Dr Ben Alcott, which followed 4,300 adolescents into adulthood, found that those who said their teachers were encouraging were 8 percentage points more likely to enter higher education than those who said their teachers were not, rising to 12 points for students whose parents lacked post-compulsory education.[34]

Over recent decades, governments across the political spectrum have introduced policies to improve the quality of teaching. (Having had bad experiences, Maria is unsurprisingly a fan of these: 'it's great that kids are expected to learn certain things'.) There have also been improvements made in the standards of behaviour expected from pupils themselves. This shouldn't be understated: the focus and determination of policy-makers, teachers and school leaders has raised the standards of education enormously.

One of the results of the increased political focus on education has been the encouragement of evidence-based teaching practices, through government funding of research bodies such as the Education Endowment Foundation (set up in 2011). Approaches to teaching that have been assessed and championed by such bodies include 'metacognition', giving pupils tools to plan their own approach to learning[35] (and thus encouraging a sense of agency, an objective also widely shared by 'mindset' practitioners).

However, other developments are now counteracting this. Teachers are much less likely to have the time to offer extra lessons like those Dean and Joanne talked about, or to keep up-to-date with research on effective teaching practices. The average teacher in England works longer hours than their colleagues in almost all other developed nations (OECD data shows only Japan and the Canadian province of Alberta have longer hours), with one in five working 60 hours a week or more.[36] Three-quarters of teachers suffer from work-related stress (a far larger proportion than in the workforce as a whole), and almost half of these say it affects their ability to teach properly.[37] The typical teacher is too tired, too busy and too stressed to identify and develop the potential of able children from non-privileged backgrounds.

Even if a teacher does spot a child's potential, they may not be around long enough to nurture it, due to high turnover rates[38] and the frequent use of supply teachers. Squeezed school budgets are not likely to help the situation.[39]

Unsurprisingly, this affects children's experiences of school. US studies have shown that overstretched teachers (like overstretched parents) tend to inadvertently undermine any efforts to build 'positive mindsets' and social skills: 'teachers who reported higher levels of stress and lacked basic resources had students who were more likely to report mental health problems.'[40]

The stresses and shortages that undermine teachers' ability to nurture their pupils are widely distributed, but they are not *equally* distributed. Initiatives such as the Pupil Premium, which aim to ensure that sufficient resources are available to pupils who most need them, are being overpowered by larger forces. Research on 'social inequalities in access to teachers' by the Social Market Foundation and Education Datalab found that state schools with the most affluent pupils are substantially more likely to have teachers with the most experience and the highest qualifications[41] and Alcott's study (cited above) found that 'students from more advantaged backgrounds were likelier to report being encouraged'.[42]

Good teachers can make an enormous difference to the life chances of children, but the children who have access to those teachers are not likely to be those who need them.

The cost of a free education

Politicians like to be able to say that they got to where they are today by overcoming the odds. One of the most effective political adverts ever made was broadcast as part of Bill Clinton's successful presidential campaign in 1992. It begins with Clinton saying, 'I was born in a little town called Hope, Arkansas, three months after my father died.... I lived with my grandparents; they had very limited incomes....' In the UK, a large part of 'the Thatcher myth' was her origins as a 'grocer's daughter', with the (misleading) implication that she came from 'humble beginnings'.[43] It's surprising, then, that Jackie Doyle-Price, a politician with a genuine social mobility story, should tell me that she got into a good secondary school because she had friends in the right places.

Jackie's 'friends in the right places' were 10 years old; they were the children who sat next to her in her primary school. Jackie grew up in a council estate in the Wisewood area of Sheffield, and the vast majority of her classmates 'usually, automatically, would have gone to the former secondary modern', but Jackie found herself 'at the swotty end of class' with children whose parents wanted them to go to Notre Dame, an ex-grammar school. Two-thirds of her friends expected to go to Notre Dame and Jackie – as befits a politician-to-be – successfully lobbied her mum to request a place at the school where her friends were going.

Jackie isn't the only one whose education was enhanced by school friends from more privileged backgrounds who revealed previously unsuspected opportunities, provided encouragement and acted as guides. There is strong evidence that having more-privileged friends has a significant influence over an individual's chance of experiencing social mobility: in 28 countries studied by the OECD, children of blue-collar workers who attended schools in which they mixed with the children of white-collar workers were twice as likely to get a university degree or enter a professional or management occupation as similar children who did not have the opportunity to mix.[44] The potential of schools to widen children's opportunities appears to depend largely on whether they create social integration.

Unfortunately, many schools do not create social integration. Just as the most skilled teachers are concentrated in schools where the children least need them, so are the children who could otherwise act as friends and mentors to non-privileged children. Part of the reason why the UK has such a low level of social mobility is that our schools segregate our children according to the wealth and resources of their parents. Even in the state system, it is possible to buy one's way into an exclusive school.

The most obvious way in which privileged parents can buy their child a place at an exclusive but non-fee-paying school is by buying their way into the right catchment area, which inflates local housing costs and thereby drives less-affluent families out. In 2016, house prices close to the 'top 30' state secondary schools in England were £55,000 more expensive than neighbouring areas. In Scotland, the premium for living near one of Scotland's 'top 20' was £43,000,[45] and in the case of Beaconsfield High School in Buckinghamshire, the figure was £629,000 on top of the usual (high) cost of houses in the area,[46] a cost that excludes almost everyone. The effect spreads into primary schools; as the former government minister Lord Willetts has pointed out: 'this eventually feeds through into higher house prices around the primary schools that feed the secondary schools'.[47] Meanwhile, in a fifth of local areas, there isn't a single high-performing school within 'reasonable travel distance'.[48] If you are a parent who is unable to outspend the vast majority of other parents, your children may be excluded from the best 'free' education by the time they begin school.

But selecting-out the less privileged isn't just a matter of having the money to be in the right catchment area. Sutton Trust research found that in 85% of the 500 highest-performing non-selective state schools in England, the proportion of pupils from disadvantaged backgrounds was lower than the proportion of those pupils in the catchment area.[49] This is partly due to privileged parents having the social networks to swap information about schools and the confidence and know-how to make applications and appeals; but it goes beyond that, including the ability and willingness to bend or break the rules. This includes declaring second homes to be the main family home, or claiming to live at an address actually occupied by a relative (both of which have been found to be especially common among privileged families[50]). Increasingly, we can also expect privileged families to deploy professional help to get places in the best state schools: a *Forbes* list of 'jobs that didn't exist 10 years ago' now includes 'Educational or Admissions Consultant': people whose 'skills include the right connections with school administrators'.[51]

The costs of certain state schools don't stop once a child is admitted. In May 2016 the *Financial Times* reported that 29% of UK secondary schools (and 9% of primaries) expected parents to provide their children with laptops or tablet devices for use in school.[52] In other surveys, over a third of parents reported having been charged for (compulsory) trips, as well as numerous other additional costs including costly uniforms and travel expenses. Almost a quarter of parents said such costs influenced their choice of school.[53]

There are consequences of segregating children according to the resources of their parents. Children from the richest areas are 57% more likely to find themselves in state schools rated 'outstanding', and those from the poorest areas are more than twice as likely to find themselves in schools rated 'inadequate'.[54] Segregation also means children are less likely to have experiences like Jackie's, of meeting more privileged friends who could have encouraged and helped them to pursue 'ideas above their station'.

Some organisations, including the Centre for Social Justice, have concluded that because 'selection by wealth' is already happening, it would be best to bring back academic selection to 'help level the playing field', using something like the old system of secondary moderns, grammar schools and the 11-plus.[55] It is to that idea that we next turn.

Selection by ability

As a child, Mark Dixon was 'an "A" student in almost everything'. But Mark did not pass the 11-plus (he had family issues at the time) and was assigned to Rainsford Secondary School, a 'secondary modern'. Pupils of secondary moderns were widely said to have been 'consigned to failure at 11'.[56] But Mark is not a failure: in financial terms, he is easily the most successful person in this book.

Mark was saved from being consigned to failure at 11 by Anthony Crosland. Five years before Mark entered secondary school, Crosland, as Secretary of State for Education, had asked all local authorities to begin 'reorganising secondary education in their areas on comprehensive lines'.[57] In the few months between Mark sitting the 11-plus exam and starting secondary school, Rainsford Secondary School became Rainsford High School, a comprehensive. The conversion brought in 'a lot of new teachers who wanted it to work', says Mark, 'It was a fresh start. The overall standard was really good.'

Stories like Mark's are rarely heard. Much more common are stories like Paul's, in which the 11-plus was 'the biggest break of my life'. (Paul scored so well in the 11-plus that he won a scholarship to a private school.) The grammar schools, to which children who passed the 11-plus were usually sent, are frequently described as having been an 'engine of social mobility' for 'brighter children from poorer homes'.[58] Stories like Paul's are supported by data showing that the generations who went to school in the era of the 11-plus experienced the greatest upward social mobility in recent history.[59]

However, to take the above evidence and conclude that a re-expansion of selective education would increase social mobility would be misleading. Paul was one of the 'brighter children from poorer homes', but he was also an anomaly. Despite the inspiring stories, the data overwhelmingly demonstrate that grammar schools 'show a huge bias against poorer pupils' (99% of grammars have an unusually low proportion of pupils from low-income backgrounds).[60]

The high incidence of upward social mobility in the post-war era did *coincide* with the grammar school era, but it wasn't *caused* by it (it was caused by the huge number of new white-collar job opportunities[61]). In the supposed golden age of grammars in the 1950s, even if a child whose parents were classified as 'unskilled working class' did make it into a grammar school, their chances of entering university were only a fifth as good as those of their middle-class classmates.[62]

There is a wide consensus of opposition to the expansion of selective education, which includes education experts, head teachers' organisations, Conservative think tanks and the Chief Inspector of Schools (who said, 'The notion that the poor stand to benefit from the return of grammar schools strikes me as quite palpable tosh and nonsense'[63]).

Evidence and expertise, however, have little effect on policy-making in this area. During the 2017 General Election campaign, the Conservative manifesto included a proposal to expand selective education. During a break from campaigning, Theresa May attended Maidenhead Duck Day, an annual event in her constituency in which toy ducks are raced down the Thames. One of the other attendees was Karen Wespeiser, a local resident who'd taken her children to see the race. Ms Wespeiser, who at the time worked for the National Foundation for Educational

Research, chanced on Mrs May and took the opportunity to confront her with the evidence. 'You can have all the evidence in the world', Wespeiser was told, 'but head teachers have told me grammar schools are good for disadvantaged pupils'[64] (in fact, polling of teachers and head teachers shows 82% are opposed to new grammar schools).[65]

Theresa May is right. You can have all the evidence in the world and still lose. Many people, including some policy-makers, are more influenced by the mythology of grammar schools than the evidence, because substantial numbers of people who went to grammar schools (like Theresa May herself and her former Special Advisor Nick Timothy) went on to positions in which they could make their opinions heard. Grammar school alumni's judgement is skewed by the fact that their schools had an interest in making them believe that the school was indeed 'the making of them', and by the universal human tendency to avoid thinking about any evidence that suggests we're the beneficiaries of unfair advantage or blind luck.[66] Moreover, the mythology of grammar schools works because it makes a heart-warming story, of poor-but-virtuous people whose talent overcame adversity.

But the mythology of grammar schools also overpowers the evidence because opponents of the selective system are failing to make their case anywhere near as effectively. This is something that besets a lot of areas of policy around widening opportunity: much use of evidence, but not much use of the evidence about how to make evidence persuasive.

Opponents of selective education tend to respond to memorable, inspiring stories of talent overcoming adversity with forgettable, dry statistics showing that so-called 'selection by ability' is even less fair than 'selection by postcode', but facts are a poor tool of persuasion. (I've been testing this, using Twitter, by searching for tweets that refer to grammar schools as 'engines of social mobility' and replying to them, with a friendly message attaching research findings. The most common responses are to give an anecdote about someone who benefited from a grammar school education or to say that the research was conducted by people with a 'left-wing bias'. No one has said 'thank you, having seen the facts, I have now changed my mind'.) This is entirely in line with research conducted by psychologists and neurologists showing that human brains reject facts they don't like, by triggering an emotional rather than intellectual response.[67]

The opponents of selective education also make the mistake of using their opponents' language. All sides in the debate refer to 'the grammar school system', which, if you think about it, is an odd name for a system in which the vast majority of children *don't* go to grammar schools. Referring to 'the grammar school system' inclines most people to focus on the popular aspects of the system and forget the less-popular (but larger) elements of what is, in reality, the 'secondary modern system'.

Another way in which opponents of the secondary modern system inadvertently help the system's supporters is by excessive focus on the question of whether 'bright but poor' pupils have fair chances to enter a grammar school. The problem is that the vast majority of voters don't think of themselves as 'poor' (even those who are); they think of themselves as middle income. The children of middle-income families don't have a good or fair chance of getting into grammar school either, but the terms of the debate imply that only 'the poor' are excluded and therefore middle-income families don't have anything to worry about. What middle-income families are rarely told, and should be, is that only the most-privileged tenth of the population have a better-than-evens chance of avoiding the secondary modern, largely due to children who have attended a private 'prep' school being twice as numerous in the grammar schools as in the general population. If you're a child from a middle-income family in the secondary modern system, the odds are against you, four to one.[68]

Spend to segregate...

Maria, like Paul, was one of the anomalies, a child from a low-income home who passed the 11-plus. She passed with a high enough mark to gain entry into the prestigious Manchester High School for Girls. But she still wasn't allowed to go there.

What kept Maria out of Manchester High School for Girls was that although her academic ability was high enough to meet the school's requirements, her parents' income was not: Manchester High School for Girls is a private school. Theoretically, school fees don't have to be an insurmountable barrier for 'brighter children from poorer homes', because bursaries are sometimes available, but Maria's high 11–plus score wasn't quite high enough to qualify for a bursary.

Maria's experience is far from unusual. There is a long history of attempts to make private schools allow access to the 'bright but poor', and there is a long history of these attempts being at worst counterproductive and at best a way of diverting large amounts of money and effort from more effective initiatives.

One of the more notable attempts to allow more non-privileged children into private education was the Assisted Places Scheme created by the Thatcher government. Under this policy, the taxpayer would meet all or part of the school fees of 'bright children from modest backgrounds'.[69]

Having just read about grammar schools, you'll have little difficulty guessing what happened next. Some bright children from modest backgrounds did gain places at prestigious private schools, but lots of privileged parents also found ways to ensure that their children benefited (or that they got a subsidy towards school fees they would have been willing and able to pay anyway). Half of the beneficiaries' fathers were in middle-class jobs, whereas fewer than one in ten were the offspring of manual workers (eligibility was by income, which can be temporarily low – following divorce, for example – or hidden by a skilled accountant).

As with grammar schools, admission to selective private schools is easier for children whose parents have social and cultural resources as well as financial capital. (Maria's failure to qualify for a bursary, for example, may have been avoided if her school or parents had a better idea how the system worked: 'I'd had no preparation. If I'd have seen a couple of past exam papers....') Stuart Alford, whose own social mobility has given him a good perspective on how social confidence rises in line with social status, told me of a relative whose son had a talent for cricket but who narrowly missed out on a prestigious school's sports scholarship, and accepted the decision as final, whereas a more privileged person would have thought 'it just needed a push: challenge the decision'.

While the privileged found ways to take advantage of the Assisted Places Scheme, numerous 'bright children from modest backgrounds' were deterred from applying. Sometimes the deterrent was hidden costs (private schools, like grammar schools, are less numerous than other schools, and are further apart as well as usually being in high-income areas, so the travel costs can be high, as can be other costs such as expensive uniforms and equipment, which privileged parents are affluent enough not to notice and are therefore likely to be regarded as 'not an issue' by the school).

But there are also social and cultural deterrents. Michelle Brook, a Cambridge-educated biochemist now working in policy and research, was persuaded by her family not to take up a scholarship she had been offered 'because "I wouldn't get along with those types of kids"'.[70] The perceived and real potential for humiliation is high if you don't understand the social norms and hierarchies of your new 'tribe' and are too embarrassed to invite potential friends to a home you fear they'll consider 'chavvy'. Paul, whose 11-plus performance *was* good enough for the bursary, says he 'struggled for a couple of years to fit in' but still 'seemed to make the social adaptation more easily than some of my friends.'

Most children whose parents can afford to send them to one of the better-performing private schools can expect them to benefit from plentiful resources[71] and to leave with higher marks than those whose parents cannot – in other words, to use finances to overcome fairness. Beneficiaries of bursaries, however, appear to struggle to attain the benefits as fully as their more-privileged classmates (perhaps an inability of the school staff to understand the needs of pupils unlike themselves?), with the result that, as the author of a long-term study of the Assisted Places Scheme found, 'overall these pupils did worse than might be expected'.[72]

As we have seen (and will continue to see in subsequent chapters), the segregation of pupils of different social and economic classes into different schools is a major barrier to widening opportunity, and attempts to segregate children by ability rather than privilege have tended to backfire. In the next section, we look at some attempts to widen opportunity by *desegregating* schools.

... or invest to integrate

At the beginning of the 21st century, London's state schools were the worst in the country. GCSE results lagged well behind the rest of the UK. There was a general consensus, says the former Commissioner of London Schools, that they were 'places to be avoided if you wanted a good education for your children'. The proportion of London parents sending their children outside the state system was almost double the national average.[73] Today, London's school children achieve the *best* GCSE scores in the country, and the least-advantaged children have made the most improvement. The way this was done holds lessons that apply way beyond the M25.

Various ways have been tried to overcome the forces of segregation, in which children's options are narrowed in the pursuit of widening parents' choice. Allocating children to schools within their local authority by purely random lottery has its downsides (such as long travel times for some), and requires politicians to have the grit to face down a well-resourced and media-savvy minority who argue that 'Middle-class families[74] are being penalised because of political correctness'.[75]

Measures such as requiring schools' catchment areas to be redrawn to ensure mixed intakes should be implemented, so that our children's freedom to choose their futures are not constrained by a narrow insight into the lives of others, and so that children whose parents have the social and cultural resources to enforce high standards are present in all schools. But these are not the measures by which London improved.

London improved as a result of political will, driven by Estelle Morris (then Education Secretary), and with the collaboration of others in government and elsewhere, which secured significant funding for strategic, evidence-based programmes such as the London Challenge initiative of 2003-11,[76] and combining that support for schools with putting them under 'relentless pressure'[77] to raise standards.

The experience in London demonstrates the need for and benefits of investing in schools. But 'more money' isn't enough. In recent decades, investing in schools has meant that minimum standards have risen, but the attainment gap at GCSE between the most-affluent and the least-affluent children has hardly narrowed, because everyone has moved forward at a similar rate, leaving the best-off about as far ahead as they always were.[78] Various policies have been introduced to try to level the playing field, such as Every Child a Reader (introduced under the Labour government in the late 2000s, to help pupils who initially struggled with reading, like Dean, to catch up[79]) and the Pupil Premium (introduced by the coalition government in 2011, giving extra funding to schools for each 'disadvantaged' child[80]).

These initiatives to help 'disadvantaged' children are also beneficial to the other children with whom they go to school: international data show that countries who have been most successful in keeping the gaps between the test scores of children from different income groups low have also been most successful in keeping overall performance high. We can also see this phenomenon in the UK, where the distribution of state spending on education – which in the 1980s disproportionately went to children from better-off backgrounds – has been shifted, so that the less well-off now get a fairer slice[81] and, as a result, there have been across-the-board improvements in educational attainment.[82]

These initiatives are, however, vulnerable to funding pressures. Pupil Premium, for example, is now widely used to offset schools' overall budget gaps rather than being specifically targeted where it is needed.[83]

Properly funded and well-targeted spending on education is necessary, but it isn't a panacea. The US state that spends the lowest amount per pupil on education also has some of highest rates of social mobility (the capital of that state, in fact, has the highest rates of absolute upward social mobility in the whole country). In the next section, we'll find out why.

Battles won on playing fields...

In 2017 Alvin Carpio became one of *Forbes* magazines' '30 under 30' of 'the brightest young entrepreneurs, innovators and game changers'. He is a member of the World Economic Forum's 'Global Shapers' group, and already has a more impressive CV than most people will have at retirement. I first met him when we were both speaking at UpRising, a leadership development organisation working with people like Alvin ('talented young people from diverse and under-represented backgrounds'[84]). His father died when Alvin was nine, leaving him and his sister in the care of his mother, a Filipina ex-pat who worked as a cleaner.

Alvin's mum, like my dad, could have been accused of pursuing 'ideas above her station'. As is often the case with migrants (international or inter-class), their ideas of 'respectability' can appear old-fashioned to natives (always wearing a tie, for example). In Mrs Carpio's case, respectability was to be gained by spending some of what little money she had on piano lessons for her son. Improbably, the investment paid off. Alvin's piano teacher happened to be a sixth form student at the – non fee-charging but very prestigious – London Oratory School, known for having taught the offspring of prominent politicians, including Tony Blair and Nick Clegg. That boy encouraged Alvin to apply, successfully, for entry to the school.

What David Lammy calls his 'Billy Elliot moment' was also the consequence of his extra-curricular activities. As a boy, David was a talented chorister. The church he attended knew how to spot talent and also knew how to grow it, by helping David apply for, and win, a scholarship to 'a quite posh school'. The quite posh school in question was The King's School in Peterborough (also known as the Cathedral School), a part-selective state school with boarding facilities for out-of-town pupils like David. It was 'a passport out of one of Britain's toughest communities', he says, and into an 'academically strong' environment with 'lots of role models'. In David's case, the academic resources, and academic expectations, were not the only benefit of being a King's boy. Being a chorister provided an experience that sounds remarkably similar to a 'positive mindset' programme, what David describes as 'experiencing excellence' in a sustained and immersive way: 'You know what hard work is, practising as a chorister twice a day, every day for four years.'

David is not unique in finding that extra-curricular activity contributed to the development of an outlook conducive to social mobility. Long-term studies in the US have found students who participated in such activities had a stronger sense of control over their lives, a more positive attitude to school and were held in higher regard by teachers.[85] In the UK, 'outdoor adventure learning' projects focus on teamwork and problem-solving rather than academic learning, but they also have an academic benefit: pupils who participated were found to make 'approximately four additional months' progress over the course of a year', with 'vulnerable' learners gaining the most.[86] The management expert Louise Ashley suggests that some extra-curricular activities can allow participants to engage assertively with authority in a way that is otherwise impossible for children who have a difficult relationship with school (as children from underprivileged backgrounds often have).[87] In addition, participation in such activities can help with applications to universities and employers who regard them as evidence of a 'rounded character'.

But although extra-curricular activities can offer alternative routes to opportunity, which circumvent some of the psychological or social barriers often found in education, there are barriers to accessing these routes. When I asked Maria if extra-curricular activities played a part in her story, she pointed to an obvious barrier: 'Oh, God no. We didn't have the money.' Music lessons were available at Maria's secondary school, but 'you had to provide your own instruments. The only reason I can swim is because junior school offered free swimming lessons.' In surveys, 40% of parents report having to pay for their children to participate in schools' extra-curricular activities.[88] Unsurprisingly, the highest-income parents are almost four times more likely to pay for such activities than the lowest-income group.[89]

Ruth Holdaway, Chief Executive of the charity Women in Sport, reels off a list of barriers to participation, which include some financial factors (membership fees, travel costs, equipment, access to a car), but also other barriers. If your parents' working hours make them unable to drive you around, if you live outside of a big city, or if you are female (there are fewer sports clubs for girls) or have a disability, then the range of activities accessible to you will be much more limited, so you're less likely to find something you like.[90] Holdaway also mentions another factor: social confidence. A study of the Duke of Edinburgh's Award scheme pointed out a similar effect, that 'the motivated and self-confident are more likely to become involved'.[91] Unfortunately, children and young people from less-privileged backgrounds are most likely to lack this confidence, especially in situations that involve interacting with those of a different class.

Another deterrent to taking part in an extra-curricular activity can be a well-meaning parent who discourages their offspring from taking part, in a misguided attempt to improve their life chances. Lewis Iwu, formerly Director of the Fair Education Alliance (and himself a notable example of social mobility), has encountered this problem, personally and professionally. Many parents, says Iwu, have a 'relentless focus on education', telling their children not to be distracted from schoolwork, not realising that '"what exams does my child need to pass?" ... is the wrong question.' Paul, whose having won a bursary to a private school put in him an environment where the value of extra-curricular activity to personal development was championed, contrasts the two cultures: in his private school 'it was made clear that focus on exams was not enough, you had to play music, to be an army cadet or whatever', whereas in state schools 'there's kids working their arses off but not getting jobs in places like this [gesturing at the offices of the City firms whose offices surround the cafe in which we're sitting] because they weren't captain of rugby.'

Even when non-privileged children do overcome the many cultural and financial barriers to participation in extra-curricular activities, they are likely to find themselves separated from their privileged peers, who are likely to be involved in different activities in different places. Privileged parents use their social networks to find activities patronised by families with similar backgrounds, and use their money to give their children experiences that are out of reach for others, reducing the chance of cross-class meetings like the one that led Alvin (among others) towards previously unsuspected opportunities.

But extra-curricular activities can be delivered in a way that isn't segregated. The US state I mentioned, the one that spends the lowest amount on education but has some of highest rates of social mobility, is Utah. As you probably know, Utah is the home of Mormonism, and the idea of community is one the Mormons take very seriously. Volunteering is strongly encouraged, as is social mixing. According to economists in Utah's Brigham Young University, one of the keys to Utah's success comes down to 'exposing [school] students to social networks that aren't like theirs', giving examples such as an affluent church ward that had 'recently deliberately expanded its boundaries to include a nearby trailer park'.[92]

The conditions prevailing in Utah cannot be replicated in the UK (and liberal-minded atheists like me wouldn't want to try: Utah is very religious, very conservative and ethnically very homogeneous). This raises a question of whether social integration can be improved in a more pluralist setting such as the UK. One organisation that is trying is The Challenge, one of the providers of the National Citizen Service (NCS) programme. In addition to building young people's confidence and employment skills, The Challenge's main focus is on building a more integrated society. The Challenge's Fiona Stone tells me that the organisation creates 'intentionally socially mixed' groups, and gives an example of a youth club at Stepney City Farm, which includes private school pupils alongside those who've been permanently excluded from school. The work of The Challenge is rooted in 'contact theory', which posits that building a team ethos helps people relate to each other, and to get a (hopefully inspiring) insight into each other's aspirations: 'someone like them is doing it, so they think they can'. NCS can also point to results, including that pupils from disadvantaged areas who participate in NCS are 50% more likely to go to university than their classmates.[93]

These figures should be treated with some caution: it may be that NCS disproportionately attracts participants who may live in 'deprived' areas but whose families *already* have greater financial, social or cultural resources than their neighbours and are therefore more likely to go to university anyway. Nor is the social mixing facilitated by NCS an adequate substitute for the longer-term social mixing that can – but too often doesn't – happen in schools, but there are grounds for hope that it can play a part.

Basic provisions or extra rations

A typical mid-morning break at Minsthorpe, the high school in which I spent the late 1980s. A 1960s comprehensive whose monochrome modernist buildings were supplemented with pre-fabricated 'temporary' classrooms, which remained temporary for decades. By the admin office there's a line of teenagers, displaying a downcast anxiety that suggests they're about to be disciplined, but the group lacks the defiant swaggerers usually found in such a gathering. This is the free school meals queue – not the queue to get the meal, the queue to get the vouchers to be presented at lunchtime – which is in full view of everyone in the schoolyard. The public humiliation these teenagers are suffering is a punishment for being brought up in a 'deprived' household.

Research published in 2012 found that of the million children in the UK eligible for free school meals, almost one-in-three did not actually take them, largely to avoid the shame.[94]

Providing free school meals to all pupils, regardless of income, is controversial because it involves significant expense, and is unlikely to be as cost-effective as other programmes such as breakfast clubs.[95] However, when free meals have been introduced on an experimental basis, one of the results has been to show that it isn't just families eligible for free school meals who are struggling to keep their children properly fed. When local authorities in Durham and Newham piloted free school meals for all primary school children in 2009-11, take-up was approximately 90%. Following the pilots, the standard of schoolwork improved because children were better nourished and therefore better able to concentrate. This did not just improve the schoolwork of the pupils who were eligible for free meals; the schoolwork of children *not* usually eligible for free meals also improved. At Key Stages 1 and 2, the *overall* progress of pupils in the pilot areas was between four and eight weeks' ahead of those in neighbouring areas.[96]

Food isn't the only basic human requirement that many families struggle to provide and that affects children's ability to fully benefit from education. According to Shelter, more than four in ten Britons live in homes that do not reach acceptable standards of cleanliness, safety and space.[97] Children in low-quality housing are at increased risk of respiratory illnesses and sleep problems, which can mean lost school days and reduced ability to concentrate in class.[98] For a high and rising proportion of families, including those who would never consider themselves 'deprived', providing each child with their own bedroom where they can focus on their homework is simply unaffordable. For families in receipt of Housing Benefit (most of whom are in work) the 'Bedroom Tax' rules mean children are expected to share with a sibling until they're 16 years old.[99] Some of my interviewees, like Joanne, told me that their local library had been a refuge of 'peace and quiet', but libraries may not be conveniently located, and in many cases, funding cuts are restricting their opening hours or closing them completely.[100]

Parents' influence on their children's performance at school isn't limited to their ability to provide a clean, safe, spacious home with a well-stocked kitchen. It includes their ability to play a role in the educational process itself. Research by numerous academics has found 'at-home good parenting' to have a huge influence on children's attainment, which, at primary level, is 'much bigger than differences associated with variations in the quality of schools'.[101] For some parents, their commitment to 'good parenting' is undermined by circumstance. Their desire to help their children through school can be frustrated by anti-social working hours and health problems that are disproportionately associated with low-status work. Parents with few academic qualifications may find it hard to help their children with homework in subjects they themselves found intimidating, and inadvertently convey a confidence-destroying message to their child that 'this is difficult, even mum/dad is struggling'. Initiatives such as 'family learning' programmes (involving both children and parents) have been shown to help families to support their children's learning and development[102] and less-educated parents are responding positively: they are now almost as likely to help with homework as their more highly educated counterparts.[103] However, while both middle-income and low-income parents have raised their game, high-income families can stay ahead by buying in 'extra rations' in the form of one-to-one tuition.

An additional difficulty faced by parents in low-status jobs is more subtle. Without realising it, they are being trained to help their children learn in a not-very-effective way. Low-paid, low-status employees are typically expected to do as they are told (and behaving otherwise can have serious consequences), but doing as you're told isn't a particularly effective strategy for learning. Pupils who *don't* just do as they are told, but instead set goals for their own learning outcomes and devise their own strategies to achieve those outcomes (what to read, who to ask and how to marshal the information) tend to learn better. In one experiment in West Yorkshire, 10- to 12-year-olds in selected schools were trained in this 'self-regulated strategy development' technique, and were found to have made nine months' additional progress compared to those in schools that did not participate. It helped the children to feel, and to be, more in control of their learning.[104]

The effect of children's home lives on their education, including the effects of the living standards and working conditions of their parents, can be hard for policy-makers to fully comprehend. Strategies to improve children's education tend to focus on matters within the remit of the Secretary of State for Education. However, a child spends more of their 'school years' in the home than in school, and children's home lives affect the education of children in the UK to a greater degree than is usual for a developed country. Professor Garaint Johnes, one of an international team that analysed pupils' performances in different countries, writes that in the UK, 'educational performance is very much driven by social factors. So while tweaking educational policy may help or hinder at the margin, it is social policy that really has the power to secure large gains in educational attainment'.[105]

But one more thing also plays a role in how well children do at school, something neither in the home nor the schoolyard....

Neighbourhood

In the mid-1990s the US Department of Housing and Urban Development ran an experimental initiative called 'Moving to Opportunity'. As part of the initiative, families living in 'high-poverty housing projects' were randomly assigned into groups. One of the groups was given nothing, and continued to live in high-poverty housing projects. Another group was given housing vouchers, which could only be used to move to specific areas selected for their lower poverty rates. The researchers who had designed the experiment expected to find that the neighbourhood makes a difference, and in some ways, these expectations were confirmed: within a few years, the mental and physical health of the families who had moved to lower-poverty areas was 'greatly improved'. However, the researchers were also expecting the people who moved to lower-poverty areas would have better chances of getting a well-paid job, and they found no such effect. There was 'no significant impacts on the earnings and employment rates'.[106] If anything, people were being paid *less* after the move than they were before.

The experiment appeared to have demonstrated that the neighbourhood in which we live affects how healthy and happy we are, but not our financial life chances. Until 2015, that is, when three economists carried out a new study that found that people who had moved *were* earning more – lots more – than those who had stayed: they were being paid 31% more and were also more likely to have a college education.[107] So what explains the very different results? Which sets of studies are correct?

Both are correct. The different results are explained by the fact that the different researchers had studied different groups. The earlier researchers had only looked at people who had made the move when they were adults, whereas the later study only looked at people who had done so as children.

For adults, changing neighbourhood (even to a more affluent one) can damage their earning power by, for example, severing ties to people who would otherwise be a source of word-of-mouth job opportunities. For children, however, wellbeing and development improves if their neighbourhood feels safe and friendly and offers places to play and explore, whereas wellbeing is damaged by living in places that are ugly, polluted, noisy or where people and traffic feel – or are – threatening.[108] Where we live shapes our mental and physical fitness, which, in turn, shapes our life chances.

Another way in which our neighbourhood determines our life chances is through the people we meet. Across the world, neighbourhoods that are more segregated (that is, that offer little chance of meaningful interaction with people from other social and economic classes) have lower rates of social mobility.[109] There are efforts to address this: local authorities such as Hackney are not only working with private sector partners to create neighbourhoods with a mixture of social housing tenants and homeowners,[110] but are also requiring that services are shared, so that facilities such as the nursery at the Woodberry Down estate caters for all the residents' children.[111] But existing housing, and some new-build developments, are becoming more segregated along class lines. The geographer Danny Dorling has written extensively of Britain's 'growing social class segregation',[112] in which the most privileged are increasingly living apart from the rest of us. This means that if you are a middle-income or low-income family, the odds of your children mixing with privileged children, let alone striking up a firm enough relationship to accompany them on the paths to opportunity (as Jackie did), is lessened.

Those paths to opportunity, and the choices our children make about which path to choose as they prepare to leave their school years behind, are where we will look next.

FOUR

Choosing a path

Inspiration and aspiration

London, 2012: something remarkable happened. It happened at Elizabeth Garrett Anderson School, an all-girls comprehensive secondary school 15 minutes' walk east of King's Cross station. Surrounded by social housing estates, nine-tenths of the school's pupils are from a black or minority ethnic background and a high proportion are the children of refugees or asylum-seekers. The remarkable thing that happened in 2012 was that its pupils' GCSE results went up, and they went up dramatically: equivalent to each pupil moving from eight 'B' grades to four 'A' grades and four 'A★' grades. Girls who'd never mentioned university before began talking of their intention to study at Oxford.

The story behind the remarkable rise in educational attainment and academic ambition at this particular school begins three years earlier, when the pupils of Elizabeth Garrett Anderson attended an assembly that included a guest speaker. It isn't unusual for schools to host such speakers, but it is unusual for the guest to be First Lady of the United States, which Michelle Obama had recently become.

We have to be careful not to jump to conclusions. Just because Michelle Obama's visit *preceded* the school's booming exam results doesn't mean it *caused* them, but Professor Simon Burgess – who has published an analysis of the phenomenon – thinks it did. Burgess' study of the effect of Michelle Obama's visit concludes that the increase in exam performance following Michelle Obama's interaction with the school is no coincidence, and that this demonstrates that 'inspiration and aspiration and effort are important, potentially very important'.[1]

Also in London in 2012, a far larger project was underway, also intended to inspire. One of the reasons national and local politicians had been keen for London to bid for the 2012 Olympic Games was the potential that such events had to raise the nation's sporting aspirations. When the bid was launched eight years earlier, a target was announced to motivate a million extra people to play sport regularly, and by 2015 there *were* more people taking part in athletics, cycling and gymnastics. But the rest of the Olympic story wasn't so good: the number of people taking part in 15 other sports actually declined. Even in Stratford, where the Olympic Park is located, researchers found 'no difference' in activity levels.[2] The Olympics have had an undeniable legacy, prompting huge redevelopment of the Lea Valley area of East London, but inspiring people to take up sports? Not so much.

So what was the difference between Michelle Obama and the Olympics? Why do some things appear to have the power to inspire people to change the course of their lives while others do not? That's what this chapter is about. Specifically, it is about the choices we and our children make in our teenage years – typically between the ages of 14 and 18 – which often set the direction for the rest of our lives and careers. The next two sections look specifically at the role of 'inspiration' and 'aspiration'.

'Someone like me'

Michael Sheen is a famous British actor, as you probably already know. You might not know that he was brought up in the same town that produced (among others) Rob Brydon, Anthony Hopkins and Richard Burton. It's not unusual to find 'clusters' of actors who were brought up in the same place, because actors disproportionately come from certain (affluent) areas. But Sheen, Brydon, Hopkins et al are not from an affluent area; they are from Port Talbot, a South Wales steelmaking town that the BBC has described as 'one of the most deprived communities in the UK today'.[3]

Port Talbot's unlikely status as a breeding ground of famous actors (and a few opera singers) is the subject of a book by a history professor from the same town. Professor Angela John says one of the reasons Michael Sheen became an actor was *because* Hopkins and Burton had also done so. In Port Talbot, knowing an actor wasn't unusual, and becoming an actor was something that seemed attainable, something that could happen to 'someone like me'.[4]

This is part of the explanation for Michelle Obama's ability to inspire the girls of Elizabeth Garrett Anderson School. Most people don't think of the former First Lady as 'someone like me', but she was able to persuade the schoolgirls that she was like them, for two reasons. First, Michelle Obama is a world-class politician, whose part in her husband's campaign for the presidency was a big part of its success, and part of the reason she is so effective a politician is her ability to 'connect'. Second, she came from a background the girls could recognise; like most of them, she was from a minority ethnic community and (as she told them), 'wasn't raised with wealth or resources or any social standing to speak of'.[5] In studies of young people who plan to pursue 'ideas above their station' such as entering medical school, the importance of having encouragement and guidance from 'someone they identified with (and who could identify with them)' crops up repeatedly.[6]

Way before Paul Monekosso Cleal became a partner in a major international company, he had his own 'someone like me' to act as a role model. I have already mentioned that Paul's mum was, in Paul's words, a 'very poor' single parent after Paul's father, a medical student from Cameroon, returned to West Africa. What I didn't mention is that although his father was mostly absent, his influence wasn't. 'I had some notion that my dad was a doctor with a job of some importance', says Paul of the man who would later become the Cameroonian Health Minister, 'and that made a big difference to my self-esteem as a child, reinforced by the very occasional meeting with him and books on Africa that he left me. All of this certainly helped me to cope with racism at the time and I think made me more determined to progress.'

Stories of deprived individuals with high-status relatives are surprisingly common among socially mobile individuals. In

2016, Kidane Cousland, a boy who was 'raised in a Tottenham council house' and who 'spent time living in a bug-infested bed and breakfast' made the news when he was awarded the Sword of Honour for graduating top of his cohort at Sandhurst, the British Army's officer training academy.[7] Cousland's story was even more newsworthy because he wasn't the only high-achiever in his family. One of his brothers, Solomon, was the first black British dancer in the Royal Ballet and the other, Amartey, is an artist whose paintings hang in the royal palaces of Dubai. By any measure, what the brothers have achieved is impressive for a family from any background, let alone a 'tough housing estate'.[8] But theirs wasn't a typical family on the estate. Their mother, Maryam Golding, is a social worker and historian, a former convent school girl, herself the daughter of a military officer and journalist.[9]

What is happening in these cases is that although the families involved experienced a big drop in their financial or occupational standing, they retained a lot of their non-financial resources (cultural knowledge, expectations, social confidence or contacts) that their children can draw on to persuade themselves and others of their potential and to navigate through the un-signposted roads to opportunity. The families that are rich in these non-financial resources – which sociologists refer to as 'cultural capital' and 'social capital' – are usually also rich in financial terms,[10] but there are some people (like Kidane Cousland and the actors of Port Talbot) whose low financial status belies some valuable cultural or social assets. This is surprisingly common among the children of ex-pats, who are more likely to experience upward social mobility than the 'white British' population because their parents typically took lower-ranking jobs in the UK than they had in their country of origin: the 'social climbing' of individuals is actually 'social rebounding' for families. Simon Burgess, whose study of the 'Michelle Obama effect' opens this chapter, suggests that the higher incidence of upward social mobility among the children of ex-pats may also be at least partly related to the 'mindset' effect of having a parent who, by overcoming the considerable challenges of migration, is an ever-present demonstration of the possibility of taking control over one's own life.

But Kidane Cousland and the actors of Port Talbot are anomalies. Most children from ordinary towns throughout the UK don't get to see people like themselves becoming commissioned military officers or members of the Royal Ballet or actors. (Sometimes, people from ordinary backgrounds are found in such roles, but their background is hidden, as with the working-class actor Maxine Peake, who was told to 'sound more posh' when portraying a barrister.[11]) Lynne Truss, the novelist and author of the unlikely-sounding 'bestseller about punctuation', *Eats shoots and leaves*, and who grew up in 'a small council house', expresses this feeling that some careers are not for 'people like me' when she says, 'I always wanted to write, but thought I hadn't been born with the right certificate'.[12]

Children looking for relatable role models may find their parents and teachers have few examples to present them with. An example is Joanne Martin, now a student at the University of Aberdeen School of Medicine, who was raised in Glasgow, in 'a flat in a small block in a council estate' that had 'a bad reputation'. Joanne's school, which she describes as 'one of the lowest performing in Glasgow', made efforts to highlight the accomplishments of past pupils, but had a limited range to draw on: 'there was a wall in school, with achievements of people who'd done things previously. One or two dentistry, not really medicine. A few had been to university.' Another of my interviewees, Stuart Alford, now a barrister, remembers similar attempts by his school to showcase past pupils' achievements, including someone who had gone into law as a legal executive (which has a rather less glamorous-sounding job description than a barrister). Stuart contrasts this with the experience of his wife, Sylvia, who's 'what you might call posh. Very expensive private school.' At Sylvia's school, he says, 'they all wanted to become lawyers and there was a presumption they could.' Sylvia's classmate's parents included 'a minister in government, a lord chamberlain, people in the foreign office, lawyers, judges....'

Role modelling starts early. 'When we were very young', says Maria, 'we had to draw pictures of the jobs we were going to do. But we weren't given a choice, we were told. All the boys had to draw a footballer. All the girls had to draw a nurse. I remember thinking, who are you to tell me what I'm going to be?' Another of my interviewees, Stuart Sime, tells me that a teacher discouraged his brother's interest in a medical career, 'because nursing was almost entirely a female occupation': the idea that a working-class child might become a doctor was apparently even more unthinkable than the idea that boy might become a nurse. On the other hand, *positive* messages can also start early. A project in a primary school on a large council estate in the former mining town of Barnsley, for example, drafted in volunteers to help children with reading, but it achieved much more than an increase in literacy. The fact that the volunteers came from a range of professions helped the pupils see that their schoolwork could actually be a path to a career. The main benefit of the project was not in technical reading skills, says the founder of Education and Employers, the charity that ran the pilot, but in 'improving their motivation and attitudes to learning'.[13]

It's easy to dismiss people's tendency to follow the same career paths as their family, friends, classmates and neighbours as 'aspiration failure' or 'herd mentality'. But herd mentality isn't confined to poor or middle-income families (although I've never heard a privileged person's decision to follow the same highly paid career path as their parents dismissed as bovine passivity). And this fear of stepping outside the norms of our group exists for good evolutionary reasons: for early humans, unfamiliar paths through the forest presented serious risks,[14] and today, taking unfamiliar educational or career paths can entail serious financial and social risks (as later chapters will show). We all tend to forget that our own comfort zones are only comfortable because they are familiar. In the next section, we will see one of the ways that the fear of the unfamiliar territory of aspiration can be broken down.

'Yes we can'

Joanne Martin, whom we met in the previous section, didn't let the lack of relatable role models hold back her aspirations. At the age of 16 she had decided to be a doctor. But when Joanne mentioned her ambition to her teachers, 'some laughed, said "don't be silly". I had to say "I'm being serious".' Some academics have been equally 'encouraging'. One professor, for example, has written that 'UK medical students tend to come from higher socioeconomic classes, perhaps not surprisingly, as social class correlates with intellectual ability'.[15]

What Joanne was encountering is a common experience of people from non-privileged backgrounds, not just a lack of 'people like me' to act as role models but also some explicit or implicit messages that certain career paths are beyond their capabilities.

This may be another reason Michelle Obama appears to have had a genuinely inspiring effect on the girls of Elizabeth Garrett Anderson School: her ability to persuade them that getting into prestigious universities and 'elite' careers was *within* their capabilities. She did this by not only presenting an aspiration – which the girls could have interpreted as empty feel-good rhetoric – but by also mapping out some of the landmarks along the route to achieving it. Michelle Obama didn't just deliver the usual feel-good speech to her audience, she also arranged for some of them to accompany her on a visit to the University of Oxford, to demystify the place and to tell them, in her own words, that 'you belong here'.[16]

Mapping out some of the landmarks along the route to a destination that previously appeared unreachable is another key difference between Michelle Obama's success in inspiring schoolgirls to raise their aspirations and the Olympics' failure to inspire Brits to rise from the sofa. The broadcaster and psychology lecturer Claudia Hammond has written that Olympians may make us feel more intimidated than inspired. Hammond says that she was very aware, while watching sprinters 'moving at speeds which I had never before seen humans move', that their unattainable feats 'had nothing in common with the extra sprint I might do when I go on a jog and am in sight of home'.[17] For Hammond, the takeaway message from the Olympics was 'yes they can, but you can't'.

The spoken and unspoken messages we pick up about what constitutes a realistic ambition are subtle and pervasive, barely understood by those who hear them or those who deliver them. For example, the high proportion of instances in popular culture in which the word 'scientist' is preceded with the word 'brilliant' appears to intimidate some people away from scientific careers:

most people aren't immodest enough to consider themselves brilliant. This effect is especially strong for individuals whose perceptions of science have not been coloured by interactions with real scientists who display human flaws rather than alien brilliance.[18]

So it appears that a lack of relatable role models and a lack of encouragement are creating limited aspirations in young people from families with limited incomes, and therefore aspiration-raising should be used to improve their life-chances, right?

Apparently not. The frequent warnings about a 'collapse of aspiration'[19] appear to be based on assumptions, and are contradicted by a wide range of studies showing little or no difference in the ambitions of pupils from different social and economic groups (for example, 95% of 10- to 15-year-olds from both high-income and low-income backgrounds want to continue in full-time education after leaving school).[20] The idea that raising aspirations is the key to improving outcomes is also at odds with evaluations of aspiration-raising initiatives, which have found them to have 'little to no positive impact'.[21]

At first glance, this seems contradictory. The evidence of high aspiration among non-privileged children appears to be inconsistent with the low numbers of such individuals entering 'elite' careers and educational institutions, and the ineffectiveness of aspiration-rising initiatives looks to be at odds with the examples of the power of encouraging relatable role models.

Part of the answer may be that young people's aspirations are strong, but their knowledge and confidence about the steps necessary to achieve those aspirations is weaker. Another part of the answer is that high aspirations are frustrated by practical barriers that stand in the way of the would-be socially mobile. The following sections explore the practical barriers faced by people from ordinary backgrounds pursuing extraordinary aspirations.

Improbability drives

On the House of Commons terrace, overlooking the Thames, David Lammy was telling me how one of his teachers had discouraged him from 'unrealistic' career aspirations: 'at seven years old I wanted to be a barrister. Mrs Parker tried to convince me I wanted to be a fireman. My reaction was to prove her wrong. Some people couldn't get past their own perceptions of....'

It took me a moment to realise that he'd said something odd. How did he know he wanted to be a barrister when he was seven? Surely most seven-year-olds don't even know what a barrister is?

The reason David knew what a barrister was at seven years old is that his mother left him to watch television when she was busy (which, as a single mum with multiple jobs, was quite often), and one of the programmes David watched was the ITV drama series *Crown Court*. The seven-year-old David decided to be a barrister, and as an adult he actually did become a barrister before becoming an MP. If David's mother had set the television to the BBC, things might have been very different.

David's experience might not appear to offer useful lessons about how today's seven-year olds could be inspired towards ambitious career plans. Most seven-year-olds who watched *Crown Court* did so under sufferance, and were not inspired towards a legal career. David's story is idiosyncratic and improbable.

But David wasn't the only one of my interviewees for whom something improbable played a pivotal role in their lives. The more people told me their stories, the more it became apparent that it was normal for the plots of their stories to hinge on an unlikely encounter, an anomalous experience, or an unusual decision. It is highly probable that socially mobile people have had something improbable happen to them.

In Jane's case, her becoming the only girl in her school year to go to university hinged on the right teacher having been assigned to her English class, and to that year's curriculum including a book that caught her imagination. 'We did Austen: *Persuasion*. I loved it. I told Mr Clarke I loved it, that it was like I could hear her speaking like she'd speak now, like she was transcending time. That woke him up, like, "what did you say?!?"... I wrote an essay one day on Jane Austen. He said "that essay was brilliant".' It just so happened that Mr Clarke also taught part time at the University of York. 'He said he'd taken it to his university class and said "this is what you're aiming for". From that moment onwards the word "university" popped into my head. When he praised the essay so much, I was being told that my perception, my understanding was at a degree level. It gave me a lot of confidence ... that's when I realised I had ability.'

For Mark Dixon, a boy feeling restricted by life in small town Essex in the 1970s, his paper round offered a glimpse into another possible life. Mark had access to broadsheet newspapers, and – unusually for a schoolboy – he found the business sections interesting: 'I'd read the *Sunday Times* business news. It looked exciting. Looked like real life.'

For others it was about the right people being in the right place at the right time. For Jackie Doyle-Price, the people who were in the right place at the right time to help awaken the political consciousness that would eventually lead to her becoming a Conservative politician were the left-wingers who controlled Sheffield City Council in the 1980s. Those left-wing councillors did 'everything they could', says Jackie, 'to bully my parents into not buying their council house.' Jackie was encouraged to develop her political consciousness into political involvement by another '1980s-style left-winger': a teacher who engaged Jackie in 'vigorous discussions' and told her, '"you ought to go out and participate in democracy".'

But others went through their entire school career without finding their inspiration. Jackie's fellow MP Angela Rayner, the Shadow Education Secretary, 'left school with nothing', and only found educational inspiration years later, through Unionlearn (a TUC programme): 'once I found something I was interested in', she says, 'I excelled.'[22]

The prevalence of improbable opportunities playing pivotal roles raises the question of whether the improbable can be made more probable. Can we create what the education and careers expert Johnny Rich calls 'planned serendipity'?

Yes we can.

The chance events that captured the imagination of my interviewees, which set them on the path to opportunities in education and careers that they previously hadn't suspected the existence of, are really just examples of people being presented with new ideas in an interesting way.

Encouragingly, in recent years, teachers and educationalists have been putting in a lot of effort to present new ideas in a way that catches the imagination. Take chemistry as an example. My own experience of chemistry lessons in the 1980s was of attempting to remember facts about the properties of various substances, occasionally enlivened by the teacher setting fire to something; none of which seemed to have a practical application, let alone a relevance to possible careers. But more recently, when I was sitting in on a chemistry lesson at Canons High School in Edgware, West London, the teacher opened the lesson with a mystery: why was a used disposable nappy the only object not to be destroyed in a house fire? I found myself wanting to know the answer, and it was explained that the nappy contained a moisture-retaining polymer that prevented it from becoming dry enough to burn, a fact that had prompted chemists to develop non-evaporating sprays to extinguish fires. I started to think that chemistry sounded like an interesting job.

However, the children who stand to benefit most from experiences that make subjects like chemistry relevant, practical and fun are the least likely to be given the opportunity. The less privileged your family is, the less likely your children are to be offered 'informal science learning experiences' such as trips to museums or factories, because the trips cost money and because 'lower-attaining' students are least likely to be offered the opportunity to participate.[23] In arts subjects, too, the opportunity to experience inspiration is restricted, and often becoming more restricted. Michael Sheen, having been inspired by the famous acting alumni of Port Talbot, was able to develop his interest in acting classes at school, but as he recently explained to the All-Party Parliamentary Group on Social Mobility, the school's drama department has now been cut; 'these opportunities', he says 'no longer exist'.[24]

What to study?

I didn't realise it at the time, but at the age of 14, I inadvertently decided which subject I'd study at university.

It happened like this. When my classmates and I were 'choosing our options' to study at GCSE, there was little sense that the implications of our choices might stretch beyond the next two years. Some of the teachers had mentioned that some subjects, like Maths, would 'stand us in good stead', but apart from that, we didn't have much to go on. The day we made our choices, we were each given a form with a choice of subjects (subject to some restrictions: at least one Science, at least one of the 'Humanities'...), and left to tick our preferred boxes. One of the lads in my class asked me 'what's Sociology?' My answer was informed by something half-remembered from that week's news (which, in retrospect, was probably reporting on the *British Social Attitudes* survey): 'it's about whether people think it's alright to have kids if you're not married, that sort of thing.' There was a brief pause while he processed this information, then, 'that sounds alright', and he put a tick against it. I chose the subjects I knew I liked and a new one, Economics, which I liked the sound of. Two years later, like the majority of the minority of my classmates who stayed on into sixth form, I chose A-levels based on which subjects had given me the best GCSE scores (in my case, English, Economics and History). Two years after that, like most of the few from my school who planned to go to university, I chose between degree courses that reflected my A-levels, and having got the idea that English didn't offer many career prospects, I narrowed my options to 'Economics and History' or 'Economic History'.

Five years after my classmates and I conducted our life-changing exercise in ill-informed box-ticking, I was at the University of Hull, studying Economic and Social History. I was talking to someone taking an Economics degree. He told me he had had a plan to work in finance since he was 15, and with the help of his parents and teachers, he'd identified which degree course would advance that plan, and what to study at school to best prepare him for that course. This struck me as a clever and novel idea.

The experience of inadvertently making decisions as a teenager that will later restrict your choices is a common one. Like me, Maria hadn't been encouraged to develop a long-term career plan, and made important decisions based on little more than an assessment of which of the subjects she'd recently studied she felt suited to. As a sixth former she'd been good at Maths, but wanted something that felt more practical, and therefore applied to study Engineering at university, having had little chance to consider whether she really wanted to be an engineer.

Large numbers of individuals who attempt to access opportunities (such as applying to certain university courses) are informed that they really ought to have made a different decision some years ago. Researchers who interviewed would-be medical students from non-privileged backgrounds found that despite having the academic ability and interest in studying medicine, they 'had hazy perceptions of the steps needed to become a doctor ("Do you need any sciences?").'[25] The individuals concerned were in Years 10 and 11, beyond the age at which GCSEs are chosen, so their 'hazy perceptions' are likely to have already led them to inadvertently make subject choices that made them ineligible for their preferred course at their preferred institution.

This is not a problem restricted to medicine. Lord Willetts, the former Universities Minister, wrote in 2016 that 'by the age of sixteen 93 per cent could not become an engineer without a dramatic change of track'.[26] Overall, the higher your social class and income, the more likely that your children will choose GCSE subjects (or, in Scotland, Nationals) that allow them to go to university (and an 'elite' university in particular), regardless of their academic ability.[27]

In Jane's case, the fact that she had inadvertently excluded herself from certain options didn't become apparent until she went to university open days and interviews. It was impossible to fulfil their academic requirements, she discovered, because she was only studying for two A-levels rather than three. She hadn't known three was the expectation. Luckily one university, Lancaster, was willing to take her anyway.

In some cases, young people make choices designed to improve their odds in education and careers, but which actually achieve the opposite. Those with aspirations to go to an 'elite' university but who come from backgrounds in which this is unusual or unknown tend to regard these aspirations as a rare and precious thing, to be protected against any possible threats. This frequently includes dropping out of extra-curricular activities that could have helped strengthen their university applications, in order to concentrate on study (financial pressures to have a part-time job also don't help).[28] They are also likely to avoid certain subjects, including sciences, in a misinformed effort to prevent career limitation. As Katherine Mathieson, Chief Executive of the British Science Association, says, 'People from lower-income backgrounds who are unaware of the range of possible science careers might see it [choosing to study sciences] as a high-risk gamble'.[29]

These well-intentioned acts of accidental self-sabotage could easily be avoided if high-quality careers advice were available, but many of my interviewees got little or no careers information at all. When I ask Maria if she remembers any such advice (including at her predominantly middle-class secondary school), she is emphatic: 'No! Well … there was a questionnaire thing. It got put into a computer. For me it said "embalmer". I didn't take any of that seriously. A waste of time.' (Since Maria mentioned this, I've been asking around to see what career suggestions others were given as a result of this test, and the answers are similarly odd, including 'bee-keeper', from the research director of a think tank, and 'vicar', from a Jewish atheist.)

These stories of being ill-equipped to make major life decisions are not the chronicles of a pre-enlightenment past. In fact, as recently as 2017 a report by the All-Party Parliamentary Group on Social Mobility noted, 'a marked decline in the quality and quantity of the career guidance in schools from what was already regarded as a low base',[30] and a few months earlier the outgoing Chief Inspector of Schools, Sir Michael Wilshaw, described careers education in schools as 'a shambles, a disgrace'.[31] By Year 11 (that is, 15- to 16-year-olds), having already made some big decisions about what subjects to study, barely half of all students are satisfied with what careers education they have received, which for more than a third of them (disproportionately the least-privileged) is none at all.[32] This should be a national scandal, because careers advice – especially early and sustained careers advice – is important: each additional careers talk that 14- to 15-year-olds are given is associated with an increase in the amount they can expect to be paid as adults, whereas for those a year older, there is no apparent effect.[33]

Meanwhile, at the top of the social scale, things are very different. At Eton there is a whole career education department, dedicated careers space in the library and support in the form of work experience, seminars, advice and mentoring from 'parents, Old Etonians and other well-wishers'.[34] Not that the boys of Eton (and Harrow, Fettes, Gordonstoun et al) are likely to be reliant on such resources, because they usually have access to information about careers from their parents and family friends. Almost half of parents classified as being of 'high socioeconomic status' know a university or college lecturer personally, compared to only one in seven 'low-status' parents.[35] (Michelle Brook, a Policy & Research Director from a working-class background who got into Cambridge against the odds, points out that parents like hers couldn't help her because they have 'no way of knowing how to understand the systems you are facing'.[36]) My guess is that this is one of the main reasons why careers education in the UK has been treated with such scandalous negligence: the people who make and influence policy disproportionately come from families who didn't need their schools' help to access careers information, but instead had it provided, literally in-house, by their families.

But even the most brilliant careers provision – which starts early and is sustained, which gives an insight into the rewards and realities of a wide variety of careers, which gives opportunities to investigate and space to consider and re-consider, and which makes clear what is required to enter those careers – is useless if individuals can identify the path to their aspirations but are prevented from following it. Joanne Martin, having already had to overcome the lack of role models and face down the scepticism of adults, then encountered a further barrier: the courses she had to study at school in order to be eligible to apply for medical courses weren't offered at her school. But Joanne didn't let that stop her. She had the initiative to ask whether she was allowed to take courses elsewhere, the luck to find somewhere willing to let her do so, and the endurance to travel three hours a night, four nights a week, across town to the University of Glasgow, where the courses were run.

Joanne's school isn't unique in channelling individuals towards 'class-appropriate' options. In England, Sir Michael Wilshaw's successor as Chief Inspector of Schools, Amanda Spielman, reports that some pupils 'did not have any opportunity to study a language or some arts subjects'.[37] A separate study showed that 'triple science' GCSEs – regarded as the best preparation for a scientific career – are much less likely to be offered in schools serving lower-income areas, which is one of the reasons why disadvantaged pupils are almost three times less likely to study triple science than their more-advantaged counterparts.[38] A study by Dr Jake Anders et al at the Institute of Education summed up the situation, concluding that 'we should be sceptical of considering young people's subjects of study purely in terms of "choice". They are, at most, constrained choices'.[39]

Joanne would not have got as far as she has without heroic levels of tenacity. She had to fight to be given choices, to be told that those choices even existed. She had to take substantial risks, gambling that the long hours travelling across town to lessons wouldn't ruin her ability to concentrate on those lessons, and that she'd be able to handle subjects that no one she knew had ever studied before. But while Joanne had to swim against a rip tide, others found themselves carried into elite universities and high-status careers by the same currents that carried their parents there.

Work experience

In my own case, the chance encounter that allowed me an insight into a previously unimagined career was a consequence of one of the perks of Dad's job. When I was a teenager, an extension was built on the side of our house, to accommodate the ridiculously outsized boiler required to burn the solid fuel he got free as an employee of the National Coal Board. The extension required an architect, who came round to our house – a quiet man, but nevertheless willing to talk to me, and to show me some architectural drawings. A plan for a small extension isn't Frank Gehry's design for the Guggenheim, but it was enough to catch my imagination. To an uncool kid like me, the ability to call buildings into being with a pencil seemed very cool. Shortly afterwards, Mr Hilton – my school's careers teacher – mentioned that he would be assigning each of us to a two-week work experience placement. I asked if he could arrange for me to do my work experience in an architect's office. He went through the architects in the local *Yellow Pages*, starting at 'A'. Most said no. It took him until 'R' to get a yes, from Mr Smith at the Reid, Smith Partnership in nearby Pontefract. I loved it. I had my own drawing board, was taken on site visits, and invited back to spend the summer holidays there. It was a view into what goes on in one of those businesses that occupy the discreet brass-plaqued Georgian townhouses at the 'posh' end of town.

I was very lucky. Most of my year group hadn't experienced a visitation from an inspiring member of the professional classes, and even if they had, Mr Hilton – for whom being a careers teacher wasn't his main job – wouldn't have had the time to have made the calls. Typically, my classmates were allocated to a local employer without much choice on their own part, shelf stacking in the local Asda or making tea at the warehouses on the Langthwaite Grange industrial estate.

My classmates' uninspiring experience of work experience isn't peculiar to working-class northerners who grew up in the 1980s. If anything, the experience of the average pupil from a middle-income family today is even worse. Almost half our young people do not experience a work placement while at school or college, and almost four-fifths haven't had visits from businesses to their school. Friends and family are the most influential source of information in helping young people decide on a career,[40] with the result that the insights available are all too often 'class-appropriate'.

Nor is the situation likely to improve; in fact, the Children's Commissioner has expressed concern that school funding cuts are leading to further cuts in work experience placements.[41] Access to the sort of work experience that will help pave the way to a professional career is still mostly reserved for children of the privileged classes, disproportionately in the South of England, whose parents' social contacts allow them to arrange high-quality placements for their offspring.

If children and young people are to properly understand the range of careers and education opportunities that exist – including what they involve, what they require, that they are attainable by people like themselves, and how their studies are relevant to these careers – they need to be personally exposed to them. Merely being told about these opportunities isn't enough. One of the teachers at my school once arranged for someone to give a presentation about working for Midland Bank (now part of HSBC), which did give an insight into a previously unknown world, revealing that there was more to banking than the clerks stamping deposit slips we could see in our local branch, but it didn't make that world feel relevant to me and my classmates; like a presentation about the Yanomami tribespeople, we now knew they exist, but it didn't occur to us that we might grow up to *be* one of them.

Exposure to the range of careers and post-compulsory education needs to start early and needs to be sustained. That means starting in primary school, and it means a range of hands-on work experience for teenagers (crafts, professions and business; in private, public and third sectors). The importance of providing children and young people with multiple encounters with employers is well-known by experts in the field,[42] and some organisations are now making this happen, such as The Brilliant Club, which sends PhD researchers to work with primary school children who wouldn't otherwise know what 'PhD' stands for, and the Social Mobility Foundation, which arranges work experience and mentoring in the 'professions'. But those organisations are constrained by their limited funding and their requirement for the collaboration of school staff (who may be unaware that those organisations exist, or be too overworked, overstressed or under-resourced to take advantage of what they offer). Those organisations are doing a heroic job, but they are only able to offer to some children what all deserve.

So what happened to me, having been inspired by the thought of a career in architecture and given the opportunity to have an equally inspiring hands-on experience of that career? Well, my school's lack of a proper careers teacher meant my work experience placement wasn't followed up by any further encouragement or advice about the practical steps towards my aspiration. The memory faded, and, like most of my classmates, I was carried along in the current of the options I'd chosen at 14, a current that didn't flow towards architecture.

Choosing higher education

Barbara Stocking, the daughter of a Warwickshire postman, went on to have a remarkable career. She won a place at Cambridge to study Natural Sciences, before working on a World Bank Commission in Washington and later becoming Director of the King's Fund and then Chief Executive of Oxfam. She is now President of the same Cambridge College in which she was an undergraduate.

But the remarkable rise of Barbara Stocking was not an inexorable one. Like so many others, the plot of her story turns on a chance encounter that created a cross-class friendship. 'The only reason I got into Cambridge', she told me, was because her best friends at school came from a very different family to hers.[43] The friends in question were the twin daughters of one of the directors of AEI, a large engineering company that happened to be based in her hometown of Rugby. The twins' parents had the confidence and assertiveness concomitant with their place in society: 'the family attitude was that the twins were going to go to Cambridge', and the school was 'expected to make it happen'. Because Barbara was friends with the twins, and at a similar level of academic attainment, she was 'swept up in the updraft'.

Barbara had the reassurance of knowing that she would not be completely away from her friends at Cambridge, because friends were going there too. But students from communities in which going to university is unusual can feel that their friendships could be put at risk by the process of applying to university. As one prominent commentator on higher education, Jim Dickinson, puts it, 'those 18-year-olds who do go are those who're prepared to undergo a reinvention, a rite of passage, a break away from your previous life. Away from family and friends and community. People who are prepared to transform themselves into something else'.[44]

Although Barbara's friends helped reassure her that she should brave Cambridge, her family was less confident. Barbara's father wasn't a man who wanted to constrain his daughter's aspirations (in fact, quite the opposite − she describes him as a man who 'opened possibilities', who valued education and had high expectations for her). But he'd had a personal experience that made Cambridge seem too high an expectation; as a 14-year-old he had left home to work in the kitchens at St John's College, Oxford. He remembered most of the students having good meals while the 'scholars' (the poorer students) had toast. He also remembered the scholars as being so intellectual as to be otherworldly, telling Barbara that they 'were so clever they'd trip over their own shoelaces; if you're from a normal family, you have to be a genius to go there.' His experience was so intimidating that he told his daughter, 'I really don't think you should apply, you're not clever enough.' Luckily, Barbara's school friends helped again: their mother's background meant she was familiar enough with the idea of Cambridge not to be intimidated by its reputation, and she helped reassure Barbara's father that Barbara was up to scratch. (The intimidating reputation of Oxbridge doesn't just deter the working classes. Another of my interviewees, Stuart Alford, was encouraged by his school to apply to Oxford, but his parents were 'very sceptical'. Even though they were 'solidly middle class', his family 'thought it was pitching beyond where I should be pitching.... Oxford was for people who weren't us. I think they were motivated by fear of failure, that I'd make a fool of myself, would struggle and not cope.' Stuart was persuaded to go to university in Reading instead.)

Stuart and Barbara's experiences are from 1986 and 1969, but 'protective discouragement' continues. Almost a quarter of secondary school teachers still say they never advise pupils, even 'academically gifted pupils', to apply to Oxford or Cambridge.[45] Some of this reluctance appears to be an attempt to protect them from failure (18% said 'I think they are unlikely to be successful in their application') or a fear that they would fail to thrive if they were admitted (13% said 'I don't think they would be happy there' and 9% 'I don't think they would perform well academically there').[46] In 2004, academics conducting focus groups with would-be medical students found similar fears from the students themselves, who regarded medical school as 'geared towards "posh" students' and consequently 'greatly underestimated their own chances of gaining a place and staying the course'.[47] Sometimes, these doubts and fears are inadvertently exacerbated by those who wish to broaden access to higher education, by, for example, focusing attention on the disproportionate number of privately educated students at elite universities to such an extent that would-be students assume that their state school background would put them in a minority (which it wouldn't).

The demoralising doubts that beset students and their families about their ability to cope in an academic and social environment that is 'above their station' are partly rooted in the fear of humiliation, of having to return home amid the shame of hubris. But there are other bases for doubt. Justine Greening, a Rotherham steelworker's daughter and now a Cabinet minister, was one of those who had financial worries about going to university: 'It felt like a risk', says Greening, 'because I was putting off when I would start earning money'.[48] Around the developed world, sociologists have found that families with low or insecure incomes are forced to put their immediate financial needs above their longer-term aspirations and 'spur their children to abandon school in favour of a job'.[49]

Having decided she would take the financial risk of going to university, Greening faced another challenge. Navigating through the process of choosing and applying for a particular institution and course was, says Greening, 'a step in the dark; when I asked my parents for advice on where to go, what to study, it was new to them too'.[50] Very often, in the face of absent or baffling information, non-privileged students will fall back on their gut feeling, and choose an institution and course that 'feels right'. Paul Monekosso Cleal is an example. He 'had no idea which was a good or a bad one', he says, and chose Warwick on the basis that 'I liked the culture'. Choosing an educational institution by 'feel' is common, and tends to stream students into 'class-appropriate' directions. Based on interviews with students, education researchers have suggested that 'post-1992' universities (former polytechnics etc) and further education colleges provide 'a comfort zone where the working-class students feel they are accepted'.[51] But that this socially comfortable environment comes at a price, including that it cuts down course choice: courses like Economics, for example, which produce graduates with high average salaries, are being withdrawn from the post-1992 universities.

Luckily, there are a growing number of projects and organisations trying to guide potential students through the fearful unknowns surrounding university applications and university life in general, and those of Oxbridge and other 'elite' universities in particular. The Sutton Trust, which takes students to Oxford and Cambridge for Summer Schools, is one example, as is the Social Mobility Foundation, which aims to provide non-privileged students with the support and know-how about university that their more privileged peers get from family and friends. These interventions have impressive results: young people from non-privileged backgrounds who have experienced their programmes are more likely to go on to study at selective universities than those who have not.[52]

We have to be careful not to conclude that the barriers to entering university can be overcome by giving young people 'a bit of information about it'. Very often, giving would-be students a bit of information doesn't help at all. An experiment in the US, in which potential students from low-income and middle-income families were given information about financial aid available to study at college, found they were no more likely to make applications than a similar group who had not been given the information.[53] Sometimes, having 'a bit of information' only makes us realise how much we don't know. People who were the first from their family to go to university, or the first to go to an 'elite' university, can find it difficult to know where to go for answers to their questions (there are guides and rankings that purport to help prospective students to choose the 'best' institutions and courses, but how do you know which of the many guides and rankings will be helpful?). Sometimes questions are not asked for fear of looking stupid.

If we want non-privileged young people to get into higher education institutions (or another path) that are appropriate to their interests and their potential, rather than their level of privilege, we have to accord them the same support and reassurance that is offered to the privileged. The experiment that found potential students were not encouraged to make college applications by being given information on college costs and grants also found that offering help to fill in the application forms *did* have an effect: a 15% increase in applications. The programmes that appear to work, like those delivered by The Sutton Trust, Social Mobility Foundation and The Brilliant Club, are the products of a lot of research, experiment, evaluation and improvement, and they are also intensive. In Australia, a larger (publicly funded) programme called TRiO also employs a sustained, holistic approach to supporting non-privileged students into college, including tutoring, counselling, mentoring, financial guidance and other assistance, and it works: students in one of TRiO's programmes are six times more likely to complete college than their peers.[54]

Policy-makers in government, universities and elsewhere (who disproportionately come from privileged families and attended elite universities themselves) often struggle to grasp that part of the reason why people like themselves choose to go to elite universities is that their families, friends and schools have, subtly and subconsciously, been persuading them to do so for years. The process of persuasion includes exposure to relatable others who have followed the same path, which assuages any social and financial fears. If the decision-makers believe in equality of opportunity, they have to ensure that we are *all* provided with enough reassurance, exposure and guidance. Projects already operating in the UK and elsewhere that aim to provide such reassurance, exposure and guidance can show significant, independently evaluated results. Projects like those can and should be scaled-up. They wouldn't guarantee that everyone was able to choose an elite university but they would be an improvement on the current reality of under-informed, mis-informed and constrained choices.

Of course, choosing higher education is no guarantee of being accepted, and chances of being accepted also vary by background. The next section asks why.

Admissions of failure

A civil servant friend of mine, knowing I was writing this book, emailed me to suggest I interview his colleague, Charlotte Dring. 'She is not a big cheese yet', he wrote, 'but probably will be.' When Charlotte, the daughter of a marine electrician at Grimsby Docks, enrolled in sixth form college, the college vice-principal took one look at her GCSE grades and said 'Oxbridge, then?' This came as a shock to Charlotte: 'I'd never entertained the idea.... I went home to my mum and said "what's he on about?"' But the idea took hold; she joined a group the college had created for students considering the elite universities, which took them on visits and, for those who were offered interviews at Oxbridge, conducted mock interviews.

The mock interview is where Charlotte got another, less pleasant, shock. 'I remember them saying "they will probe your wider knowledge".' Charlotte hadn't been taught any wider knowledge than was on the syllabus, and hadn't previously been told this was a problem: 'I did what I was told to do as perfectly as I could.' In a panicked attempt to broaden her knowledge, she sat up late in the library, 'randomly reading science journals', but this just 'made me think I couldn't do it ... this process wasn't for people like me. I didn't want to put myself through that.' On the day of Charlotte's real interview at Cambridge, she tells me, 'I went into college as normal. The teachers said "aren't you meant to be at your interview?" I already had an unconditional offer from Durham, I took that.' Academically strong students from non-privileged backgrounds, having swum against the hidden currents that push them away from elite universities, often find that interviews (and admissions processes in general) are, as Charlotte says, 'set up for a private school experience, where, from what I have seen since, they are taught so much more about the world.'

Joanne Martin was another would-be student who was wrong-footed by university interview questions that appeared to bear little relevance to the course for which she was applying. In her case, this happened in the interview itself, her school not having had the know-how to prepare her). She says, 'I was traumatised, I was thinking "why are you asking me this?"' Others were discombobulated not so much by the questions they were asked, but by the alien-ness of the whole experience, which can be overwhelming even to those with no shortage of 'strength of character'. Stephen, who later rose to become chief executive of a large multinational company, told me that despite his middle-class background, interviews at Cambridge proved 'too much for me: you turn up and there are kids in tweed jackets drinking sherry!' Even Lucy Hunter-Blackburn, formerly the Scottish Government's Head of Higher Education – whose own parents went to Oxford – remembers feeling 'like a gatecrasher the whole time, awkward and scruffy and excluded' at an Oxford Open Day, where she was the sole attendee from her 'average sort of local comprehensive' amid 'gangs, buses even, from the big public schools of southern England.'[55]

Interviews can also constitute a financial barrier[56] for some students, because they involve incidental costs that some can't afford but others regard as so 'trivial' they don't really notice them. Tom Stocks, now a young actor, struggled to meet the travel and accommodation costs of auditioning for entry to drama schools. But Tom also mentions an additional cost that I hadn't imagined existed: 'Drama schools charge you for an audition; you go to maybe eight auditions at about fifty quid each, that's four hundred quid.' Upfront fees like this can be difficult if not impossible for some students to find, reducing the number of drama schools they apply to, which reduces their odds of being accepted. It also increases the psychological pressure in each audition to 'make it count'. To add insult to the financial injury, says Tom, there is not normally any feedback from failed auditions. Nor is Drama the only course to charge for tests: Joanne had to sit an aptitude test to study medicine, which cost £80, as well as the cost of travel to interviews (which she was only able to afford because she had a part-time job). Some universities are willing to help with the costs of getting to open days or interviews (the columnist Dawn Foster says the fact that the University of Warwick sent her a National Express voucher was an important part of her decision to go there[57]), but such assistance is not always publicised or even available.

The interviews, auditions and other tests that are a common part of admissions procedures for elite universities may have flaws, but they can also tell selectors something that exam results and other data simply cannot. In a study by Theodore Sarbin, the ability of trained university staff to predict the end-of-year grades of students (based on a 45-minute interview) was compared with statistical predictions based solely on data from exams and tests. The statistical predictions did not match up to those made by trained, experienced humans who had had the chance to personally interact with the students. Unfortunately for the humans, where the statistical predictions differed from the humans' predictions, the humans were the ones who got it wrong. Of the 14 professionals in the study, 11 (that is, 79%) were beaten by the algorithm.[58] The extra information that can be gleaned from interviews was worse-than-useless information, such as the social confidence that people typically equate with competence but is often just a mark of background. The interviewers were overruling useful data in favour of misleading impressions.

Another example of the effectiveness of interviews as a tool for assessing academic potential came from the University of Texas in Houston (UTH). In 1979, more than 2,000 students had applied to study Medicine, of which the university interviewed 800 and admitted 150. Soon after, the Texas state government passed legislation requiring the university to increase its intake. Fifty extra students were required. The medical school contacted those students who had just missed out and offered them places. But Houston had a problem: by the time the almost-successful interviewees could be contacted, some had already accepted places at other medical schools. UTH therefore had to accept students who had been rejected not only by their own interviewers, but also by other interviewers at other universities. Seven years later, a team of academics were able to track the performance of the 50 initially rejected students as they progressed through medical school into postgraduate training, in academic work and in clinical practice, and compared this to the performance of the 150 students who had passed the interviews. They found no meaningful differences at all.[59]

Those misleading impressions don't just favour those from certain social and economic backgrounds. Research into admissions procedures for Art and Design courses found 'admissions tutors' construction of "having potential" and "being creative" are informed by ... racialised perspectives of what counts as legitimate forms of experience and knowledge'.[60]

Charlotte, Joanne and Stephen did well even to be offered interviews for elite universities; most students from non-elite backgrounds don't even make it that far. They don't make it that far because (as well as having been less-effectively coached to pass exams, and being channelled into more 'class-appropriate' directions) their teachers tend to under-predict the grades of non-privileged individuals, with the result they are less likely to be offered a place at high-status institutions.[61] Their chances of being offered interviews are further reduced by universities' 'personal statement' that students are required to write as part of the university applications process. In these statements, applicants are advised to say 'what interests you about the subject', as well as outlining their 'sporting, creative, or musical' interests and 'any relevant employment experience or volunteering'[62] Unsurprisingly, the personal statements written by the most-privileged students can typically draw on the most impressive experiences. (One well-connected 18-year-old cited in research on personal statements could point to work experience for a fashion designer, a brokerage, a BBC radio station, a city law firm and as an events planner in a five-star hotel.[63]) Those who are educated in the most prestigious private schools can also count on help with their applications (and interviews) from their school's in-house tutors who have a *lot* of experience of successful applications to elite universities.

Once A-level results are announced, students who didn't get the grades they expected have a second chance, by applying to other universities and courses through the 'clearing' system. Again, the privileged families are at an advantage. As Sir Peter Lampl, of The Sutton Trust, says, 'A lot of well-off parents are on top of this as soon as their kids' grades come out. They're talking to universities, they're getting their kids into the best courses. Kids from low to moderate income backgrounds don't have parents who can play the system and they're not at schools geared up to getting kids into Russell Group universities. So in that sense, clearing is unfair'.[64] (If higher education institutions made offers to students after exam results were known, it would solve both this problem and that of non-privileged students' grades being consistently under-predicted by their schools. As the former editor of *Schools Week* points out, this would create a longer delay between results and enrolment, which would be a good time for students to participate in CV-enhancing initiatives such as the National Citizen Service.[65]

When Joanne's applications to study Medicine at elite universities were not successful, (despite having the necessary grades), she decided to study another subject, namely, the admissions procedures themselves, so that the following year she would be ready. Some of the expectations, such as that candidates would have relevant work experience, were difficult to fulfil. 'How do you get medical experience', she asked me, rhetorically, 'if you didn't know any doctors?' Joanne resorted to cold-calling doctors, trying 60 of them before being offered a single day in a biochemistry lab. To supplement this, she got herself onto an international placement via the government-funded International Citizen Service, but still had to do some fundraising to 'show commitment'. Whereas the first time around Joanne had been under-prepared, the second time around she says, 'I knew how to play the game a bit better, knowing how different universities mark applications, what institutions I have best chance of getting into; I was more confident … second time around the place is a bit more familiar, you know how to formulate answers … after I got in, I realised that was the aim of work experience: to give you answers.' Second time around, Joanne was accepted at Aberdeen.

Widening participation in higher education

Almost everyone involved in higher education – government, education experts and the higher education institutions themselves – agrees that the underrepresentation of students from non-privileged backgrounds, especially in the elite universities, is a problem. And having recognised the problem, they are spending substantial amounts of money addressing it (universities and colleges in England alone are estimated to have spent £833 million on 'widening participation' programmes in 2017-18).[66] In England, institutions are obliged to report on their 'widening participation' plans as a condition of being allowed to charge increased tuition fees. Specific targets have been set by the UK government and the devolved administrations to increase the proportion of students from 'underrepresented' groups.

(Before continuing, it should be pointed out that 'underrepresented' groups include more of us than we might imagine. For example, official guidance for higher education institutions classifies more than 80% of households as 'low-income'.[67] Typically, policies to widen participation are described by their opponents as a threat to 'middle-class' families. They don't say middle-*income* families, because it is those with well-above middle incomes who are really the most likely to have their advantage reduced by any effective 'widening participation' initiatives.)

How universities and colleges actually go about widening participation is up to them, being regarded as 'an important part of academic autonomy'.[68] As a result, there are a wide range of approaches. Some of these are intended to make the institutions more attractive to students, such as offering bursaries to those from low-income backgrounds, running promotional events in low-participation areas and using sport as 'outreach'. Others focus on making students more attractive to the institutions, including working with schools to raise academic performance and coaching people on how to navigate the admissions process (as distinct from making the admissions process more navigable).

Substantial time and effort has been invested in 'widening participation' initiatives and some, such as that at King's College, London, can demonstrate substantial success based on evidence and evaluation.[69] Numerous others, says John Jerrim, Professor of Education and Social Statistics, 'go out and spend money but they don't know if it works'.[70] In the worst cases, some institutions apparently don't *want to* know if it works. The Sutton Trust reports having offered to evaluate a 'widening participation' scheme being run by 'a highly prestigious UK university' but had the offer refused.[71]

Even where universities can point to evidence of an increasing proportion of their students coming from 'underrepresented' groups, the headline data can hide a lot of important detail. It is possible to see how many students from various groups are admitted to each institution, but not how many are admitted to each *course*. 'The stats look alright', says Jim Dickinson, of the University of East Anglia, where he was previously the Student Union's Chief of Staff, 'because they're padded out by people doing nursing courses, where you find the kids from Yarmouth [Great Yarmouth ranks among the 10% of boroughs with the worst deprivation figures in the country].... People from Yarmouth aren't coming here to do Law.' In fact, the Government's Office for Fair Access told him that it is *legally prevented* from analysing subject-level data on admissions.[72] In Dickinson's view, if universities had to demonstrate action on widening participation for each course, there would be an incentive for universities to take much more meaningful action: 'medical courses would be sending medics to Yarmouth, might do an experiment on a body. Instead what happens when the university sends people off to Yarmouth is there's a general talk given on the general experience of being at university.' As Dickinson has written for the Higher Education Policy Institute, 'despite general progress on higher education access, there appears to be little or no impact on the diversity of those entering Dentistry, Medicine or Law.'[73]

One way that *is* demonstrably effective in helping non-privileged students into prestigious educational institutions is to make 'contextualised offers': taking a candidate's background into account, and adjusting the required A-level (or equivalent) grades accordingly. This approach is now being championed by the Scottish Government,[74] and by 2017, 60% of Britain's most selective universities were (in at least some cases) making adjustments to entry grades for applicants from 'under-represented' backgrounds.

Unsurprisingly, this is controversial, especially among those who send their children to private schools and fear that the odds won't be stacked in their favour to the same extent as they are used to. Nigel Farndale, a privately educated author and columnist, warned that some students faced being 'discriminated against because, through no choice of their own, they had the privilege of going to a public school'.[75] Liz Smith, the education spokesperson for the Scottish Conservatives, supported the idea of more 'deprived' students being offered a place, except when it comes 'at the expense of those from other backgrounds'[76] (but the number of university places in Scotland is capped, so the number of non-privileged students cannot rise *unless* it comes at the at the expense of 'those from other backgrounds').

Warnings that mediocre-but-privileged students will miss out on university places, in favour of bright children from ordinary homes, are signs that contextualised offers are effective. But the effect is hardly revolutionary. The quote from Liz Smith above was prompted by the news that 18-year-olds from the most privileged areas of Scotland were now 2.90 times more likely to enter university than 18-year-olds from a middle-income area (and almost 10 times more likely than those from the least privileged areas), representing a tiny change from 2016, when the figure was 2.96 times.[77]

Contextualised offers are not a panacea, but most experts in education and social mobility agree that they are necessary, because exam results now indicate 'how well prepped and drilled the privileged few have become' rather than academic merit.[78] Those experts who are unhappy with contextualised admissions tend to say that entry grades are *not adjusted far enough*. In a joint article, three academics noted that the University of Edinburgh, whose use of contextualised offers is more radical than most, reduces offers for the most disadvantaged applicants from a requirement for AAA★ to a requirement for ABB, whereas to properly reflect the difficulty involved for such an applicant, the offer would be more like CCC.[79]

One objection to the use of contextualised offers is the argument that universities and colleges should provide higher education to people who have the ability to benefit from it, even if they do have that ability because they have been 'well prepped and drilled'. Most of us can see the strength of such an argument (would you want to find yourself undergoing brain surgery at the hands of someone who'd got a place at medical school in compensation for their background rather than in recognition of their ability?). But what if the beneficiaries of contextualised offers find that their abilities increase, once they are studying in the same environment as their more privileged peers? We will look at the evidence for whether that happens – or whether non-privileged students in higher education face further disadvantage that causes them to fall even further behind their privileged peers – in Chapter 5.

Pressure points

So far, this book has been perpetuating an inaccurate stereotype. By talking about higher education choices within a chapter focused on the teenage years, I'm reinforcing the misconception that the 'typical' student is someone who begins higher education in their late teens and studies full time at a university; whereas in reality, the majority of students are part-time, 'mature students' and/or studying at college.

As part of my research on part-time and mature students' experiences of higher education (which you can read in Chapter 7), I went back to my hometown of South Elmsall to interview an old school friend, Trevor. During the interview, I asked him why he'd decided not to go to university straight from sixth form, when he'd obviously had the academic ability and, as far as I remembered, the inclination. He looked a bit sheepish, and told me his grades 'weren't brilliant' because he was 'romantically distracted' during his A-levels, so he left school for a job in a warehouse. A few weeks after talking to Trevor, I heard another version of the same story, but it had a very different ending. I heard the second story in a cafe in London, from another friend, whose brother, Richard, also got A-level grades that 'weren't brilliant' due to his having gone 'a bit off the rails' that year, so he repeated his final year of sixth form, re-sat the exams, got much-improved grades and went to university.

Why did Trevor and Richard's stories have such different endings? There are a couple of likely reasons. The most obvious is financial. Richard was a middle-class boy from suburban North London, but Trevor was a working-class lad from the South Yorkshire coalfield. Trevor's parents 'didn't have much money at that time', he didn't think there'd be enough financial support, and most of his friends had already left school ('they'd got an income and I hadn't'). These pressures are especially acute for the one in twelve young people who act as carers for relatives, around half of whom are prevented from studying at college or university by their caring responsibilities.[80]

Another reason Trevor's story ended so differently to Richard's is expectations. Having done badly in his first attempt at A-levels, Richard's parents 'made him pull himself together':

as far as they were concerned, the poor results had been an aberration caused by peculiar circumstances. Trevor, by contrast, came from a community in which higher education was not a normal expectation, A-levels had been his never-to-be-repeated opportunity to go to university, and he'd missed it.

If you feel that that your future depends on your performance in a never-to-be-repeated opportunity, the pressure can be overwhelming, especially if you see university as your one chance to escape poverty, or to escape an environment in which you feel uncomfortable or threatened. This was the case for Dean. Some of his neighbours were hostile towards his sexuality, and to make matters worse, Dean's father had been laid off by the closure of the car factory in which he worked; the struggle to find a job became a struggle with alcohol, and Dean's father took it out on his family, making Dean's need to leave more urgent, but also more difficult: 'The violence at home was so bad I couldn't revise, I was terrified, "if I don't pass I don't know what options there are, I can't go into the factory, I'm in trouble, if I don't get this what do I do?" it was desperation.' Luckily, Dean was able to focus when it mattered ('I switched on in the exams'), but for others, the tremendous pressure focused on a small point in their lives causes something to break.

The experience of living in a one-shot world, where appraisal of our performance comes not as feedback but as verdict, is toxic to the development of a growth mindset in which mistakes are seen as learning experiences.

One policy that relieved at least some of the financial pressure to abandon full-time post-compulsory education was the introduction of the Education Maintenance Allowance (EMA). The scheme was piloted in 1999, with up to £30 a week being paid to 16- to 18-year-olds from low- and middle-income families in full-time education.[81] In areas where EMA was piloted, the number of eligible 16-year-olds participating in full-time education rose by 4.5 percentage points in the first year and by 6.7 points in the second. Accordingly, the scheme was rolled out across the UK in 2004. But it came at a cost: the coalition government elected in 2010 cited a cost of £580 million, and also cited research suggesting withdrawal of EMA would not deter 88% of eligible students from continuing their studies. The devolved administrations in Northern Ireland, Scotland and Wales retained the scheme, but in England it was scrapped in 2011. Six years later, the drop-out rate for 16- to 18-year-old students from disadvantaged backgrounds was almost twice the rate for their non-disadvantaged peers.[82]

Further education colleges can also relieve some of the pressure by offering a 'second chance' to enter higher education, but their ability to do this is declining. Restricted funding means colleges are focusing on vocational routes rather than allowing another shot at A-levels. Just 2.4% of students who entered further education via vocational routes then go on to higher education at Level 4 or above, and 'consequently face careers which often have little chance of meaningful progression'.[83]

A phrase from a 1997 report commissioned by the Further Education Funding Council still has resonance today for too many students from non-privileged backgrounds who aspire to higher education: 'If at first you don't succeed … you don't succeed'.[84]

Choosing a different path

As an MP, Jackie Doyle-Price has frequent opportunities to speak to school children. Her background means she is relatable to the children of Thurrock, which remains a largely working-class area. She uses her position to encourage them to aspire to well-paid jobs. Sometimes, their teachers disapprove of this.

Among the well-paid jobs in her constituency to which Jackie is encouraging the children to aspire are those at the Port of Tilbury where, Jackie tells me, career peak pay is at £40,000-£50,000 plus a final salary pension scheme, with an average wage of around £36,000 (that is, better-paid than two-thirds of full-time jobs in the UK). The reason the teachers disapprove of her encouraging the children to consider such careers is that they can be accessed via apprenticeships so, as Jackie tells the schoolchildren, 'you don't have to go to university'.

An apprenticeship can be a better career choice than a degree, but – as Jackie can attest – anyone who says such a thing to children is likely to encounter resistance from their parents and teachers. Despite widespread agreement that the UK needs more people becoming apprentices, 96% of mothers want their own children to go to university[85] (although recent, if patchy, evidence suggests this may be changing[86]). As the economist Alison Wolf says, everyone thinks apprenticeships are 'a great idea for other people's children'.[87]

David Lammy, as well as being one of my case studies, also has experience as a government minister with responsibility for higher education and skills. He sees the low esteem in which vocational education is held as being the consequence of policies and developments that favoured the service sector over manufacturing, especially under the Thatcher government. But David says his own party's policies also played a role, particularly Tony Blair's goal that half of all young people should go into higher education (commonly misinterpreted as 'half of all young people should go to *university*'). This sent a message to young people from working-class homes, says David, that they had failed if they did not go to university.

This lack of esteem for 'non-academic' learners has consequences for individuals. The lack of attention paid by the political establishment to vocational learning enabled a situation in which almost one in five apprentices are – illegally – paid less than the Minimum Wage and the majority don't receive the off-the-job learning to which they are entitled.[88] It also has consequences for vocational learning as a whole. Whereas the UK spends more per head on education than most other developed countries, we lag well behind our competitors on funding vocational education.[89] In some cases, the lack of funding – especially of further education colleges – is causing labour shortages. In Derby, for example, demand for welders exceeds supply, but Derby College can't pay enough to recruit instructors with up-to-date welding skills.[90]

The lack of esteem doesn't just lead to financial underinvestment; it allows a general neglect of vocational education that, like an untended garden, leads it to become impenetrable, tangled and chaotic. This hasn't been helped by deregulation of the sector, which was meant to encourage competition and therefore drive up standards, but, in fact, drove standards down.[91] Careers advice for vocational routes is even sparser than it is for academic routes. Just one in ten apprentices learned of their course from a careers adviser or teacher; most had to do the research themselves.[92] Those who did do the research themselves would have found that it involved more complex data than anything encountered by the typical undergraduate, because by 2017 there were 13,000 separate vocational qualifications.[93] Paul Johnson, Director of the Institute for Fiscal Studies, has said that even he, a Professor of Economics, found it 'staggeringly hard' to help his son find a suitable apprenticeship.[94] The UK, says Johnson, 'stands out in international comparisons' in its neglect and underfunding of vocational education.[95]

The outstanding levels of neglect of vocational education create a problem for employers, who struggle to recruit staff with the skills they need. It also creates problems for people who are highly able but not academically inclined. Such people (of whom there are many) are turned off apprenticeships by lack of guidance, lack of information about the options and where they might lead, and a widespread belief that apprenticeships and other vocational routes only ever lead to poor-quality jobs. In being turned off, these people are missing out: while it is true that the lifetime incomes of the average graduate exceed those of the average apprentice, it is also true that large numbers of graduates end up in non-graduate jobs, and that some apprenticeships lead to good, well-paid jobs (such as those at Tilbury, or BAE Systems, the UK's largest defence company, some of whose apprentices have become directors[96]).

Part of the reason for vocational education's neglect is that policy-makers – and their officials and advisers, and the journalists whose articles they read – tend to come from privileged families, and therefore tend to be graduates of one of the elite universities. Vocational education is outside their direct experience, and consequently out of mind. There are no shortages of organisations (the Learning and Work Institute, for example) proposing measures that would improve vocational education, such as a shift of government focus towards the quality rather than quantity of apprenticeships, an industrial strategy that gives preference to high-skilled sectors, and initiatives to improve the pay and esteem of 'non-graduate' careers. But the number of areas to which government can give substantial attention is limited, and vocational education is in the blind-spot of the policy-making classes.

To give credit where it is due, some politicians do put an effort into checking their vocational education blind-spot (helped along by lobbying from organisations like the CBI, whose members need skilled workers). One example is George Osborne, who, in 2015, as Chancellor of the Exchequer, introduced the Apprenticeship Levy (a scheme in which large employers are levied an amount equivalent to half a per cent of their payroll bill, which is then granted back to employers to pay for apprentice training). In 2017 Osborne's successor, Philip Hammond, set out plans to improve vocational and technical education in England, including simplifying the 13,000 post-16 vocational qualifications down to 15 routes and creating maintenance loans for students in further education or technical college.[97] But there are still significant problems arising from policy-makers' unfamiliarity with vocational routes. The majority of apprenticeships for young people are still not giving them a higher level of qualification than those that they already hold,[98] the skills gained are not always 'portable' into other jobs, and the number of people starting apprenticeships *dropped* after the Apprenticeship Levy was introduced, sparking fears that it was being seen by employers as a tax benefit rather than an incentive.[99]

One way to address this perennial vicious circle neglect is to break down the barriers between academic and vocational education. Many of the distinctions between what is currently taught in universities and what is taught in higher education colleges or in workplaces are based on snobbish ideas about the differences between blue-collar and white-collar jobs (whereas in the real-life world of work, almost everyone uses a mixture of practical skills and theoretical knowledge). Moving away from the current snobbism-based system to one in which practical and academic education are combined within the same courses and institutions would help reduce the odds that our children's destiny is decided at the age of 18, by putting them into institutions where previously unimagined, class-inappropriate options are apparent, allowing them to amend their own course (in both senses of the word). It would facilitate the integration of both theoretical and practical elements into each individual student's experience, which would make it less likely that those who currently study 'academic' subjects would leave university – as they very often do now – with good grades and poor employability. And it would reduce the tendency for vocational learning to be neglected and under-resourced, because it would be integrated into institutions that the policy-making classes know and care about.

The system of further and higher education and training we currently have, by contrast, is beset by silos and social stratification, which creates problems for the would-be socially mobile, as we will see in the following chapter.

FIVE

Higher education, and other higher education

Strangers in paradise

The last time we encountered Dean Hanley, he had passed his A-levels with grades good enough to get him into university, something he'd wanted so desperately that the pressure had almost broken his chances of achieving it. For students like Dean, higher education can feel like a promised land, an escape from poverty into a place where swots and misfits are no longer misfits. For Dean, that promise was false. 'I was on a course with people from much more privileged backgrounds. I always made a social faux pas, always said the wrong thing.... I expected it to be friendlier, more diverse. The working-class people dropped out ... one boy – I liked him, really polite – just disappeared one day, turned out he'd had a breakdown.' Dean stuck it out for longer, but 'had problems adapting' and also dropped out, during his final year.

For others, stepping out of a life in which they are something of a misfit into one where they find they are still a misfit – but for reasons of background rather than of aspiration – isn't so traumatic. Rozina Ali, the Liverpudlian daughter of a Pakistani factory worker, studied medicine at London's St Thomas's Medical School, among a tribe that to her was exotic: very male and very privileged. Rozina was able to treat it as an adventure, a chance to broaden her horizons and her network of connections, a chance to reinvent herself: 'Every ounce of manners, confidence and chutzpah I developed was because I went to "a boys' public school" that happened to be a medical school', she says, 'it was fun'.

For most people who are the first from their family to go into higher education, the experience is mixed. Dean and Rozina each told me they'd had both ordeals and adventures. For too many students from working-class backgrounds who get into a university – or those from middling backgrounds who get into an 'elite' university – the ordeal overwhelms the adventure so much that they struggle or drop out. Why universities fail to retain these students is being discussed more and more in higher education circles.

In some cases, students' personal attributes make them more or less likely to be welcomed by their fellow students. Dean found that many of his course mates struggled to see past his sexuality, and Rozina tells me it probably helped to be 'good-looking'.

However, individual attributes such as sexuality and perceived attractiveness don't explain the differences between more- and less-privileged groups. One theory that attempts to explain the difference is that non-privileged students lack 'resilience'. In Dean's case, this appears to be a poor explanation: he'd had the resilience to face down the low expectations others had had of him since childhood, and performed well in his A-levels despite violence at home. Nor does this theory stand up well against wider evidence. A sociological study of students from working-class backgrounds who make it to 'elite' universities found they had, in fact, 'developed almost superhuman levels' of resilience (they'd had to, to get to such a university at all), but despite this resilience, nearly all the working-class students interviewed 'had a crisis of confidence on arriving at university'.[1]

For some students, the crisis of confidence may be accompanied by a family health crisis (as happened to Jane: 'In my first year I nearly came home. Mum was really ill.' Luckily, Jane was – just – persuaded to stay.) The risk of higher education being discontinued or disrupted by family health problems is higher for those from less-privileged families, whose working lives and financial insecurities mean they tend to experience health problems earlier in life than their more privileged counterparts.

Another explanation – and one frequently alluded to by my interviewees – is that students from 'non-traditional' backgrounds are liable to accidentally behave in ways that mark them out as weird, and lead to their being excluded. There are rules they're meant to stick to but haven't been told, rules about what to do, what to wear, what to talk about. Jane remembers inadvertently breaking the rules by styling her bedroom 'like a prison cell'. This arises from Jane's lack of preparation: 'I knew I was going to go to university, but I didn't know what it meant. I had no picture in my head, I'd never had a discussion with anyone who'd been to university … other people brought nice food, they brought cushions, headache tablets, things for their lives…. Their rooms were nice…. I had a box of food and a Snoopy poster.'

Mercifully, a growing number of students whose family and friends can't brief them on the social and cultural protocols of life in higher education are being briefed as part of projects run by social mobility charities such as The Sutton Trust, which runs Summer Schools to acclimatise participants to life in Oxford, Cambridge and other 'Russell Group' universities.

For some of my interviewees, mentoring was provided informally, by a 'posh friend', such as the school friends who went to Cambridge with Barbara Stocking. For Stuart Alford, now a Partner in a City law firm, that mentor was his sixth form girlfriend, Emma, a girl who wouldn't normally have gone to a school like his, but who had transferred there from a private school that didn't offer the mix of A-levels she wanted. Socialising with Emma and her friends effectively acted as a 'finishing school' for Stuart: 'rounding off the edges. It changed my vocabulary, the way I dressed, like a stone on a beach, tumbled and tumbled, more and more smooth, subconsciously changing my language, changing the things that interested me.' Stuart hadn't been especially 'rough' to begin with (he came from a solidly middle-class family), but his state school education would put him in a minority in his hall of residence at the University of Reading ('each hall had a very strong social identity', he says, 'mine was regarded as most like an Oxford College'), and the cultural makeover he'd had as a sixth former still didn't impress the 'sloanes':[2] 'I remember one of them commenting on the fact my shoes had plastic soles.' Stuart might have found himself living in the clubhouse, but he wasn't about to be granted membership of the club.

Jane had to wait until she had arrived at university before she found a native guide to privileged society, a fellow student called Carolyn. It didn't start altogether smoothly: the first thing Carolyn said to Jane was, 'sorry, I didn't understand a word you just said', but soon they were getting on well enough for Jane to be invited to Carolyn's family home. 'I went to visit her at her house in Bristol, in Clifton', says Jane 'Her dad was a lecturer and her mum was a macrobiotic therapist or something. I didn't have a clue what that was. All the family had been to university. She lived in a big mansion! I didn't recognise it as a house.' The Bristol visit was another opportunity for embarrassment: 'I'd had my tea on the train, at five, but when I arrived I was told that dinner would be at eight. I didn't know what they meant – I thought dinner was at lunchtime – I said "what do you mean? I've had my tea" and they didn't know what I meant, they thought tea was a drink. So I had two teas.... Everybody was dressed down, in holey jumpers and jeans. I'd changed into my best dress, from Laura Ashley. I didn't look like them.'

It is exhausting being the odd one out, feeling that everything you do and say is scrutinised, and treated with, at best, anthropological curiosity and at worst, censure. Maria Solomon found out her culture was, as she puts it, 'not just different, but wrong' when she repeated an anecdote about her dad. Working in his chip shop one day, he saw a woman leave her empty lager bottle on the shop's step, chased her down the road with it and gave it back to her by plonking it in her cleavage. This story got a different reaction to the one Maria was used to. Someone 'told me he could have been up for sex discrimination. Different sense of humour. Now, when I mix with middle-class people I edit what I say.' It is also exhausting to constantly have to explain simple things to 'sophisticated' people. (Jane's friend, Carolyn, again provided an example, by asking 'why are all the people in this launderette? I can understand why we, as students, are here, but other people, why don't they just buy a washing machine?') And it is exhausting to have to find excuses for yourself (Jane, having to withdraw her invitation to Carolyn for a reciprocal family visit, after her dad pointed out that they couldn't afford to host her: 'it was in the miners' strike and he didn't know when he'd next earn money').

Most of my interviewees said they benefited from finding 'friendly natives' who were willing to guide them through the confusing protocols of a more-privileged culture. But they also spoke of the value of finding someone from a similar background to themselves, with whom they could be themselves, who understood, who didn't require explanations. For Maria, that someone was Dean: 'I was lucky I met Dean. Thank God! There was a connection right away ... behaviour and language ... you don't have to constantly explain yourself ... it's a relief, a burden off your shoulders.'

As the number of students from 'non-traditional' backgrounds increases, as it has done, each individual student is less likely to experience the loneliness of long-distance social mobility (although the social mix of students in certain courses at some institutions has changed less than others). In some universities, however, more proactive innovations are being put in place to make those institutions feel more welcoming to a wider group. A number of students' unions are now creating 'working-class officers', representatives elected from among the student body, partly to bring people together, to increase the sort of chance encounters by which Maria met Dean. These representatives also allow working-class students a means of advocating for ways in which their needs can be met by educational institutions overwhelmingly run by people from very different backgrounds. The idea of 'working-class officers' is still relatively new – and as Stuart's experience illustrates, in some institutions it is not just working-class people who feel excluded by lack of relative privilege – but it is a positive development, recognising that all of us who find ourselves in alien environments not only need someone to guide us, but also someone to understand us.

Out of class

When I arrived at university, eight years after my sister, I had no problems adapting to the rarefied social environment – because it wasn't a rarefied social environment. By that time (1990), in that university (Hull), there were enough working-class students around to make me feel far from alone. The roommate I'd been assigned by the university was Ed, a cook's son from Barnsley.

In lectures I sat with Caroline, the daughter of a warehouse manager. I went to the pub with Chris, an engineer's son from Essex. This is entirely normal. Despite universities' promotion of the student experience as a 'chance to mix with a wider group of people',[3] higher education experts recognise that in reality, students tend to gravitate towards people who are in their cultural or social 'comfort zone'. (If you've read the previous section, you'll appreciate why this might be.)

The social divisions in higher education institutions aren't just between working class and middle class. Stuart Alford remembers that at the University of Reading there were four tribes, distinct enough to have commonly agreed names, which he listed, in declining order of poshness, as 'Sloanes, Pissheads, Meatheads and Whitesocks', only the latter of which was working class. The people I lived and studied with at university did not open up previously unimagined lives and aspirations, because their lives and aspirations were remarkably similar to my own, until the start of my second year, when something changed.

I joined a student society. Specifically, I joined the Hunt Saboteurs Society, a group that got up early on Saturdays to drive around rural East Yorkshire in a hired Ford Transit minibus ineffectually attempting to impede the Holderness Hunt. As a working-class lad, I was in a minority in the 'hunt sabs' (my sixth form friend Gail Bradbook had introduced me to ideas like animal rights, environmentalism and radical feminism; ideas with a misfit militancy that appealed to me, but weren't wildly popular in a socially conservative mining town). My background had little in common with my fellow hunt saboteurs, but thanks to Gail's influence, I had enough common ground to build the foundation of friendships on.

However, the mere foundations were not enough. From the subtle signals of social feedback, I soon developed a nagging suspicion I was somehow embarrassing myself, and sometimes those suspicions were confirmed. One Wednesday afternoon, after the hunt sabs' regular weekly lunchtime meeting, I'd invited some of them to my student house for coffee. One of them, seeing me pick up a jar of 'instant', asked if I had any 'proper coffee'. 'It is proper', I told him, 'it's Nescafé' (pleased with myself for knowing it was posher than Mellow Birds, and for not pronouncing it 'Nescaffy'). I learned that day of the existence of non-instant coffee. I also learned that buying Nestlé was frowned upon. Most of the time, I felt uninformed rather than unacceptable, but I was aware that when my new friends talked about their shared pre-university experiences, many of those experiences weren't shared with me, so I had little to bring to the conversation and was therefore in danger of being seen as 'hard work', the sort of person who isn't exactly shunned, but who also isn't invited. But then something else changed.

Eventually, someone had a conversation I *could* bring something to. Something I'd found while doing my Saturday job as a shop assistant in the Leeds branch of Concept Man (now rebranded – together with Chelsea Girl – as River Island). The shop had an upstairs stockroom where we all occasionally went to collect something or skive out of sight of the manager. A lad called Rodders worked up there, and he had a stereo. Unlike the chart pop that was piped onto the shop floor, Rodders' tape deck played the Velvet Underground, the Pixies, and the Jesus and Mary Chain. To the 16-year-old me, it was as glorious as the hallelujah chorus and much more cool. I became a fan, and *that* gave me what sociologists call 'cultural capital', something to talk about with my new friends. It was just enough to tide me over until we built up enough new shared experiences for our backgrounds not to be a barrier.

I moved from the hunt saboteurs to an environmental group, and later got involved with the students' union. This extra-curricular activity, rather than the academic aspects, was the way in which university allowed me to develop and attain aspirations 'above my station'. Unlike lectures, it *did* open up previously unimagined lives and aspirations. I became friends with people whose parents were managers and professionals and entrepreneurs and aristocrats.[4]

I'm far from the only one for whom extra-curricular activities were the primary means by which their student years allowed them to form friendships with people from other social classes on a common ground of shared values and shared enterprise. A friend of mine, who initially felt an outsider in her Russell Group university, found an enclave of people she describes as 'normals' in the Labour Club. (It was also the basis for a friendship with the daughter of an MP who, by acting as a mentor, helped my friend on her way to a career in politics.) In other cases, though, student clubs or societies can make some students feel excluded. Writing of his own experience of Cambridge in the early 2000s, Dr Peter Matthews – now a Senior Lecturer in Social Policy – said 'being a member of a drinking society essentially meant you were in the in-crowd and had friends and connections for life.... If you were excluded then you were one of the bullied geeks around the place'.[5]

As well as contacts, these sorts of activities can develop career skills. My own involvement in the student union was what got me my first 'proper' job after university (as a member of staff in a student union). In some careers, the skills and experiences developed in extra-curricular activities are not just useful but necessary. Over the last 20 years of my own working life, I've interviewed lots of candidates for graduate jobs, and – because there are lots of graduates – the ones who get the jobs are those who have demonstrated practical organisational ability, very often as an officer of a student society or in a student union role.

While these extra-curricular activities can act as a route to opportunity, that route is often blocked for the students who could benefit most. Sometimes this is just because it feels alienating. Despite his provincial middle-class background, Stephen – the CEO-to-be – wasn't posh enough to feel welcome in the Labour Club at his Russell Group university: 'I left within six months', he says, 'Lots of politicians' children, lots of people from public schools'. (But other student societies can be more approachable than expected. Some student Conservative Associations have a reputation of being less-than-welcoming towards working-class people, but Jackie Doyle-Price's experience did not bear this out: 'although Durham had a lot of more traditional Conservative people', Jackie told me, 'they weren't involved in the Conservative Association. The officers were people like me and Graham Brady' [Brady was a state-educated Salford lad, also now an MP].)

Sometimes, what stops non-privileged students from participating in extra-curricular activities is lack of prior experience of the activities themselves. Ruth Holdaway, Chief Executive of Women in Sport, points out that whereas some schools have 'good playing fields, enough money to employ sports specialists, maybe bring in coaches', in others, budget constraints are constraining interest in sport. 'However creative and brilliant the teachers are', she says, 'it's harder to make sports fun.' Holdaway offers herself as an example. She almost joined the women's rugby club at university 'but chickened out because I never played rugby at school. I didn't have the confidence to do it.'

More often, such activities are just unaffordable. Partly because membership of clubs and societies can run into hundreds of pounds a year,[6] but mainly because students from less-affluent backgrounds are more likely to have to take part-time jobs in their 'extra-curricular' hours. They are also more likely to have caring responsibilities for family members, or to live with their families and therefore have longer commutes to campus.[7] Almost one in four students are 'commuter students', but the timetabling of extra-curricular activities (and often of academic teaching) typically ignores them, perhaps because the decision-makers in universities disproportionately come from more privileged backgrounds, among whom being a commuter student is much less common and therefore tends to be overlooked.[8]

Another barrier preventing students from non-privileged backgrounds participating in extra-curricular activities is that they are deliberately avoiding such activities, seeing them not as a means of personal and career development, but rather as a waste of time, a distraction from the academic elements of student life that are seen as the 'real' engine of opportunity. Students from non-privileged backgrounds are often told by their families to concentrate on the academic work and not to waste time on sports and societies or getting involved in the students' union. I was told this too. Luckily, I ignored this advice.

The seminar room

Durham's University College is unofficially known as the 'Castle', because that's what it is. (The College is housed in Durham Castle, a UNESCO World Heritage Site.) You can find a photo-feature of University College's June Ball in *Tatler*.[9] According to one of its recent students, it 'very much feels like

a public school boys club' (it didn't' admit women until 1987).[10]
Jackie Doyle-Price, arriving fresh from her Sheffield council
estate, was not University College's typical student, as she found
out on her first weekend: 'We were invited to the Master's
house for drinks', she says, 'A tutor was saying his wife was a
comprehensive school teacher, and that for comprehensive kids
"the best you can hope for is YTS".'[11] When Jackie – herself
educated at a comprehensive – interjected with 'that's not quite
true ...', he responded with 'ah, you must be Jackie.'

Other state-schooled students who went to 'elite' universities
also found themselves treated as peculiarities by academics.
Sometimes this took the form of well-meaning but clumsy
attempts to make them feel included, such as the academic
who offered to introduce one of my interviewees to 'other
poor students'. In other cases, it appeared more hostile. Jim, a
working-class drama school student, told researchers 'one of my
lecturers said to me, "have you ever considered going back and
being a plumber?"... That really fucks with your confidence.'[12]

Being given the impression that 'this place isn't really for you'
is common among students from non-privileged backgrounds,
especially in 'elite' universities. Beccy Earnshaw, Director of the
social mobility charity Voice 21, says even students who were
'probably one of the strongest speakers in your school, one of
the people most likely to contribute' find themselves in seminar
rooms with privately educated classmates who are 'so much more
confident than you and speak in a way that you don't speak.'
The result of this shock, says Earnshaw, is that 'You spend a
good two terms building your confidence back up to be able to
participate'.[13] Dean Hanley's experience exactly reflects this: 'I
didn't volunteer ideas, didn't answer questions', he says, 'I was
horrified when the lecturer spoke to me. I thought "they'll see
through me right away". Eventually I did adapt, but it was tough.'
This silence is often interpreted by academics as indicative of a
lack of ability, and they – consciously or unconsciously – treat
the student accordingly, further undermining their confidence.

Students who are the first from their family to enter some of
the more prestigious universities could be forgiven for thinking
someone is deliberately trying to confuse them. In Joseph Heller's
classic Second World War satire, *Catch-22*, the novel's hero

and his fellow airmen conspire to discombobulate a military education officer by asking apparently nonsensical questions: 'Who is Spain? Why is Hitler?'[14] At the University of Oxford, students may find themselves with an equally disconcerting query: 'When is Hilary?' ('Hilary' is the second term of Oxford's academic year, running from January to March, named for the feast day of the not-very-well-known Saint Hilary of Poitiers.) Rushanara Ali, now an MP, has memories of being baffled by another example of Oxford's arcane terminology in her first year as a student, when she was told to expect 'collections'. Having initially being told this referred to a meeting with the college president (which it also, confusingly, does[15]), it was only later, having been asked by a fellow student if she was 'preparing for collections', did she find out that it in fact meant exams, exams for which she should have been preparing.[16]

In addition to being 'put on the back foot' by the academic arcane, students from non-privileged backgrounds find themselves struggling to cope with costs their more-affluent classmates (and the academic establishment) struggle to notice. As Jim Dickinson tells me, 'there's a range of activity that goes with being on one of the prestigious courses and costs money: law society balls, "optional" trips and so on.' Advisers at the University of East Anglia Student's Union, where Jim was formerly Chief of Staff, 'spoke to one student who was considering dropping out, partly because of the expectation to participate in all that' and another 'whose dad had proudly bought them a stethoscope, which apparently wasn't good enough: the tutor laughed at them.' Another problem, says Jim, is academics who don't edit their reading lists, but rather 'just keep adding to them, more and more books to buy.' Jim and his colleagues raised the issue with university authorities, but 'if you bring that up you're told "it's not really an issue for our students".' (Polling released in 2018, however, suggests it is an issue for a lot of students. One in four said they'd had an unwelcome surprise when they found out 'how much everything would cost', especially accommodation and extra-curricular activities, but also field trips and 'books that you "have to have" but only look at once'.[17])

The costs of studying that aren't included in tuition fees are, theoretically, covered by 'maintenance loans', which are also meant to cover living expenses. For two-thirds of students, however, maintenance loans aren't enough to live on. In some university cities, they aren't even enough to cover rent, leaving nothing for food or other expenses.[18] In some cases, accommodation costs, and especially accommodation costs that have to be paid in advance, are reported to have prevented students taking up their university place at all, especially for those who were offered a place through 'clearing', which meant they missed out on university accommodation and were expected to find private rented accommodation, which requires upfront rent and deposits.[19]

The result of inadequate maintenance loans is that many students find themselves reducing the time they might otherwise spend studying or in extra-curricular activities by taking part-time jobs,[20] although this is not always an option at, for example, Oxford, where 'term-time employment is not permitted except under exceptional circumstances'.[21]

Compared to the cost of tuition fees, this aspect of student finance is rarely mentioned, probably because the more affluent students, who disproportionately go on to influence debates about higher education, are accustomed to extra handouts from their families. As Joanne told me, among her peers in an 'elite' Scottish university, 'no one pays their own bills, I'm the only one.'

The effects of struggling with finances, combined with the effort of adapting to a cultural and social experience designed for someone unlike oneself, will inevitably sap the mental 'bandwidth' of non-privileged. This being the case, you're probably now expecting a depressing statistic showing how this undermines the academic performance of non-privileged students, so that the privately educated score higher than their state-schooled counterparts?

There is no such statistic. In fact, privately educated students who entered university with the same A-level grades as their state-schooled course mates do significantly *worse* in their final exams.[22]

The explanation for this phenomenon is not that the most-privileged students are somehow put at a disadvantage by university: they still have an advantage, just less of an advantage than they had at school. Academics who carried out case studies of university students reported the 'striking finding' that, in contrast to their state-educated peers, 'none of the student participants who had attended a private school were achieving a first by the end of the second year.' The academics' suggested explanation was that 'without the support offered by their schoolteachers they lacked the self-discipline to adapt to a less monitored teaching and learning environment'.[23] The performance-enhancing effects of an elite schooling, which allowed the mediocre-but-privileged to keep pace with their less-privileged counterparts' exam performance up the age of 18, start to wear off when both groups are in the same institution, with the result that the less-privileged students begin to outpace their peers.

This throws light on one of the key objections to the practice of making 'contextualised offers', in which the required exam results to enter a particular university are adjusted downwards for less-privileged students (the hypothetical risk proffered in Chapter 4 that we might find ourselves undergoing brain surgery at the hands of someone who'd got a place at medical school in compensation for their background rather than in recognition of their ability). Universities will be offering places to students whose exam performance reflects something other than their potential if they *don't* adopt contextualised offers: students from privileged backgrounds will be given places in medical schools and other prestigious institutions as a result of the performance-enhancing effect of their schooling (which will recede over time) rather than as a result of any natural ability, with obvious implications for any brain surgery you may undergo.

This doesn't mean contextualised offers are without problems. It is true, for example, that non-privileged students who are admitted to elite universities are more likely to drop out than their privileged peers (but that problem would be better addressed by making the university experience less culturally, socially and financially hostile to non-privileged students than it would by keeping them out). It is also true that work should be done to remove the *need* for contextualised offers, by helping non-privileged students achieve better marks in sixth form and in colleges (and many universities are funding programmes to do just that: they account for a large chunk of the £833 million that universities are spending on 'widening participation' programmes). However, due to it being implausible that any of these initiatives could create a totally level playing field, some adjustment will remain necessary if we are to reward potential rather than privilege.

And it is true that contextualised offers are sometimes clumsily designed. The definition of disadvantage used by the Scottish government, for example, is based on a student's home neighbourhood, but as Lindsay Paterson (the University of Edinburgh's Professor of Education Policy) points out, almost *two-thirds* of Scottish young people in low-income households don't come from low-income areas.[24] The criteria on which contextualised offers are based in such cases are unacceptable, and urgently need reform to make them fit for purpose, but otherwise the imperfections of contextualisation are dwarfed by the huge unfairness of the old system, which unfairly keeps students with more potential than privilege out of good universities and courses.

The old system is also unfair to the privileged students who, as the result of what amounts to a parentally funded social engineering project, find themselves in prestigious courses and careers for which they are intellectually ill equipped.

Creating or hosting prosperity?

What's the best university in America? Harvard? Yale? MIT?

On the basis of new research, which tracked the careers of over 30 million former students, the best American university is probably CUNY (the City University of New York). It cannot claim the most Nobel laureates, as Harvard can, or to produce the most billionaires, as Princeton can (where 23% of graduates go on to be members of the wealthiest 1% in the USA). But CUNY can claim the best record of improving the incomes of its students. Whereas Princeton – and the other 'Ivy League' colleges – mainly produce rich graduates by disproportionately recruiting students whose families are *already* rich, CUNY recruits the poor and makes them rich. It has the best record of taking students whose parents were in the country's bottom 20%

of household incomes and turning them into graduates whose incomes are in the top 20%.[25]

In the UK, the elite higher education institutions are more like Princeton – what *The Economist* calls 'rich-in, rich-out'[26] – than CUNY. Even among students who graduated with the same grades in the same degrees from the same institutions, the graduates who get the most highly paid jobs tend to be those who had the most highly paid parents, [27] and almost half the people sociologists categorise as 'elite' don't have a degree at all.[28] In contrast, graduates from lower-income regions like the North East tend to be paid less[29] and graduates from lower-income backgrounds disproportionately struggle to find graduate-level jobs.[30] (This, says Rushanara Ali MP, is something a new generation of potential students in her constituency have noticed, prompting them to ask 'what's the point?')[31] As researchers who studied graduates' career prospects have concluded, 'It has historically been assumed that participation in higher education has a social levelling effect: once you're in, you'll get ahead. This is a myth.'[32]

This doesn't mean the institution and course in which children study won't make any difference to their future careers. Higher education institutions provide marketable qualifications, some give students an opportunity to make valuable social contacts, and certain employers only recruit from 'elite' universities (the typical employer's UK graduate recruitment programme focuses on a limited number of prestigious universities, ignoring four-fifths of higher education institutions.[33])

The added value that comes from higher education – and especially the elite institutions – makes it important that non-privileged individuals are able to get into them, and using the usual headline measures, participation has been improving since the late 19th century (when the 'higher education participation rate for the "lower class"' was 'estimated to be zero').[34] The rate of 'lower-class' participation in higher education has increased especially quickly in recent decades, whether class is measured by income, neighbourhood, occupation, parental education or eligibility for free school meals. Ninety per cent of school leavers entering higher education are now from state schools.[35] This still leaves state-educated individuals significantly underrepresented in higher education, because they make up rather more than 90% of the overall population of school leavers, and if we include students as a whole – that is, not just school leavers – the numbers from non-privileged backgrounds have recently dropped back, for reasons that will be explored later, but overall, there has been nothing short of a revolution in access to higher education.

However, not everyone has been swept up in this revolution. Almost half of all young people now enter higher education,[36] but the odds are much higher for those living in London and Northern Ireland than they are for those living in, say, Wales, and much lower for those with experience of the care system, of whom only 7% enter higher education.[37]

There are also stark differences *within* the higher education system. The average privately educated school leaver is approximately one-and-a-half times more likely to go into higher education than their average state-educated counterpart, but they are almost four times more likely to go to one of the 'elite' universities that make up the Russell Group (whose graduates are typically paid 40% more than other graduates[38]).

The odds are yet more uneven for some individual institutions. For example, the privately educated are 8 times more likely to get into Cambridge and almost 10 times more likely to get into Oxford (Professor Les Ebdon, former Director of the Office for Fair Access, said, 'Do I think there's fair access at Oxbridge? Well, obviously not'[39]). But Oxford and Cambridge aren't the worst: the privately educated are *17* times more likely than anyone else to get into the Royal Academy of Music.[40]

Within institutions, the students studying subjects associated with the highest-paying jobs tend to be those with the highest-paid parents. And even when students from non-privileged backgrounds do manage to get a place on the most prestigious courses at the most elite universities, it is far from guaranteed that they will be able to benefit from the career-boosting effects that friendships with their more-privileged classmates could bring them, partly due to students being segregated by their accommodation (as researchers from two universities found, there is 'a social chasm between private and state school students, often exacerbated by university accommodation costs'[41]).

All this segregation of the classes, between and within institutions, means a student from a privileged background is likely to get more benefit from their years in higher education than their less-privileged peers. But their tuition fees will probably be the same, because almost all universities have set their tuition fees at the maximum allowable level. It has been proposed that 'less prestigious universities' and 'courses with poorer outcomes' should not be allowed to charge as much in tuition fees, to reflect the reduced financial benefit their students receive.[42] This seems superficially attractive but, as Nick Hillman of the Higher Education Policy Institute points out, would create a 'pupil premium in reverse', underfunding the under-privileged.[43]

Alternatively, the problem of the least-privileged students getting the least-valuable higher education could be addressed by tackling the root cause, that is, the unfair advantage that the most-privileged students have in accessing the most-valuable education. Again, this suggests a need for admissions criteria to move away from a reliance on interviews and raw exam results that can be influenced by 'performance enhancers' such as are provided to students in elite private schools.

Careers services

My interviewees' recollections of their student days (for those who went into higher education) make up a disproportionately large section of my research notes. Their memories varied between adventure and endurance, but the memories were invariably strong ones. Except when I asked about university careers services. Most couldn't remember anything at all. One of the more vivid memories (Maria's) was, 'I think there was a university career event? I might have gone? It obviously made no impression.'

Reports from large-scale research into university careers services were hardly more impressed than my interviewees. A report by The Bridge Group found 'effective practice in this area is emergent at the most committed institutions, and a worryingly low priority at the least committed.' This was, apparently, an area in which the most prestigious institutions were not necessarily providing the best service ('institutional investment in Careers Services appears to vary wildly across the sector, and not only by expected factors such as university income or league table position'). Damningly, the report found it hard to identify much benefit – 'almost half of 130,000 participants in the research had never visited their careers service', and said there was 'little evidence' that students who had used university careers services had better career outcomes than those who had not.[44]

Universities are keen to point out that their alumni have 'significantly enhanced job opportunities',[45] so it is odd that they aren't better at helping students identify and take advantage of those job opportunities. It is also a lost opportunity, because when university career services are effective, they 'can contribute to social mobility, improved retention, attainment and progression to employment, as well as to enhanced career management skills'.[46]

One of the reasons why students who were the first from their family to go to university – or the first to go to an 'elite' university – can't take full advantage of careers services is their tendency to start thinking about their post-graduation life too late in their university career. (Maria remembered the shock of realising, in her final year, 'you don't know where you're going.') The underlying reason for this may be found in recent research from the US, which suggests the idea of 'university' represents very different things to people from different backgrounds.[47] For some students, universities – and especially elite universities – are so far outside the experience of their friends and family they take on a fairytale quality. Lynsey Hanley, writing about her own preconception of university, says, 'If I could just get there, I believed, my life would be transformed utterly.'[48] For those of us who as teenagers regarded university as a promised land, it takes time to adjust to the dream becoming reality – and to deal with the sometimes jarring reality of the place – let alone start preparing to leave.

People from privileged backgrounds – who disproportionately go on to positions of influence over policy and practice in higher education – can have trouble grasping that others' ability to fully prepare for their careers during their student years could possibly be suppressed by something as absurd-sounding as having a fairytale notion of something as *normal* as higher education.

The privileged also tend not to notice whether their university careers service was fit for purpose because they didn't really need to use it. Instead, their family and friends could give them access to advice and contacts from people with first-hand experience of working within the sorts of careers to which they aspire. Such students are more likely to take advantage of CV-enhancing opportunities to study or train abroad, spend vacations in the sorts of internships that have good odds of turning into post-graduation jobs, or in the sort of extra-curricular activities that impress employers. It appears that some academics assume their students will have families who are able and willing to help, such as the head of department who told researchers there was no need to help students find work experience placements because 'We've a much more middle-class student body here. It's much easier for them to obtain placements: they have contacts'.[49]

For students studying the most prestigious subjects, the quality of the university careers service is of little consequence, because many academic departments effectively provide their own in-house service. 'The law department knows how to get students into law jobs; through introductions, getting dressed up in suits to drink wine with canapés', says Jim Dickinson, 'the impact of the university careers service on getting people to the Bar [that is, to become barristers] is probably negligible.'

But change may be coming. There is pressure to demonstrate that students are getting good value for their tuition fees. The Government's Office for Students is pushing for 'widening participation' plans to go beyond outreach and admissions. Institutions are increasingly being assessed on students' post-graduation outcomes. Some universities, such as Loughborough, are exploring ways to help students develop 'employability' skills as well as just qualifications.[50] The University of York now enrols all undergraduates, during their first year, on to a 'Strengths Programme', designed to help students develop 'a vision of where you might want to go' and 'ideas of how best to use your time as a student to help you get there'.[51] Queen Mary University of London is integrating hands-on employability opportunities into the curriculum, in recognition that some students lack the finances or knowledge to participate in initiatives that are offered as 'added extras'.[52]

But there are forces holding back the development of high-quality careers support. Many new initiatives are still at the trial-and-error stage, so there is 'minimal evidence base about what works'.[53] Regulators like the Office for Students have limited powers to compel university authorities to improve their careers services, and the managers of university careers services are constrained by their lack of seniority within the university hierarchy (to address this problem, The Bridge Group recommends giving a senior member of university management, such as a pro-vice-chancellor, responsibility for student careers outcomes).

The development of high-quality careers services is also subject to a backlash against the idea of employability among some commentators in and around academia, who object to the 'neoliberal notion of employability'.[54] The idea that universities should be 'judged on how successful they are at getting students into postgraduation employment', they say, is indicative of a 'market-driven philistinism that privileges economic returns to education above all else.' This objection – that the purity of academia shouldn't be sullied by mucky materialism – is not one I have heard from people who were the first of their family to go to university: they mainly felt the careers advice and experience they received at university was too little, too late; none said receiving little or no careers support and advice had been a lucky escape from neoliberal notions of employability.

The cost

In 2010, the government decided to increase the cap on tuition fees for English[55] students entering higher education, tripling the amount from £3,000 a year to £9,000. Within two decades, tuition fees in England went from zero to being among the highest in the developed world.[56] In advance of the cap being raised, protests flared up around the country, with campaigners warning 'education will become a privilege for the few that can afford it'.[57] In the years that followed, however, the number of school leavers entering university increased, and the gap between the number of students from advantaged and disadvantaged areas narrowed.[58] It appears that the increase in tuition fees did not profoundly damage social mobility. An academic assessment published in 2018 concluded that the English approach to tuition fees had had the effect of 'increasing quality, quantity [of students enrolled], and equity in higher education'.[59]

But the bigger picture is not so simple. The paragraph above refers to the number of *school leavers* entering university, a group whose numbers have increased, but the number of part-time students dropped by more than half between 2010-11 and 2015-16.[60] If both part-time and full-time students are included, the number of people from 'low-participation backgrounds' entering higher education has fallen.[61] And while tuition fees may not have stopped increasing numbers of school leavers from disadvantaged backgrounds getting into university, repaying tuition fee loans (plus interest) does make it harder for those students to get on in life after they graduate by, for example, reducing their ability to save for a deposit on a house. It is also suggested that, even for full-time school leavers, fear of debt may not have reduced the numbers applying for higher education courses, but could have suppressed an *even bigger* rise that would have otherwise taken place.[62]

Taking into account the effect of tuition fees on restricting the opportunities of people in their mid-twenties and older, the case for the UK-wide adoption of the Scottish approach – where free tuition in higher education is a cornerstone of the government's commitment to building an 'inclusive, fair, prosperous, innovative country'[63] – becomes stronger.

However, the Scottish experience suggests that shifting the cost of tuition from the student back to the taxpayer would not, on its own, give students from non-privileged backgrounds a better chance of entering higher education. New students from the most-privileged fifth of localities in Scotland are 53% more likely to enter higher education than those who come from an average area, and 143% more likely than those from one of Scotland's most-deprived areas.[64] What's more, the introduction of 'free' tuition fees has been accompanied by a cap on the number of places available (to prevent universities and colleges from creating a high number of low-quality courses, knowing the taxpayer would pick up the bill) and the students excluded by the cap are disproportionately those from non-privileged backgrounds.

The weight of expectation on the Scottish government to keep tuition fees at zero is increased by almost a tonne by a sandstone block the former First Minister Alex Salmond had erected in Edinburgh, inscribed with the words 'The rocks will melt with the sun before I allow tuition fees to be imposed on Scottish students.' Unfortunately, this weight causes undue pressure elsewhere in the student finance system – grants to cover living expenses have been cut back drastically in Scotland – which leaves students, especially those from low-income backgrounds, struggling to pay their way. Loans to cover Scottish students' living expenses also have a lower repayment threshold than similar loans in England, which means students who find themselves graduating into in low-paying 'non-graduate' jobs (disproportionately those from non-privileged backgrounds) are more likely to find themselves making repayments they can ill-afford.[65]

Tuition fees have dominated the debate on student finance throughout the UK. Scrapping tuition fees has been a flagship policy of both the Labour and Liberal Democrat Parties within the last 10 years, but amid the noise about tuition fees, the issue of living expenses – which has a greater impact on students from low-income backgrounds – has been neglected. In England, the loans that are supposed to cover living – including rent, bills, food, travel, books and some sort of social life – are so inadequate that in 2017 the average student overspent their maintenance loan by £221 a month.[66] In the absence of parents who are willing and able to help meet the shortfall, none of the remaining options are ideal: get a job (which reduces the time available for studying and/or extra-curricular activity) or take on the sorts of debt that aren't written off if your income is too low. In surveys, some students reported other approaches, including skipping meals or leaving higher education altogether.[67] Unlike tuition fees, which have an impact on students' finances after they graduate, inadequate provision for living costs can make it unaffordable to enter higher education in the first place, and result in the poorest students leaving with the most student loan debt.[68]

The idea that spending money on higher education in general, and the abolition of tuition fees in particular, would 'inaugurate a new era of social mobility',[69] also means that proposals for opportunity-enhancing initiatives outside of higher education are neglected. While politicians and activists are making the case for spending an estimated £8 billion[70] on tuition fees, other proposals are going unfunded, including those that would have a far greater impact in terms of improving opportunity and reducing poverty. There is no shortage of such initiatives, but a few examples include removing the caps and freezes on social security that are the cause of so much of the child poverty that undermines life chances from the outset; making good-quality pre-school education available to everyone; increasing the Pupil Premium; providing free extra-curricular activities in which young people can develop both skills and social connections; addressing the acute underfunding of education for 16- to 18-year-olds to counteract the reduced subject choice and resources available to non-privileged students; restoring the Education Maintenance Allowance; funding the creation of a national careers service that employs trained specialists and guarantees high-quality advice, guidance and experience to everyone; and filling the numerous gaps in finance available for career development training.

The politicians and commentators who set the terms of political debate could be accused of over-focusing on tuition fees out of cynical self-interest: the groups who would benefit most from the abolition of tuition fees are overwhelmingly the better-off (because people from low-income families typically don't go into higher education at all, and lower-paid graduates aren't required to pay back their loans unless and until they meet an earnings threshold). However, I don't think that most of the people who regard tuition fees as a priority issue – and the best use of £8 billion – are driven by selfishness, but rather by short-sightedness. Influential people tend to come from families that are affluent enough to be unharmed by the closure of a local children's centre or a freeze in social security payments (it is noticeable that one of the few politicians to have overtly said that Early Years provision is higher priority than tuition fees is Labour's Shadow Education Secretary, Angela Rayner, a non-graduate with experience of the social security system as a working mum.[71]) The influential and affluent also don't tend to notice the inadequacy of students' living cost loans, because their parents could easily pay an additional allowance.

Tuition fee debts can reduce the incomes of graduates in later life, but they do not prevent anyone from accessing higher education. And until all students are allowed to compete for entry to higher education on fair terms, cutting tuition fees will be a subsidy that disproportionately goes to the privileged, for a service to which they have preferential access.

An alternative higher education

Graduates have a higher income than non-graduates, on average, but of all the people interviewed for this book, Mark Dixon, who never went to university, has easily the highest income. He has experienced, in financial terms, the greatest degree of social mobility.

Having narrowly escaped a secondary modern education owing to his school becoming a comprehensive just in time for his arrival, Mark got 'a good level of secondary education' and 'very good O-levels'. His teachers told him, 'you could go on to the best universities in the country'. He considered university but rejected it: 'at 16 I knew they couldn't teach me fast enough. I felt held back. It wasn't *practical* enough. I wasn't doing anything … my plan was, in five years, to get as much practical education as possible.'

Getting as much practical education as possible didn't start at 16. At 14, Mark got a Saturday job in a bakery, owned by a local businessman called Peter: 'he paid less than Woolworths, but was one of the most inspirational people. Larger than life. I thought I'd learn more there.' Mark did learn more there. Peter is still a friend of Mark: 'he was an early mentor, very creative, good at seeing holes in the market, an observer of detail, super-ambitious, looked at life in a different way.' At the bakery, Mark learned to make bread. He also learned, from Peter, about 'dealing with circumstance, dealing with opportunity, dealing with people'. Peter hadn't been to university either, but 'he'd had lots of businesses. It looked like fun. He made things happen.'

Once he'd left school, Mark started his own business, Dial-a-Snack, making and delivering sandwiches. He promoted the business door-to-door, 'just walked into offices with a price list'. His sandwiches proved popular, and takings were good, but profits were not. Mark was spending too much, putting a lot of chicken in the chicken sandwiches and buying the ingredients from shops rather than wholesalers. He learned that 'in most businesses, selling is the easy bit. The problem is sourcing.'

Having completed his 'sandwich year', the next stage of Mark's alternative higher education was 'studying abroad'. Ignoring the advice of his father to 'play it safe, stay at home', he hitch-hiked to Saint-Tropez: 'I'd read something about the place in a newspaper, with a picture of Brigitte Bardot; I thought "that looks interesting".' In Saint-Tropez Mark had two 'strokes of luck'. The first came as soon as he arrived, when he asked directions to a campsite from a character known locally as 'the commandant': 'He took me there in his car, asked did I want some lunch, took a shine to me.' The commandant also helped Mark get a job, cleaning boats in Bertrand's Boatyard. Later, sitting in a bar, covered in blue dust from sandpapering the bottom of a boat, he met a man who told him that Le Papagayo – a restaurant-cum-nightclub – were desperate for staff: 'They said have you worked in a restaurant, I said yes – I hadn't – I started that night.' Mark says he wouldn't have got the job if they hadn't been desperate, 'any amount of decent interviewing would have shown that I hadn't worked in a restaurant, I'd hardly *been* in a restaurant, and couldn't speak French.' Mark says Le Papagayo was 'the busiest place in St Tropez, which was busy.' Its clientele included Brigitte Bardot. 'It was good money, and I didn't have to clean the underside of boats.' It was also, as Mark says, 'a first class education.... I learned French. You get good at talking to people, working hard, being reliable.' From France, Mark travelled on, to Thailand, Singapore and Australia; he worked in an open-cast mine and as a logger; he earned and he learned.

'That practical experience', says Mark, 'has helped in everything I've done afterwards.... I haven't had any lessons since I started, but I've had some wonderful teachers – almost everyone I've met I've learned something from.'

Mark is far from being the only person for whom higher education 'wasn't practical enough'. As we saw in the previous chapter, however, anyone who shows sufficient academic ability is put under considerable pressure not to 'waste' that ability on a more vocational career.

For those who can find them, an increasing number of apprenticeships are being offered by providers with good experience in education – including Oxford, Cambridge and approximately a hundred other universities[72] – and by employers such as Rolls-Royce, whose apprentices have higher salary expectations than most graduates. But elsewhere, young people who were directed to apprenticeships by their further education colleges have found themselves participating in schemes that are criminally inadequate, providing just a tenth of the required amount of training and none of the promised career opportunities.[73] Ofsted (the education and skills regulator) is theoretically responsible for ensuring quality, but has nowhere near adequate resources to inspect the huge number of apprenticeship providers – estimated at over 2,000 – that now exist.[74] Work desperately needs to be done to give potential apprentices a clearer idea of the range and benefits of different apprenticeship schemes, and the reassurance that providers will provide a high-quality product.

Anyone wanting something similar to Mark's apprenticeship in entrepreneurial skills without putting together a DIY version as he did has a more limited number of options. 'Work experience' for aspiring entrepreneurs is offered by Young Enterprise, which works with teachers and universities to guide participants through the process of setting up and running a business over the course of a year. Young Enterprise's programmes are not delivered as apprenticeships, but instead run alongside students' college work.[75] For those ready to start a permanent business – and aged between 18 and 30 – The Prince's Trust offers support with business planning and mentoring. But attempts to develop an official apprenticeship standard for entrepreneurs appear to have been discontinued.[76] A handful of colleges offer entrepreneurship diplomas, but nothing equivalent to the (degree-comparable) higher apprenticeship levels. The level of provision for aspiring entrepreneurs is surprisingly low, and many potential entrepreneurs will never become aware of the potential support available.

One development that can remove the need to choose between an academic and practical path is the recent development of 'degree apprenticeships', combining a degree with on-the-job training for which participants are paid a wage and not charged tuition fees.

Degree apprenticeships are still a minority pursuit: fewer than 10,000 young people take up apprenticeships each year, compared to 33 times that number who begin traditional degrees.[77] There is a concern that the name may be a deterrent to potential applicants who assume anything with 'apprenticeship' in the name will lead to lower-quality jobs. One proposed solution to degree apprenticeships' branding problem is to change the name to 'career degrees'.[78]

A better solution would be to call them 'degrees', but not to make them more like existing degrees. As proposed in the previous chapter, the distinctions between academic and vocational routes should be broken down, with academic courses being the ones to change most, so it becomes the norm for degrees to provide a more balanced mixture of knowledge, analytical skills and practical abilities. This would also bring a wider mixture of people into higher education institutions, helping demystify such places, so 'non-traditional' students feel more confident in applying and more at home when they arrive.

SIX

Into a job

Unexpectedly unready, again

In November 2008 a Cabinet minister, Hazel Blears, warned that too many of her colleagues were 'career politicians', who had arrived in their jobs as a result of 'a "transmission belt" from university activist, MP's researcher, think-tank staffer, special adviser, to Member of Parliament and ultimately to the front bench'.[1] Jackie Doyle-Price – who was elected to Parliament 18 months later – had, as Blears described, been a university activist, and shortly afterwards she, too, became a researcher, but not the sort Hazel Blears was thinking of. The research Jackie was doing paid £1.31 an hour, and consisted of 'sitting outside bus stations, counting how many people used them'. After 18 months of similar temporary jobs and unemployment, one of the temporary jobs – with South Yorkshire Police – became her first 'proper' job.

While Jackie was struggling to find a direction for her career, Maria was realising her career was already heading in was the wrong direction. Two months after graduating with a degree in Civil Engineering, she was on her way to catch a bus to an interview for an engineering job, a bus that had already left. Her late arrival at the bus stop, Maria tells me, was 'probably subconsciously deliberate' and made her realise that she didn't really want to be an engineer. Her dad, she says, was furious: not only had Maria left home to go to university (despite there being local universities), chosen Civil Engineering (despite being a woman), she now didn't want to do engineering (despite having a degree in it). To top it all, Maria didn't know what she *did* want to do.

'I was adrift for maybe a couple of years', says Maria, before she 'stumbled on advice work' and began volunteering at the Citizens' Advice Bureau (CAB): 'I spent three years unemployed, two of which were virtually full-time CAB.' Eventually Maria found paid work as a welfare adviser in Oxford, working alongside an employment adviser who was a qualified solicitor. Until then, the idea of becoming a solicitor 'hadn't been on my radar, I didn't think I was bright enough', but the job in Oxford gradually 'gave me a lot of confidence because I was trusted in my abilities.' To become a solicitor, however, Maria had to go back into higher education, for a year of a law conversion course followed by another year getting a Legal Practice certificate, and had to find the money herself: 'I had to save the money. I saved £10,000, from a salary of £19,000 or £20,000.' This still wasn't enough, so Maria chose a law course in Manchester, allowing her to live with her parents and work 15 to 20 hours a week in addition to her studies, at her dad's chip shop and at a hospital records department. Most of Maria's course mates, however, weren't spending their evenings frying haddock: 'It was a shock how many people said their parents were paying', says Maria, 'I'd never come across parents putting so much money into their children's lives.'

Following her academic training, Maria got her first hands-on experience: a trainee position with a firm of solicitors in Brixton, South London. 'It helped', she says, 'that the person who decided who got the training contract was from Manchester – the first time in my life I've felt that my background put me in good stead.' Unlike many trainee solicitors, Maria had her Legal Practice course fees reimbursed (on condition she qualified as a solicitor and worked in the Legal Aid sector for at least two years), because the cases she was working on were funded by Legal Aid (a system that has since been severely cut back[2]).

Elements of Maria's experience – and Jackie's – recur in my other interviewees' accounts of entering the jobs market. Some of these have been touched on in previous chapters, such as a feeling of having had little understanding or control over the direction in which their education was taking them, leaving them qualified for a job they didn't really want. (Jane, for example, talks about 'decisions happening to me rather than being made by me', and says 'I loved studying Sociology, but to this day I wouldn't have done that degree if I'd have known I'd have to be a social worker.') A postgraduate experience of their career being 'adrift', and only finding a direction as a result of something 'stumbled on', was also common: Paul was prompted to investigate accountancy by a suggestion made by his mother's then-employer, who happened to be an accountant, and Charlotte was made aware of the existence of the local authority's graduate scheme – which she entered prior to working as a civil servant – as a result of her mother working in a school.

Like Maria, several of my interviewees also reported having to face down family opposition to new career choices. Stuart Alford, having decided to change direction towards law after first studying something else, found this decision 'greeted with dismay' by his parents, because Stuart had already been offered a job with IBM, and his family saw no reason not to stick with the safe, steady option: 'My father worked for Kodak', says Stuart, 'he took such security from the career and pension … the consensus among him and his friends was that you join a company and stick with it.' (In non-privileged families, who are more likely to have experienced financial insecurity, the aversion to risky career choices is more than understandable.)

Another common experience among upwardly mobile jobseekers is the shock of discovering that a degree is a not the golden ticket to a good career they had been led to believe. As one former law student put it, 'you get this kind of perception, like if you've got a good degree from a good uni you'll come out and people [that is, employers] are going to be crawling all over you and it's just the absolute opposite.'[3] An expansion of university places created an increase in the number of graduates. Even a first-class degree is becoming quite common (the proportion of students obtaining a first-class degree has more than tripled since the mid-1990s: almost a quarter of degrees awarded in 2015/16 were graded as 'firsts'[4]). This increasing number of highly graded graduates has not been matched by an increase in the number of graduate jobs, so that increasing numbers of graduates (especially those from non-privileged backgrounds) find themselves in non-graduate roles.[5]

One way that some graduates are trying stand out amid the growing crowd is to get a postgraduate qualification. Such qualifications were always required for certain professions (law included), but are increasingly common in other prestigious careers such as journalism, where more than a third of new entrants now have at least a Master's degree:[6] As local newspapers have become rarer, their role as training academies for aspiring journalists has been taken over by postgraduate journalism courses, especially those at City University (London) and Cardiff.

Postgraduate study can also help improve career prospects by helping people to *not* get a job: providing something CV-enhancing to do while you ride out a recession, rather than entering the labour force at the wrong time and consequently being forced to take a job with worse pay and progression prospects.

As Maria found out, however, postgraduate qualifications can involve a great deal of expense: becoming a solicitor might cost between £25,000 and £50,000, while qualifying as a barrister can cost up to £127,000.[7] A very limited number of law students qualify for scholarships that will cover course fees, and some others are sponsored by Barristers' Chambers in return for working for them on completion (David Lammy got half of his fees this way, and borrowed the rest). The costs of a postgraduate qualification are particularly high for those who aspire to a legal career, but they aren't low elsewhere. The average tuition fees for a postgraduate course are around £11,000 plus living costs (but the maximum government loan for postgraduates is £10,000[8]). There are also fees for even *applying* for postgraduate courses: someone applying to Oxford, Cambridge, LSE, UCL and Warwick would have to find a total of £315 for the application fee.[9] Unsurprisingly, access to postgraduate courses is even more skewed towards those from privileged backgrounds than access to undergraduate courses, and becoming more so[10].

There has been increasing discussion of how internships have become the main route to a career in many sectors. Half the top graduate recruiters now say applicants have 'little or no chance of being accepted without internship experience.[11] This is especially prevalent in prestigious careers such as journalism, where in 2013 over four-fifths of new entrants had done an internship, of which almost all (92%) had been unpaid.[12] As with postgraduate courses, unpaid internships are simply beyond the financial reach of many people (there are no official figures on what proportion of internships are unpaid, but estimates range from just over a fifth to just under half[13]). Some opt to meet their living expenses by taking paid work in the evenings, but some unpaid roles don't leave enough time to do so: a 2013 study of work placements in creative industries found most participants were expected to work 'up to 12-hour to 15-hour days and sometimes weekends'.[14] And even when internships are paid, the cost of attending interviews can be unmanageable, as can the costs of living somewhere (usually London) during the internship itself, because landlords typically require rent and a deposit in advance, whereas pay is in arrears. As with the hidden costs of higher education, the idea that internships can be unaffordable for some can be incomprehensible to more-privileged others. A few years ago I was told by the chief executive of a charity – a sector where unpaid internships are also very prevalent – that 'if someone really wants to do an internship, they'll find a way'.

Nor is lack of finance the only barrier to internships faced by people from non-privileged backgrounds: a lack of connections can also be a problem, preventing potential candidates from even knowing about the majority – estimated at up to five-sixths – of internships that are not advertised.[15] Louise Ashley, an academic who has studied recruitment processes in the 'elite professions', has found that internships are often seen as currency, something to offer to sons and daughters of clients and overseas governments as a way of strengthening commercial relationships.[16] (Similarly, the former Prime Minister, David Cameron, despite his avowed interest in social mobility, admitted in 2011 to having 'my neighbour coming in for an internship', which he justified by saying, 'In the modern world, of course you're always going to have internships and interns … who come through all sorts of contacts, friendly, political, whatever.'[17])

Because internships are much discussed, they are under attack, and in some places unpaid internships are being withdrawn. The government's own Graduate Talent Pool website, for example, stopped offering unpaid positions following an investigation by the Social Mobility and Child Poverty Commission.[18] Some professional bodies such as the Royal Institute of British Architects will not allow their members to use unpaid interns, and the Conservative MP Alec Shelbrooke has repeatedly – although so far unsuccessfully – attempted to persuade the government to ban unpaid internships altogether.[19] But there are also 'internships by another name', such as the expectation of aspiring journalists to have had numerous articles published before they are deemed to have 'won their spurs' and be entitled to be paid as a freelancer (and many, many more articles before a select few will be taken on as an employee). Megan Bramall, now working at the BBC, says 'journalism expects people to work for free for such a long time, more than any other profession I've heard of'.[20]

But even when 'entry-level' jobs are paid, they can still be unaffordable. Acting is one of these, where work – perhaps in short-run theatre productions and adverts – typically comes infrequently and isn't paid anything like enough to live on. It requires aspiring actors to take the sorts of low-paid jobs that will allow the flexibility to drop everything if an audition comes up (shortly after telling me this, the actor Tom Stocks left the bar in which I had met him, to do his shift at a call centre). Unless you have family money to draw on, it isn't sustainable for long, says Tom: lots of his friends from drama school have 'given up hope or run out of money'. Aspiring lawyers find themselves in a similar position. As one told researchers in 2016, despite having been through the hard work and huge expense of qualifying, they were forced out by financial pressures: 'Unfortunately, I no longer work in legal aid … the financial anxiety was overwhelming. Working 10-hour days when you didn't know if you were going to be paid or not became too much'.[21] Ben Chu, a journalist at *The Independent*, points out that unsustainably low pay in entry-level positions in the creative sector and beyond, creates 'tournament jobs' with 'a high rate of workforce attrition'. People without pre-existing financial advantages, 'such as a trust fund or subsidised living costs from living at your parents' house', says Chu, are most likely to be forced out and for many 'it can be an unacceptable financial risk even to enter the tournament'.[22]

In addition to the implicit assumption that applicants for certain 'entry-level' jobs will have amenable parents, it is also assumed that they won't be parents themselves. For those who do have children – or other dependents – the costs, hours and risks of tournament-style jobs make them simply inaccessible. This presents particular barriers for people from sections of society where it is usual to have children relatively early in life, and for the increasing numbers of us who are expected to need 're-entry-level' jobs as we switch careers to survive and thrive in the changing employment market.

So-called 'entry-level' jobs are not the only ones that present an unacceptable financial risk. Almost 20 years after her entry-level experience of counting passengers at the bus station, Jackie was trying to become a Member of Parliament. Standing as a Conservative candidate in the Labour-held seat of Thurrock required her to leave her job to concentrate on campaigning. Because she had no family wealth to fall back on, she says, 'my level of savings wouldn't have lasted long if I hadn't won … some people have access through networks to people who can write out a four-figure cheque.… I had to bloody win!' In this case, taking the financial risk paid off, but only just. Jackie won by less than a hundred votes.

High-quality candidates

In an experiment, two groups of participants (group A and group B) were asked to rate a candidate's suitability for a job. Despite being presented with the same CV in the same way (they were handed the document on a clipboard, and given the same amount of time to consider it), group A rated the candidate as significantly better qualified and more motivated than group B.

The difference between the two groups is that although both were presented the CV on a clipboard, group A's clipboards were six times heavier.[23] Assessments of candidates' suitability were, subconsciously, being distorted by irrelevant factors. In real-life situations, the same thing happens: your chances of getting a job are skewed by factors that have nothing to do with your suitability. Louise Ashley, the recruitment expert mentioned in the previous section, says because candidates for entry-level positions have little relevant experience, interviewers tend to judge them on other indicators of personal 'quality', such as how they speak, what they wear, their posture and confidence. In a report Ashley co-wrote, a rejected candidate for a banking job recounted the feedback he'd received: 'he said you interviewed really well. He said you're clearly quite sharp, but ... you're not polished enough'; when he asked what "not polished enough" meant, he was told '"see that tie you're wearing? It's too loud. Like you can't wear that tie with the suit that you're wearing"'.[24]

It is possible to learn what sort of suit and tie are deemed suitable (although you may not have the money to actually buy them, especially if you've already shelled out for an outfit you thought *was* suitable). Other supposed indicators of a 'high-quality candidate' – such as having an air of assertive, extraverted confidence – cannot be put on as easily as a suit of clothes. Extraversion is a trait strongly associated with having high-status parents,[25] and applicants for 'elite' professions who don't have high-status parents tend to be those who, as school children, displayed the quiet compliance associated with being 'academic'. (Pupils from privileged backgrounds, by contrast, tend to be regarded as being 'university material' by default, having been 'brought up in a culture of entitlement' towards higher education.[26])

Even the more confident members of the non-elite classes can find that confidence cracking in elite environments. At his interview for a pupillage in a barrister's chambers, David Lammy was made 'very nervous' by someone he met before he even entered the room, a fellow candidate he describes as 'a posh lad, a blond haired, blue eyed, public schoolboy, wearing a pinstripe.' David then quotes me a line from *The Talented Mr Ripley* ('better to be a fake somebody than a real nobody'), and says the encounter with his pin-striped rival left him feeling 'in danger of being exposed as a real nobody'. Upwardly mobile job applicants who do try to summon up confidence – or an appearance of it – can find that it isn't as simple as they thought to appear confident rather presumptuous and brash. Jackie Doyle-Price's plain-speaking style could be regarded by some as brash, and though it didn't exclude her from standing as a Conservative MP, it did narrow down her options. 'Some constituencies find me rough and ready and abrasive; a street fighter', she tells me, 'people choose people they like, and they don't like that sort of thing in the Cotswolds.'

Sometimes my interviewees found that one of their personal characteristics – albeit one not very characteristic of others from their background – allowed them to meet the approval of employers. Dean thinks his ability to get a job in publishing may have been helped by some of the existing staff liking the idea of working with 'a nice gay man who did yoga'.

Most of us are subconsciously biased to seeing marks of privilege as indications of quality (people across the social spectrum understand 'well-spoken' to mean 'posh-sounding'). But people who make recruitment decisions – who disproportionately come from unusually privileged backgrounds and are surrounded by others like themselves – are even more vulnerable to these biases. As Stephen – drawing on his experience as CEO of a multi-billion-pound company – puts it, they are 'typically from a public school in the South of England'. Other cognitive biases to which recruiters are vulnerable include status quo bias, which inclines them 'to look for candidates who are similar to candidates they have hired before'.[27] I recently encountered an example of this when I pointed out to an employee of a think tank that a large proportion of their colleagues had graduated from the same course at the same university (Philosophy, Politics and Economics – PPE – at Oxford). Their response was that PPE provides good training in analytical thinking, which may be true but overlooks the potential benefits of introducing new and different analyses and viewpoints.

A number of organisations, aware that their recruitment procedures may be inadvertently rejecting candidates with more potential than 'polish', are now introducing 'unconscious bias training', a relatively low-cost way of addressing the problem. However, while unconscious bias is clearly a problem, it is less clear that training is an effective remedy (as academics who studied it pointed out, 'understanding the cause of malaria and understanding its treatment are two different things'[28]). Also, as Louise Ashley has pointed out, a lot of bias *isn't* unconscious:

one in ten recruitment managers openly admit that they would 'reject an applicant who went to a state school'.[29]

In some cases, the alumni of the more prestigious private schools are consciously sought out by employers who see them as possessing marketable attributes, such as the right social contacts and refinement to reassure clients. In other cases, employers are seeking people they themselves feel socially comfortable with. For example, Hashi Mohamed, a child refugee who went on to become a barrister, was told 'when barristers decide whether or not to take someone on as a member of chambers, what they're doing is saying, do I want this person as my colleague … do I want to share [conversation] with them? And the sorts of things they want to share are, often, fine wine … very often opera'.[30] The law isn't the only place where most people will find themselves struggling to meet cultural expectations; it also happens in arts and creative industries, where researchers found the dominant 'values and attitudes' to be those of 'a "creative class" quite distinct from the rest of society'.[31]

Very often, the experiences that form the basis of privileged people's conversations – and interviewers see as indicative of character – are too expensive for candidates to afford. The former Education Secretary, Justine Greening, recalls being interviewed for a role at 'a long-established City bank. Sat in a wood-panelled office, being quizzed by one of their most senior managers.' Despite having a degree in Economics, being a chartered accountant and having been one of the first postgraduate researchers to work on behavioural economics, her interviewer wasn't impressed. 'He looked me in the eye', she says, 'said he felt I didn't have enough of the "world experience" that they wanted, and pointed out that I hadn't had a gap year travelling. That was correct. At the time I was too embarrassed to admit that I simply couldn't afford one.' (Apparently Greening's stint working at a Morrison's in Rotherham didn't count as 'world experience'.[32]) Since then, these expectations have not died out. Amy Carter, a trainee solicitor who gave evidence to All-Party Parliamentary Group on Social Mobility in 2017, recounted a recent interview in which she, like Greening, was asked 'why she hadn't been travelling'.[33]

Not only does CV-enhancing experience cost money, so does the process of applying for jobs. Unless you are based in London, you'll rack up significant costs travelling to (and possibly staying in) London as part of the application process for the hefty chunk of the UK's jobs – especially the most prestigious and profitable ones – that are based there, and quite a lot of those that aren't: auditions for roles in Northern theatre productions, for example, are frequently held in the capital.[34] One of Charlotte's colleagues had to borrow money and sleep on a friend's floor while taking part in the civil service's fast track recruitment process (a process that has since been changed): he considers himself one of the lucky ones, to have had friends in London whose floor he could sleep on.

Some professions also involve other upfront expenditure. Tom Stocks reels off a list of requirements for anyone wanting a role on stage or screen, including £150 every year for a listing on Spotlight (a casting website), £200 for photos and £500 for a show reel. For someone like Tom, the time it took to save the money delayed his entry into the job market: 'so you're always behind the posh kids'. Delays like these put acting careers in serious danger, says Tom. 'I was falling behind, your twenties is your make-or-break time in acting, and I was eating into it.'

In some quarters at least, change is in the air. A growing number of employers are realising their recruitment processes are weeding out talented applicants. Approximately 100 employers are now taking part in the Social Mobility Employer Index (a joint initiative between the Social Mobility Foundation and the government's Social Mobility Commission), submitting information on employees' backgrounds and on what they're doing to widen opportunities.[35] Companies like KPMG, the top-ranking company in the 2018 Employer Index, are changing (among other things) how they attract and recruit candidates. Leading employers are widening their recruitment efforts beyond the 'top universities', offering work placements (with accommodation) to non-privileged applicants from outside London, and ending the practice of internships going unpaid and unadvertised.[36] Law firms such as Clifford Chance and Freshfields Bruckhaus Deringer are increasing living costs grants for Legal Practice course trainees, in recognition that insufficient grants have been 'a barrier to pursuing a career in law'.[37] The most prominent employers in such rankings tend to be large enough to have specialist HR staff (and recognition that their business model is heavily reliant on the talent of their staff). But some smaller employers, notably those with experience of social mobility themselves, like Jackie, are doing well: 'I've never had unpaid interns', Jackie tells me, 'and I've deliberately picked people from the constituency, who've not worked at Conservative Central Office.' (One of her former interns, who turned up 'not dressed for an interview', now works at the BBC.) Whitehall has also taken a leading role, seeking the advice of civil servants who have experienced social mobility themselves (like Charlotte Dring) on overcoming barriers their more-privileged colleagues hadn't encountered. Charlotte makes it clear that the problem is far from solved, but attitudes are changing: 'now', she says, 'if your face doesn't fit, it sort of does.'

So far, according to social mobility experts, 'there is minimal evidence that activity amongst employers is having a meaningful effect on socio-economic diversity'.[38] The proportion of privately educated new recruits in the Civil Service Fast Stream, for example, actually rose between 2013 and 2016.[39] This could be for a number of reasons, including that changes take a long time to produce results, but also because some initiatives are still at the trial-and-error stage: it is very likely that some innovative approaches won't be effective, but learning from them will help to identify which approaches will be.

One approach that already has proven results is contextualised recruitment, similar to the contextualised offers made in higher education. This works either by using data such as that that offered by Rare Recruitment,[40] showing how applicants performed relative to others with a similar background (rather than presenting recruiters with raw exam scores, in which potential is masked by privilege) and/or by setting quotas for the proportion of non-privileged candidates they recruit and promote. Grant Thornton, the accountancy firm that topped the Social Mobility Employer Index in 2017, says that more than a sixth of the school leavers and graduates it is now recruiting would previously have been unable to apply, and any worries that this might represent a reduction in the quality have proven to be baseless: once in the job, the previously excluded recruits are four times more likely to be ranked among the company's top performers than their colleagues.[41]

Because contextualised recruitment appears to be effective in reducing the advantage of the most privileged candidates, it has provoked a backlash. As the saying goes, 'When you're accustomed to privilege, equality feels like oppression'. The columnist Nigel Farndale,[42] for example, derides the 'anti-public school bias' of barristers' firms like Outer Temple Chambers, where recruitment procedures now consider 'whether the candidate has overcome difficulties to get into that interview chair'.[43] Others, such as the former *Guardian* editor Peter Preston, warned that taking steps to ensure that employees reflect the wider world is too much bother – 'newsgathering means looking outwards at the wider world, not anxious introspection'[44] – and a number of employers appear to agree: as the *Financial Times* has pointed out, those who participate in initiatives like the Social Mobility Employer Index are 'likely to be those who care most about the issue', hiding an unknown quantity of opposition or apathy. Unlike discrimination based on gender or ethnicity, legislation provides little challenge for those employers who put job applicants at a disadvantage on the basis of socioeconomic background. as *HR Magazine* reported, 'HR departments just aren't compelled to think about it in the way they are with other characteristics'.[45]

Until the 1870s, it was possible to literally buy your way into some of the country's 'top jobs', with institutions such as the Army producing price lists showing the cost of becoming, say, a Lieutenant Colonel.[46] The 'purchase of commissions' is no longer practised but, despite the efforts of some employers, there are still jobs from which your background or budget will exclude you.

Self-made

'Self-employment', says Steve Siebold, 'is the fastest road to wealth'.[47] Siebold himself became self-employed at the age of 17, and never looked back. He now writes books about how to become rich that sell in their hundreds of thousands.[48] Siebold is

American, but it is also true in the UK that most very wealthy people are self-employed. It is not true, however, that most self-employed people are very wealthy. Over three-quarters of the self-employed, in fact, live in poverty.[49]

If you are self-employed but not rich, Siebold says this is at least partly 'because you hang around people with no money'[50] rather than following his advice to 'get around wealthy people'.[51] Getting around wealthy people, however, can be easier said than done. Roger Burrows, a Professor at Newcastle University who studies the super-rich, says they 'never want to be on the same ground as the rest of us ... they're either in a helicopter or a private jet, or they're on a yacht ... we can't get to them'.[52] The offices, homes and social lives of the super-rich are separated from those of the merely-rich (who, in turn, segregate themselves from those on middle incomes, and so on). Even if you are able to get through the physical (and cultural and social) barriers that separate you from the rich, the effect on your bank balance may not be as you hoped. An example given by Rachel Johnson in *The Spectator* concerns a man who, as a wedding gift, was given the use of a rich friend's super-yacht for a week's honeymoon. Ill-advisedly, he waited until the end of his honeymoon to ask his friend how much to tip the crew: 'Oh, not too much. Just a token amount. Fifty, sixty thousand should do it'.[53]

Self-employed people who do succeed in getting around wealthy people tend to do so by being related to them. An example is Jonathan Rowland, the son of multimillionaire property developer David Rowland, who set up Jellyworks, a company that attracted enough capital to be valued at £245 million before becoming one of the dotcom bubbles that spectacularly popped in the early 2000s. Reviewing the rise and fall of Jellyworks, one City figure said 'investors believed he had the expertise because of his background'.[54] For Rowland, success was a self-fulfilling prophecy, until it wasn't.

Would-be entrepreneurs with the right connections don't just have an inherited reputation; they are also much more likely to have access to role models and mentors who can encourage and help guide them towards success. In addition, they have access to financial capital, which is the key difference between the wealthy minority of the self-employed – the 1.7% of them who get 31% of all the profits – and the majority: the latter lack capital, and have little or nothing to sell but their labour. The 'most commonly shared trait of successful entrepreneurs', as a recent study of wealth in 21st-century Britain found, was 'access to financial capital, often through gifts and inheritance'.[55]

Mark Dixon, in his early career, raised capital himself, almost from scratch. The money he saved from his year working around the world as a barman-turned-logger-turned-miner was enough to buy the equipment and stock for the business he would run as young man. Unlike the higher education path to social mobility, where some protection against financial risk is provided by loans that graduates don't have to pay back if their incomes don't meet a certain threshold, the entrepreneurial path chosen by Mark had no such safety nets. If the business had flopped, he would have lost everything. He was willing to give it a try because he has a resilient attitude to failure. 'You start again', Mark says – from experience – and he gives Abraham Lincoln as an example of someone who had businesses fail and became a great statesman because he learned from failure and had 'the ability to come back'. Mark was also in a position to fail if need be: 'If I failed I knew I could start again. I didn't have to worry about wife, family, destitution.'

Other non-privileged people with entrepreneurial tendencies also tend to prosper when they are given access to start-up capital, and to encouragement, advice and support. Louise Chalkley, an academic who specialises in entrepreneurship, points to an unlikely-sounding Channel 5 documentary, *The Great British Benefits Handout*, as an example.[56] The basis of the programme was that a group of people – who were unemployed when the show's producers found them – would be offered a sum equivalent to a year's social security payments, upfront, but would forgo any payments for the rest of the year. Despite tabloid stories suggesting the participants had taken the money and 'blown it', Dr Chalkley, who followed the participants' progress, found 'the result, without exception, has been positive. Specifically, an immediate short-term escape from the poverty trap for all the families featured, into a long-term strategy of entrepreneurship and small business ownership.' Having been given the support of a financial adviser, the formerly unemployed became market stall holders, party planners and salon owners.

The opportunity to become an entrepreneur, which Mark and the participants of *The Great British Benefits Handout* grabbed with both hands, can be offered to more would-be businesspeople. As other chapters of this book have shown, the UK desperately needs an improved system of careers advice and support, for those still choosing their career and for those changing direction. Such as system should include trained advisers able to assess business ideas, advise on improving any that have potential, access government-backed 'opportunity finance' on reasonable terms where there is a viable business plan, and find experienced business mentors for promising novices. It should also include measures to provide affordable start-up business space (as has been proposed by the Institute for Public Policy Research).[57]

But supporting people to become entrepreneurs also requires the safety net of a social security system that does not – as it currently does – create an unreasonable disincentive to reasonable risks (In fact, changes to Universal Credit are expected to result in 'grafters and entrepreneurs' being 'further impoverished, or pushed deeper into debt', according to Frank Field MP, Chair of the House of Commons' Work and Pensions Committee.[58]). It requires policies to reduce the chance of temporary setbacks becoming permanent crises of debt or eviction, as the debt charity StepChange and housing charity Shelter are urging. Without such safety nets, grassroots entrepreneurship is likely to decline, as it has in the US, where research has shown less entrepreneurship among middle-class Americans as a result of 'increasing economic insecurity'.[59]

Room at the top

In the late 1960s, says Barbara Stocking, 'It felt like the world was opening up. Society was changing. There was the pill … and the pill wasn't about sex: it meant freedom. A decade of real aspirations.' The postman's daughter would soon leave Cambridge with letters after her name and a sense of boundless possibility before her ('thinking I could go anywhere', she says). She soon *proved* that she could go anywhere. Her first job after university was at the National Academy of Sciences in Washington DC, followed by roles in London, Geneva and seven different West African countries within a few years of graduating. Barbara was living in what has been widely referred to as the 'Golden Age' of social mobility, and is an embodiment of the myth of that Golden Age: a working-class girl who rose through grammar school and Oxbridge to join the establishment.

But Barbara was an anomaly. People of her generation are more likely than their parents to have risen up the occupational scale, but as a report by the University of Oxford's Centre for Social Investigation put it, 'education, in many cases, had little to do with it'.[60] The increase in the number of people getting highly skilled, secure and well-paid jobs was mainly a result of more of those sorts of jobs being created by the post-war expansion of the welfare state, together with new industries catering to increasing consumerism and fuelled by – as Harold Wilson never actually said – 'the white heat of the technological revolution'.[61]

The chances of social mobility are dependent on the availability of new jobs and new types of jobs to a degree that cannot be overstated. We have seen in this chapter, and in each of the previous chapters, some of the numerous ways the privileged are able to stack the odds so their own children are more likely to get the 'top jobs'. When there is limited room at the top, everyone who goes up does so at the expense of someone else who has to go down, and the privileged will fight like hell to make sure they and their children *don't* go down (a fight they are likely to win – as any soldier can tell you, it is far easier to hold a good position than to take it). All the initiatives described in previous chapters – to equip our children with the ability and information to attain their career aspirations – are necessary, and some of them will create more 'room at the top' by allowing better jobs to be created in response to the availability of better-qualified workers, and unleashing the job-creating innovation of previously-excluded people, but job creation is largely a result of the demand for workers rather than the supply of them.

The good news is that the demand for workers is high: by mid-2018 the unemployment rate was lower than it had been since the mid-1970s. The bad news is that for many people, the jobs they get are not the 'job I love' to which most of us aspire.

We have the EU's highest rate of people in jobs for which they are overqualified, [62] including large numbers who, despite having a higher level of education than their parents, have experienced downwards social mobility in occupational terms. The likelihood that children will have lower-status jobs than their parents had at the same age is now greater than their chance of having a higher-status job. Even those whose aspirations are relatively modest – a job that keeps them out of poverty – are increasingly struggling to fulfil this aspiration, because work is increasingly not a guaranteed route out of poverty: most people in poverty are now in working households. [63]

The prospect of new *types* of high-quality jobs becoming available, which have not existed long enough to have been monopolised by privileged families, looks encouraging. Across the world, new products and services – and therefore jobs – are emerging as creative industries become more prominent and as the disruptive power of the third industrial revolution is itself disrupted by the fourth. [64] Whether the non-privileged will have a fair chance of getting the new jobs opening up in these new sectors remains to be seen: there is little data on the backgrounds of people who work in these industries, and little discussion of the issue in the industries' in-house magazines and blogs (this lack of discussion itself is unlikely to indicate recruitment practices at the cutting edge of widening participation).

There is also a question mark over the UK's ability to attract and retain new industries. Much depends on the willingness of our companies and government to spend money on the sort of research and development (R&D) that creates innovative new products and services and the new jobs that go with them. The CBI (Confederation of British Industry) has been pushing the government – and the companies that make up its own membership – to raise their game, warning that 'the UK lags well behind international peers, with total spend on combined public and private R&D... well below the OECD average'. [65] And the government has responded, by adopting a target to raise the UK's R&D spend to meet the OECD average, backed up with investment and tax credits. Another positive development is that the government is – belatedly – developing an industrial strategy, with the aim of supporting innovation. Despite being open to some fair criticism (for example, for its focus on already-thriving sectors[66]), the government has finally realised something our more-prosperous neighbours have known for decades: that unless we have a plan to attract the industries you want, we'll be left with the industries that weren't wanted by someone else.

But the UK's industrial strategy has not been given the attention and commitment it requires to develop effective objectives and approaches or to become – as it needs to be – central to the thinking and decision-making of individuals throughout government. What's more, the codes of 'corporate governance' under which our large companies operate require reform if they are to reduce the tendency towards short-termism and 'extracting value' and move towards creating value, innovation and long-term sustainability of profits and jobs.[67] Other economies already have a lead on the UK, and our ability to catch up is subject to some major challenges. The prospects for economic growth are – to quote the Institute for Fiscal Studies – 'pretty grim'. The UK is expected to be outgrown by most or all of its main competitors,[68] and the government's assessments of the impact of Brexit suggest that all possible scenarios will reduce growth (by between 2% and 8%).[69] Leaving the EU is projected to reduce foreign direct investment into the UK, with 'potential loss of "good jobs"' (that is, the more skilled, esteemed and secure jobs to which most of us aspire).[70] The process of negotiating post-Brexit trading arrangements also presents further challenges, because all the UK's potential trading partners know we have an urgent need to arrange trade deals, and it is hard to get what you want – such as deals in which the UK can specialise in high-value industries – when your counterpart knows you are desperate.

There is no clear consensus on which of the UK's regions will be hardest-hit by reductions in the number of 'good jobs',[71] but getting a good deal from Brexit is particularly unlikely for regions outside of London, whose advocates are not well-represented at the negotiating table and who lack the necessary political structures and powers to effectively drive regional prosperity.[72] Brexit is also likely to restrict the UK's supply of the people needed to drive the innovation on which tomorrow's new jobs depend: falling numbers of early career researchers choosing to come to – or stay in – the UK are arousing fears of a 'Brexit brain drain'.[73]

As Barbara said, the UK's era of 'real aspirations' took place at a time when 'the world was opening up'. The challenge for policy-makers today will be how to open up opportunities for ourselves and for our children when the country's economic options appear to be narrowing down.

SEVEN

Career progression

A crash course in applied anthropology

As we know from Chapter 5, if the children of low-income families make it to university, or if the children of middle-income families make it to elite universities, they usually graduate with better grades than their more-privileged classmates. If that's the case, does the same rule apply when non-privileged individuals get into elite professions – that the talent that carried them there against the odds means they'll out-compete their colleagues from more-privileged backgrounds, rise higher and be paid more?

No.

We've already seen that the higher a family's status – in terms of occupation, income or education – the more likely it is that their children will become graduates, and that graduates are usually paid more than non-graduates. However, even among graduates, those from a high-income family can expect to be paid more than others (10 years after leaving university, women from high-income families are paid 24% more, and men 30% more),[1] partly because more-privileged students tend to have been to higher-status institutions and studied more lucrative courses.

But even among graduates from the same institutions and courses, those who come from a high-income family can expect to be paid 10% more than graduates from middle-income families,[2] partly because more-privileged students tend to enter more highly paid professions.

But even among graduates within the same highly paid professions, background affects pay; for example, lawyers whose parents were high-status professionals can expect to be paid £19,700 a year more than their fellow lawyers whose parents were manual workers,[3] partly because within professions, more-privileged individuals tend to be in more lucrative roles, with more prestigious employers, usually in London.

But even when researchers took into account the effect of different qualifications, roles, employers and the 'London effect' (as well as factors like gender and ethnicity), the offspring of high-status professionals can *still* expect to be paid £2,242 a year more than the manual worker's kid at the next desk.[4]

Until recently, the phenomenon of people beating the odds at school, university and in job interviews, only to find themselves outpaced at this late stage, hasn't had much attention. There's been a lot of research on why children from elite backgrounds are more likely to get jobs in 'elite' professions, but little on how individuals' backgrounds determine their progression in their subsequent careers.

One of the people who are now studying this is Dr Louise Ashley, whose work on recruitment to the 'elite professions' appears in the previous chapter. She has interviewed professionals from less-privileged backgrounds, trying to identify why they are more likely to fail their end-of-year appraisals than their colleagues. One interviewee in particular stuck in her memory, a young man who felt like he was juggling two full-time jobs, one as a banker and another as an anthropologist, trying to understand and adapt to the strange new social and cultural codes of the people with whom he was working.

Two weeks later, when I talked to David Lammy, I mentioned Dr Ashley's theory that people who experience upward mobility into the professions are forced to combine the usual information overload of a new job with a simultaneous 'crash course in applied anthropology'. David immediately recognised what I was talking about: 'you can spend a lot of time as a working-class kid running towards something. When you get there, the reality is you've got to adjust to the environment, and it's not your environment.... It's too much ... working out the mores, not standing out and making a tit of yourself.' This is something I've heard again and again from my interviewees. David's fellow MP, Jackie Doyle-Price, remembers feeling that she 'wasn't from this world', and recalls working at the Corporation of London, where a senior colleague 'made a point of telling me I wasn't dealing with my knife and fork properly.' Tom Stocks talks about promotional events in the theatre, of having to make an effort not to speak and act in ways that might seem inappropriate to more privileged people: 'you've got to fit in with their persona so they like you and you fit into their comfort zone.' The result of trying to fit into other others' comfort zones is that people who have proven themselves remarkable – by getting to where they are from where they started – end up looking mediocre. As the human resources (HR) expert Norman Pickavance writes, they 'spend so much time trying to fit in that they don't spend enough time trying to stand out'.[5]

The cultural codes of the elite are opaque and baffling. Even copying the behaviour of people around you isn't a reliable way to avoid a *faux pas*. For example, brown shoes can be acceptable if worn by a foreigner, but not if you're British (this example of the pitfalls of sartorial improprieties might sound old-fashioned, but comes from Louise Ashley's research in the present-day banking industry). The anthropologist Kate Fox says English social codes are 'fraught with ambiguity, knee-deep in complication, hidden meanings, veiled power-struggles, passive-aggression and paranoid confusion', and that the elite has its own complicated and hidden codes.[6] Getting to grips with the anthropology of the privileged classes, says Jackie, is bruising and time-consuming: 'we [the upwardly mobile] are more resilient, but it takes a long time to absorb knowledge.'

Jackie had had at least some grounding in elite social codes as a result of her experiences as a student: 'I couldn't have done it if I hadn't been to Durham, you need to know what you're up against.' She isn't the only one whose ability to cope with the unfamiliar and often unforgiving cultures of elite workplaces had benefited from having been 'tutored' in those codes in earlier life. Stuart Alford, as we saw in Chapter 5, received this tutoring from the 'posh' sixth form girlfriend and her friends. Once David Lammy had become a barrister, his new friendships with fellow lawyers – especially those in the Society of Labour Lawyers, with whom he had similar values if not similar upbringing – helped implant the idea that entering politics wasn't 'for other people', and gave him access to people who knew at least some of the protocols of political life.

Despite the grounding, some people – including some very successful and self-assured people – never feel like they quite belong. Stephen, despite becoming chief executive of a large company, feels like the upper echelons of business are 'a social club' of which he was never more than 'an honorary member', having to mind his behaviour 'because you can get kicked out'. Stephen thinks the usual metaphor for social mobility, of 'climbing a ladder', doesn't accurately reflect an experience that he describes as 'more like an oily ramp'. David Tran, an American software entrepreneur, describes something similar: 'our world feels very fragile; at any moment, the clock could strike midnight'.[7]

Having to abide by other people's conventions can involve becoming, or pretending to become, a different person. As Stephen says, 'people who don't really come from the right background have to change their habits, forget about themselves, or they have to bluff it.' Some of my interviewees, especially those who felt like misfits in the social circles of their youth, were happy to change their habits or other aspects of themselves, but none spoke of a desire to 'forget themselves' or renounce their backgrounds completely. However, some socially mobile people feel they are being asked to do so. Louise Ashley tells me about corporate social mobility programmes that include an element of 'cultural education' such as formal dinners and theatre trips, which make some participants suspect the organisers of trying to 'make me middle class'. Paul Monekosso Cleal talks about the risk of metamorphosing into someone different and alienating yourself from your friends: Most of Paul's close friends are not connected to his working life, and I ask him if this puts him at a disadvantage, whether he could have advanced further in his career if he had instead made friends with 'the right people'. 'Yes, probably, but I don't want to do that.'

Management training for children

In a London pub in the autumn of 2000 I was introduced to a woman of about my age. She asked me what I did for a living. I told her where I worked and that I'd been in the job for about six months. She said, 'so you'll be getting your game plan together about now, then?' I asked her what she meant. She meant that after six months in the job, I'd have identified which people are influential and which projects are likely to be successful, and how to associate myself with them with a view to enhancing my CV and my chance of promotion. I was baffled, because no one had ever suggested such a thing to me before, and she was baffled that I'd got into my late twenties without a basic understanding of how to manage my career.

Growing up, I'd heard about people trying to 'get in with the boss', or staying in touch with ex-colleagues who they didn't much like but regarded as potentially useful; but such behaviour was regarded as being scheming, not a normal part of working life. My understanding of how to progress in your career, as far as I had any notion of it at all, was remarkably similar to my understanding of how to become a fairy tale princess: be virtuous and hardworking, and wait for someone to notice and reward you.

My younger self was more than a little naive, but not uniquely so. Peter Belmi, Assistant Professor of Leadership and Organisational Behaviour at the University of Virginia, has pointed out that aspiring executives from non-elite backgrounds are more likely to believe advancement is all about hard work and team spirit, and take time to adjust to the reality of workplace politics.[8] Dean Hanley's experience is a good example of this. He initially thought, 'if I'm good at this [job], doors will open', but later found that his competence and effort weren't rewarded: 'everyone else got promoted, I eventually complained, and I was told "do you think your face fits here?" I'd made a naive assumption. You think it'll be fair.'

The tendency of people from less-privileged backgrounds to struggle at self-promotion in working environments is partly about deference to authority (Stuart Sime remembers thinking he shouldn't 'make a nuisance of myself to get anywhere'), but it is also about unfamiliarity with the whole concept of a game plan. Dean's experience of growing up in a working-class community was that 'no one has a game plan. We don't have a career, we have a job.' My own experience was similar to Dean's.

Dad had the same job when he retired as he'd had when I was born, Mum worked as a shop assistant. Promotion, let alone a strategy for achieving it, wasn't discussed.

For others, the *consequences* of promotion are something they're expected to know but aren't told. Stuart Sime is an example of this. In common with numerous others, part of his motivation to do well in his job was a desire to repay the encouragement his parents had given him. While working as an academic at the City Law School, Stuart noticed he had had more books and articles published than some professors, and thought applying to be made a professor would be a good way to make his mum proud. His application was successful, but he hadn't realised that 'professor' was anything more than an honorific title, a sort of certificate of merit, and was surprised to find that he had also been formally promoted. He was also pleasantly surprised to find that part of his new role included attending meetings about university policy.

Some 'protocols of progression' are specific to an individual organisation, but others are common to a wide range of elite careers. Like social codes and cultural reference points (and the protocols of job interviews) they are complex and not quickly learned. Jackie refers to her realisation that there was an elite workplace skillset, and 'you don't get that by reading books and sitting exams'. Ambitious recruits in the professions, Louise Ashley says, need a finely calibrated combination of hunger and ambition blended with respect for hierarchy and deference, which is almost impossible to pick up in a short time. Innocuous interactions can cause confusion: if a superior suggests going for lunch, who is expected to pay? Are you supposed to stick to work-related subjects of conversation or avoid them? What if you don't know anyone in a similar job whom you can ask? Outsiders who stand back and watch, trying to pick up the codes, may be seen as not taking the initiative. Dean, like many others, had to learn these skills 'on the job', but realises he would have been better prepared 'if we had brushed against middle-class people more'.

Many privileged people, without realising it, have had a long training in these codes, since they were children at the dinner tables of parents who discuss each other's day. Higher up the social scale, young people are encouraged to engage with respected elders, honing their skills at combining respect with assertiveness. Disproportionately, men in the top 1% are taught these protocols by their fathers. The economist Eduardo Rodriguez-Montemayor writes that there is an (international) phenomenon of one-percenters working for the same companies as their fathers, who can act as their champion as well as their mentor, creating 'dynasties' within high-status employers.[9]

A common, if not universal, feature of the socially mobile people I interviewed is parents who underwent some form of 'alternative training' in workplace protocols, which could then be absorbed by their children. Some of this came from community activism. Barbara's parents, were, like Jane's Auntie Mavis, active Methodists, 'incredibly community-orientated' people who 'helped organise things', and Charlotte's mother was the sort who was 'on the committees' in Charlotte's school. In other cases, parents had small businesses (Maria's family fish and chip shop, David's father's taxidermy business and Jackie's father being a self-employed builder). Some of the skills acquired through these activities and businesses – and the mental habits of being someone who can make things happen (rather than doing as one is told) – are useful in professional life.

Voluntary work and self-employment, however, don't teach all the protocols of elite workplaces. One of the senior bankers interviewed by Louise Ashley's team thought client-facing roles didn't *necessarily* have to be done by someone who is 'upper class' but that 'charm … is important [and] public schools are quite good at doing that'.[10] Professionals who attended private schools can expect to progress faster in their careers than those who did not,[11] and there is a body of opinion within the 'elite professions' that state schools should do more to teach the culture and codes of elite workplaces.[12] However, many of these codes take considerable time and money to learn, and are to do with fitting in rather than doing the job well, so a better solution would be to make the path to promotion more easily navigated and more closely related to competence than culture and confidence.

For some of my interviewees, their rise was made easier because they worked in organisations where progression does not depend so much on learning arcane protocols. Paul thinks PwC, the company where he made his career, 'in its nature is upwardly mobile', partly due to its core business being accountancy, where 'early progression is about collecting qualifications'. Charlotte says something similar about the civil service, with its 'clear steps, stretching objectives, the annual careers talk', and feeling able to 'discuss and be supported in career aspirations'. Neither the civil service nor PwC are perfect in this regard, and nor do they claim to be, but (in some cases) improvements are being made, as employers become more aware that clear progression plans are a crucial part of allowing employees to meet their potential.[13]

Consequences of rebelliousness

Much of the evidence about social mobility comes from 'cohort studies', which track individuals at various points in their lives, looking for links between their circumstances as children and their fortunes as adults. One of these cohort studies involved half of all the 11- to 12-year-olds in Luxembourg (2,800 children) in 1968. Forty years later, researchers looked again at these children, now in their early fifties.

Most findings of the Luxembourg research will come as no surprise if you've read the previous chapters: children whose parents had high-status jobs were more likely to have high-status jobs themselves as adults, and high childhood IQ scores were a strong predictor of income and job status. But the study did tell us something new. As well as the usual information about family background, the researchers in 1968 collected information on each child's behaviour: how attentive were they? How patient? How optimistic? Forty years later, it was possible to assess what types of behaviour were associated with higher-status occupations and higher incomes. One of the behaviours studied was rebelliousness, using information submitted by the children's teachers. In effect, not only could parents and teachers now tell naughty children that they'd pay a price for their naughtiness, they could now calculate an *exact* price for their failure to 'do as teacher says'. The surprise came when the researchers saw how large a reduction in incomes the 'naughty' children suffered. The reduction was not large at all; in fact, it was into minus figures:

the 'naughty' kids had grown up to be *better* paid than their well-behaved classmates. After controlling for IQ, parents' social class and educational attainment, 'rule breaking and defiance' was 'the best noncognitive predictor of higher income'.[14]

The researchers, speculating about the causes of this naughtiness premium, thought the higher pay of the former child-rebels was probably due to a willingness to be more demanding when asking for pay rises and promotions as adults (and possibly due to a willingness to make money by 'bending the rules').

Unfortunately, while a bit of bolshiness appears to be useful for climbing the pay scales, in the UK it is an attribute least likely to be found among people who need it most. Recruiters in the banking industry report a notable lack of self-confidence in candidates from 'non-privileged backgrounds' compared to their privileged peers.[15] The upwardly mobile individual, having earned an 'academic' reputation in childhood through studiousness and quiet compliance, can find it a shock when they get into a professional environment where pushy self-confidence is rewarded and quiet compliance interpreted as a lack of initiative. It's hard to adopt a mode of behaviour you've spent the best part of two decades being taught to regard as transgressive and insubordinate. (Happily, moves are now being made to encourage school children to ditch some of their quiet obedience, including lessons in which they are encouraged to debate and argue. These lessons also appear to have a beneficial effect on educational attainment: pupils who took part in them made faster progress in English, Maths and Science than those who did not.[16])

Self-confident assertiveness, already at relatively low levels in the upcomers who make it into the professions, can take further knocks in the workplace. Denigration of accents is an obvious example. Theatre actors from the West Midlands report being told they had the wrong accent to act in plays by fellow West Midlander William Shakespeare.[17] Working as a solicitor, Maria was told she didn't speak clearly, to rephrase, to 'recreate my language'. (Maria was the one solicitor in the practice who was always understood by clients, whereas the others usually weren't, but the constant implications of inadequacy 'really undermined me.') Even in teaching, hardly an 'elite' profession, researchers who interviewed trainee teachers from Northern England found that most had been told to change their accents, as had one from Kent who sounded southern but 'too common'.[18] Having the 'wrong' accent seems to be punished more harshly in women than in men. Dr Katie Edwards, who interviewed academics about their colleagues' reactions to their accents, says 'women I interviewed all – every single one of them – said that they felt they had to "neutralise" their accents' whereas 'the men I interviewed, although faced with similar experiences, purposefully maintained their accents, some becoming even broader in the face of ridicule'.[19] This may help explain why, for a woman from a working-class background in a professional job, the 'pay penalty' is greater than the combined pay penalties associated with a being working class (and a man) and with being a (middle-class) woman.[20]

This policing of accents has consequences for children's aspirations: teachers can be inspirational role models, especially if children regard them as being 'someone like me', but this opportunity is lost when teachers are required to pretend to be 'someone unlike me'. The same applies in workplaces where senior members of staff are required to hide any accent or behaviour that could make them relatable to junior colleagues from similar backgrounds.

The denigration of non-elite people's behaviours, and its effects on promotion prospects, can arise from unconscious bias. Signs of social background – such as accent, posture and sartorial subtleties – are often mis-recognised as 'signals of merit and talent'.[21] Sir Keir Starmer, a working-class lad who rose to become Director of Public Prosecutions and is now a member of the Shadow Cabinet, thinks a sort of unconscious bias is part of the reason why the judiciary has failure to create fair opportunities for lawyers to become judges: existing judges' honestly held notions of 'what makes a good judge', he tells me, closely reflect the qualities possessed by themselves.[22] Barbara suspects this tendency to mistake cultured confidence for competence has affected her career, when she applied, unsuccessfully, to become Chief Executive of the NHS: 'they appointed a man. He was tall, confident. He could talk strategically but I would question whether he had the management nous I had.' She remembers that the interview panel was all men, but thinks 'the class system was as much a problem for me as gender.'

The unconscious biases against the non-privileged can become absorbed by the non-privileged themselves, in a similar way to how the children in Chapter 2 adjusted their abilities to fit their teachers' expectations. 'If you're starting off in a minority', says Charlotte, 'holding your own is harder', so you find yourself 'holding yourself back'. There is evidence that individuals from minorities are less likely to over-censor themselves (and thus censor-out the new and complementary insights that diversity could otherwise bring) if there is a 'critical mass' of them. Charlotte points to the 30% Club (an organisation campaigning – with significant success– for at least 30% of FTSE 100 board members to be women) as one that is acting on this evidence.

But as we saw in the previous chapter, sometimes the undermining of the socially mobile is not unconscious bias; it is deliberate bias. Louise Ashley says it is common for upwardly mobile people to encounter hostility from more-privileged colleagues, but it is 'difficult for them to talk about, they don't want to think it matters.' It clearly does matter, though: sociologists have found countless cases of 'upwardly mobile people feeling vulnerable and inadequate'[23] or who 'exclude themselves from seeking promotion because of anxieties about "fitting in"'.[24]

Some 'upstarts' appear to face down others' hostility or their own self-doubt by making a virtue of their upstart status. Jackie describes herself as 'bloody-minded' and being motivated to 'prove people wrong'. She says, 'I speak bluntly. Some people find it refreshing and challenging, a lot of people find it uncomfortable.' But blunt personas can hide internal damage. John Prescott, a ship's steward before eventually becoming Deputy Prime Minister, gave a robust response to the constant jibes about his background and former job ('Mine's a gin and tonic, Giovanni', being Sir Nicholas Soames' favourite), but the pugilistic Prescott still felt the blows, and later confessed to struggling with stress-induced bulimia.[25] Even for people who describe themselves as resilient, the forthright approach can take a toll. As Jackie puts it: 'you can conform, you can hide what you are, or you can battle, but you have to pick your battles, because it's exhausting.'

The entrepreneurial ladder

The first business Mark set up, after learning lessons and saving money during his 'DIY higher education' among the glitterati of Saint-Tropez, was the business that would be the foundation stone of his fortune – a hot dog van on the North Circular road.

Working through the night and meeting 'all versions of the British public', says Mark, 'was socially horrible'. But he also says it was the best of his businesses, requiring low capital for a very good return and – in those days of fewer McDonald's – there was 'no competition'. Profits were good enough to buy another van, and then another. Five years later he had five vans and a small workforce. The fast-food business gave Mark enough money to set up his next venture, and showed him the gap in the market his next venture would fill. Finding a reliable supplier of hot dog buns had sometimes been difficult, so he set up his own, drawing on his Saturday-job bakery experience. The Bread Roll Company was more complex, with more staff, more suppliers and thousands of customers. It also had the pressure of an unforgiving deadline: 'a bakery is like a newspaper, everything has to be done on time every day.' Every day for 10 years.

Mark took the profits from the bakery and changed direction. Thinking 'I've done things in England, try Europe' and having read an article in the business pages about Washington DC always doing well in recessions, he headed to another seat of multi-state parliament, Brussels, where he set up a flat rental business, 'breaking houses up to rent them to secretaries'. Again, Mark's struggle to find something his business required would show him another gap in the market, in this case, the lack of office space available for small businesses in Brussels. Mark's response was to create Regus, which now provides workspaces in 900 cities across the world.[26] Mark still owns a controlling stake in Regus, as well as the Château de Berne vineyard and hotel in Provence.

At the Château, as Mark talked me through the development of his various businesses, at each stage I asked him who had provided the finance to start and expand, and at each stage he told me that he'd financed it himself. The money to set up Regus came from profits from the flat rental business, which was set up using the profits of the Bread Roll Company, which was set up using the profits of the hot dog vans, and the first hot dog van was purchased from his savings from his year working his way around the world. 'I tried to get loans. I went four or five times and never arranged a loan. They'd say "come back in six months", but in six months the business would have moved on, I needed a different amount. They couldn't keep up.... I did the whole lot for cash.' Mark's experience reflects that of many aspiring businesspeople today. According to the SME Alliance, lenders have become 'even more reluctant to lend and are even more keen to ensure terms of lending are onerous'.[27] (However, small businesses are taking collective action to open up funding opportunities. The Federation of Small Businesses has recently worked with the government to give options for alternative sources of finance to those turned down by banks, and introduced its own Funding Platform to give access to multiple lenders with a single application.[28])

By the time Mark did manage to access external investment, Regus was already a successful business, able to expand with private equity investment and later, in 2000, through a £1.5 billion flotation on the London Stock Exchange.[29] By that point, the financiers were happy to deal with his company: 'you get up in the clouds then ... they might think you're an oik from Essex but your money's as good as anyone else's.'

I met Mark when I'd already spoken to most of my other interviewees. I'd heard their experiences of trying to make their way in professions dominated by people from privileged backgrounds, in which they often felt on the back foot, undervalued and sometimes actively undermined. What I noticed about Mark's career is that he didn't need to persuade a boss (or a banker) to let him climb the next rung of the ladder: he made his own ladder. There was no help from the government's 'Great Business' advisers or the Federation of Small Businesses or any other agency: 'there was none of that. I picked things up from business sections of newspapers. I read a few books – how to do a business plan, understanding finance and accounting.'

What Mark did have were coaches and mentors, on an informal basis. Peter, who had given Mark inspiration and business training along with the Saturday job, the employers for whom he'd worked abroad, and Freddy Fox: 'Freddy Fox owned the factory I had the bakery in. He was a great mentor as well. I went and spoke to him: "how would you deal with this issue?"'

There is a similar mentor figure in Paul Monekosso Cleal's early career at Croydon Council, a manager who 'helped me think differently' and put effort into Paul's development: 'I got to do things I wouldn't otherwise have been able to do. I if I was brighter than someone 20 years older than me, I got to go to the meeting instead of them. I learned a lot from him.' This was a recurring theme in my interviews, the key role of someone who spotted, encouraged and developed people's talents. Dr Robert Maxwell, who 'spotted and nurtured' Barbara to become Director of the King's Fund; the surgeon who encouraged Rozina towards reconstructive surgery; the upwardly mobile manager who recognised a 'slightly rough' talent in Stephen.

These mentors are crucial guides through an unfamiliar world, and some employers, such as the accountancy firm Grant Thornton, are now assigning each new employee to a manager who 'provides guidance to help them advance'. But people from non-privileged backgrounds can find it hard to find such figures. Senior people tend to offer a helping hand to people for whom they feel a 'cultural affinity'.[30] Together with the tendency towards low self-confidence in people from non-privileged backgrounds, this means that Mark, Barbara, Rozina and Stephen had lucky breaks, because the talent of the upwardly mobile is less likely to be spotted, let alone nurtured.

Getting up off the floor

Some of my interviewees, in their twenties, found themselves in jobs with no better pay or status than those their parents had had at the same age (and in some cases, were a step down). Tom worked in a call centre between acting jobs or auditions; Maria worked in her father's chip shop to fund her postgraduate law studies; others took stop-gap work while they assessed their options, or because they didn't yet know of the existence of the opportunities they would later take. For privileged people, early career stop-gap jobs are not necessary. Paying to take part in overseas voluntary work, postgraduate study or just pursuing one's interests can fill the time and bolster the CV. Actors from more privileged backgrounds than Tom's can draw on family wealth to avoid the need to work between acting roles. Family wealth can also delay the day when low-paid stop-gap work becomes unsustainable. For others, if the breaks don't come soon enough, there will come a point when they have to admit that they're no longer an actor who's working in a call centre until the big break comes; they're a call centre worker who once dreamed of becoming an actor. When 'give up your dreams day' comes, a Plan B is needed.

A potential Plan B is the path of social mobility traditionally associated with the working class, to climb up 'from the factory floor' to a senior position in whichever factory (or coffee shop or call centre) you happen to be working in after leaving education. A prominent example of this career path is Karen Hester, who began at Adnams breweries literally on the factory floor (mopping it, in her role as a part-time cleaner), and is now the company's Chief Operating Officer.[31] But outside of Adnams, prospects of getting up off the floor are not encouraging: almost nine out of ten workers in low-paid jobs at the start of last decade were still in low-paid jobs 10 years later.[32]

This is partly because better-paid jobs to which low-paid workers could aspire increasingly don't exist. The proportion of the UK's jobs paid above the legal minimum has shrunk over recent decades.[33] Newly created jobs in the UK are more likely to be low-paid than the European average. But it is also because, in many companies, a cleaner like Karen Hester couldn't rise to become Chief Operating Officer because she wouldn't be working for the same company, but for an agency.

The practice of outsourcing has grown in recent years, but whether it will continue to do so is uncertain. On the one hand, the consulting firm Accenture has said that within the next decade it expects to see large companies who have no staff except senior managers, the rest having been outsourced;[34] on the other hand, the proportion of people employed by agencies and on 'zero-hours contracts' has flat-lined or fallen in recent years, because low unemployment rates have increased workers' likelihood of finding more secure contracts.[35] What will happen in the future we don't know, but for now, there are large number of 'self-employed' or 'temporary' workers, many of whom (like the Portakabin-classrooms at my old school) have been 'temporary' for years, working at the same company but never *for* the company, and therefore with no prospect of rising up the ranks within that company.[36]

Currently, the closest thing to the 'large companies who have no staff except senior managers' are 'gig economy' businesses such as Uber, TaskRabbit and Deliveroo. The gig economy phenomenon has been much discussed, and with good reason. Between 2008 and 2016 the number of people employed in the UK rose by just over 2 million, and almost half of that rise was self-employment.[37] Some of the newly self-employed are handsomely remunerated consultants, but 45% are paid below the National Living Wage,[38] and most have no prospect of rising up the ranks. An Uber driver cannot become a supervisor, because the supervisor is an algorithm. As the business consultant Steven Toft says, of the various options for self-employed workers to escape low pay, 'the one most likely to succeed is a return to employment'.[39]

Agency and 'gig economy' workers are more vulnerable than other workers to a sudden loss of income, and much less likely to be offered training to upgrade their skills or avoid becoming obsolete (because organisations have little or no incentive to train people who aren't their employees). As we saw in Chapter 2, this tends to create practical and psychological barriers to aspiration for workers, fostering an experience-based pessimism about life's tendency to be 'all snakes and no ladders' which tends to be passed onto their children.

The gig economy's tendency to leave workers and their families vulnerable to suddenly falling into poverty and with little or no means of rising into greater prosperity has not gone unchallenged. A series of cases brought by workers, usually with the support of trade unions, have established the legal rights of at least some gig economy workers to some of the protections afforded to employees.[40] In Westminster, the issue rose high enough up the agenda for the government to commission a review, which reported in July 2017. But as I write this – more than a year later – there is no indication that some of the Taylor Review's main recommendations will be implemented or enforced.[41]

The number of workers in situations of chronic vulnerability, which declined during the 20th century, has recently had a resurgence not confined to 'working-class' jobs. If Brexit produces the degree of economic turbulence experts expect, many more of us will experience this vulnerability. Large numbers will require a financial safety net and the opportunity for career development, which will, in turn, require state provision and employer responsibility. Neither the state nor employers will be keen to face these responsibilities, but they will be preferable to what will be faced otherwise.

Even where companies do retain 'entry-level' jobs in-house, it can be hard to progress much higher than entry level. One of the more obvious limits to progression is found in family businesses, which routinely reserve the most senior roles for relatives of the owners. But in other companies also, opportunities to attain the highest-status jobs are often effectively restricted to graduates from 'elite universities' who entered the company via a 'fast track' management programme. As we'll see in the next section, this is often the result of a two-caste system of access to training opportunities.

Investing in people

Dad's first employer, the Royal Air Force, enabled him to ascend to a higher-status occupation than his father had had by training him to be an electrical engineer. Dad was one of many thousands of young men who 'learned a trade' as part of National Service. The forces still have a good record of investing in their employees' skills and careers, but now have many fewer employees. A few years after Dad's stint in the RAF, National Service ended.

Of course, the armed forces aren't the only ones willing to invest substantially in their employees' skills. The housing association that employs Trevor, my school friend, paid his fees for a Housing Studies HND (equivalent to two years of university). But he thinks 'it's getting harder to get on those courses now; local authorities and housing associations are getting their budgets cut, and when [tuition] fees went up, I reckon every local authority and housing association said "I don't think so".' Trevor is currently considering management training, but wonders whether he has enough time and money: 'I can't get fully funded for this because I don't currently manage staff, so I'd have to find 50% of the cost myself, and have to do it in my own annual leave time.'

Trevor's analysis of employee education being damaged by rising tuition fees (and public sector employers' falling budgets) is backed up by data. In England, there are less than half as many part-time students as there were in 2011.[42] Because students from disadvantaged areas are more likely to study part-time than their more-privileged peers, there has been an overall decline in the number of students from these backgrounds in higher education.[43]

Justine Greening, the daughter of a Rotherham steelworker who is now a Conservative MP, was put through a Master's degree in Business Administration while working for SmithKline Beecham (now part of GlaxoSmithKline), but points out that her experience is 'not that normal'.[44] In fact, it is remarkably abnormal. Employers in the UK are investing less in their employees' skills (and therefore their own productivity) than comparable European countries, with Dutch, French and Belgian workers receiving twice as much training their counterparts in the UK.[45] This is partly due to the UK's corporate governance codes and underdeveloped industrial strategy, which together foster a short-term, low-investment management culture.[46] As the veteran business commentator Anthony Hilton has pointed out, UK companies tend to pay lip-service to employees being their 'greatest asset', but compared to their continental counterparts, they invest little time or money into making the most of that asset.[47]

What little investment UK employers do make in their workforces' skills goes disproportionately to those who need it least, exacerbating the gap in life chances. Four-fifths of workers in the highest occupational classes have undergone some form of learning since leaving full-time education, compared to only half of the lowest-skilled workers.[48] A review of low-paid sectors such as retail and social care found 'the resources dedicated to skills initiatives targeted at low-paid workers are relatively minimal'.[49] Norman Pickavance, a writer and former HR director, says this doesn't just reduce the progression opportunities of low-paid staff, but also the ability of middle-ranking workers to realise their potential (including the catch-22 that Trevor had experienced, of being unable to access full funding for management training because he didn't currently manage anyone). As Pickavance says, a business culture has developed that ascribes larger and larger importance to a 'smaller and smaller cadre of people at the top'[50] and is therefore failing to create a pipeline of future leaders.

The lack of training and education provided by employers is a problem – including for employers themselves, who would like their staff to be better trained but fear training them will just make them more attractive to other employers – and the government has realised this. In response, George Osborne introduced the Apprenticeship Levy (in which, effectively, a proportion of employers' spending is 'ring-fenced' for training staff). The so-called National Living Wage also introduced by Osborne may help, by putting a greater value on workers' time and therefore giving employers a bigger incentive to 'up-skill' them to 'get their money's worth'. Policy-makers are still some way from learning how to incentivise training in the most effective way – as discussed in Chapter 4, the introduction of the Apprenticeship Levy was followed by a fall in the number of people starting apprenticeships – but the intention is good, if the intention continues to be acted on with further policy development.

In contrast with the well-intentioned initiatives, other developments are working in the opposite direction. The steady decline of public sector jobs since 2009[51] is a likely to be a backwards step for workforce skills development, because public sector employers are almost twice as likely to have a budget or plan for staff training as their private sector counterparts.[52] There has also been a decline in the membership of trade unions, which have traditionally played a role in providing training and, for some, an alternative route to social mobility through the union's own hierarchy (including for individuals whose refusal to adopt a quiet compliance led to them being deemed un-academic as school children, but well-suited to assertive negotiation as adults). From a peak of over 13 million in 1979, the number of union members has halved (even though the total size of the workforce has grown), leaving only a quarter of UK workers now unionised.

Even when there are clear routes into higher-paid, higher-status jobs, and the training is provided to help employees to navigate them, there may be little benefit in doing so. The increased responsibility and possibly soured relationships with workmates may not be worth the small uplift in pay associated with promotion from, say, shop assistant to supervisor. That small uplift is made even smaller by the UK's tax and benefit system: senior directors may not realise this, but while someone in the highest-paid 1% keeps most of each extra pound they are paid, working parents claiming Universal Credit may lose three-quarters of it.[53] A large UK retailer found this out, when less than one in sixty of its staff took up the offer of management training: a typical reaction was 'I don't think it would be worth the hassle'.[54]

The Sports Direct effect

In the summer of 2016, the sportswear retailer Sports Direct was investigated by Parliament's cross-party Business, Innovation and Skills Select Committee. The trade union, Unite, had previously reported widespread mistreatment of workers and a high number of ambulance call-outs to the company's warehouse, including to a woman who had given birth in a toilet cubicle. Another had been told by a manager that her chances of a permanent contract depended on her granting sexual favours.[55] According to the Committee's report, the company treated its workers 'as commodities rather than as human beings'.[56] During the investigation, Professor Jeremy Baker of the ESCP business school was interviewed by BBC Radio 4's *Today* programme. Baker argued that workers shouldn't expect to get 'full middle-class benefits right from day one'. The presenter, John Humphrys, asked whether 'everyone should be treated well, whether they're middle-class or whatever, shouldn't they?' to which Baker replied, 'well, no, I, well ... there you are you see, you're being idealistic.' Baker went on to warn the Committee not to 'come all out for decency and middle-class values without seeing the cost in the global economy.'[57]

Sports Direct has promised to change its practices, and its behaviour wasn't typical of UK employers. But it is an extreme example of something that affects large numbers of low-paid, low-status workers throughout the UK: poor-quality employment that damages the mental, physical and financial health of workers; which in turn damages their ability to escape from low-paid, low-status work.

Part of the Sports Direct effect arises from insecurity. A *Guardian* investigation in 2013 found nine out of ten of the company's staff were employed on 'zero-hours contracts',[58] not knowing how much, if anything, they would be paid from week to week. The company also operated a harsh disciplinary policy, in which minor mistakes put staff at risk of dismissal. In the UK as a whole, only 3% of workers are subject to zero-hours contracts,[59] but 14% have some form of insecure contract,[60] and a quarter fear losing their jobs, the highest level since data began being collected in the 1980s.[61] This sort of insecurity can be paralysing. Lack of a reliable income makes renting accommodation harder, and buying virtually impossible. It reduces your ability to 'upskill' yourself by enrolling in further education, because you don't know whether your finances or working hours will prevent you from continuing to attend. Research shows such insecurity to be strongly connected to poor health, with effects ranging from headaches and sleep problems to mental illness. Workers in highly insecure jobs have heart disease rates 19% higher than those in the most secure jobs.[62] This can lead to a vicious circle of poor health and low income. In the UK, this sort of insecurity is not confined to a small group of workers. Research conducted for the RSA (Royal Society for the encouragement of Arts, Manufactures and Commerce) suggested that 31% are 'chronically precarious' or 'acutely precarious', and that as many as 40% of us have a low level of confidence about 'maintaining a decent quality of life, now and in future, given their economic and financial circumstances'.[63]

Although most Sports Direct staff didn't know how much they were going to be paid from week to week, they did know it would be low, in some cases, illegally low. They were obliged to undergo a lengthy security check procedure, for which they were not paid, effectively reducing their hourly pay below the legal minimum. And, like insecure incomes, low incomes aren't confined to the marginalised migrant workers typical of those in Sports Direct's Shirebrook warehouse. As mentioned in Chapter 2, 44% of households with children have an income insufficient for a 'socially acceptable' standard of living, having to make impossible choices between life's basics.[64] The problems and worries associated with insufficient or unreliable incomes, which damage a worker's productivity as well as their wellbeing, may not be fully appreciated by employers, most of whom 'don't see any evidence of a worsening situation for their employees'.[65]

This book is about our ability to achieve our aspirations, especially the three aspirations shared by the majority of us. One of these aspirations is 'a job I love'. We are unlikely to love – or even like – a job that makes us financially insecure, and less likely to attain the second of the three popular aspirations, a home to call our own. But low and insecure pay also damage our chances of fulfilling the third of these aspirations, a family and a good relationship. As international evidence has shown, not only does income insecurity put pressure on relationships (see Chapter 2), it also causes us to suspend – sometimes indefinitely – our plans for marriage and childbearing.[66] The prevalence of precarity has created what Bob Dylan called, 'the worst fear that can ever be hurled: fear to bring children into the world'.[67]

Perhaps the most disturbing element of 'the Sports Direct effect' is workers being treated as 'commodities rather than as human beings'. Levels of humiliation such as those experienced in Shirebrook can cause a range of mental and physical symptoms, from feelings of worthlessness, vomiting, lack of concentration and insomnia to suicidal thoughts, and other symptoms usually associated with post-traumatic stress disorder.[68] Again, the conditions found at Sports Direct are extreme, but a more widespread culture of disrespect for low-paid workers can lead them to experience a chronic, nagging corrosion of self-esteem. (Imagine being a fast-food worker, watching chat-show host Alan Carr jokingly put down a guest with 'whatever, your mum works at McDonalds', a jibe so popular it comes with its own hand signals.) This corrosion of self-esteem, combined with financial insecurity, is so powerful that low-paid, low-status work has been found to be worse for mental health than being unemployed.[69]

The health-damaging effects of being in a job with low pay and low esteem don't just affect workers' ability to thrive and be promoted in a workplace; they can also damage the career prospects of their children, even if those children grow up to be in well-paid and well-respected jobs. This can happen in one of two ways. The first is the impact of parents' health problems on the careers of their grown-up children (more than one of my interviewees had their careers disrupted by the death or illness of a close relative). The second is more insidious, a legacy carried internally: research published in 2018, using data from 24,000 people, found indicators of health risks to be significantly worse in people who'd experienced poverty as children, suggesting that 'childhood adversity … compromises the biological ability of our bodies to stay healthy'.[70]

Of course, low-paid workers aren't the only ones whose working lives feel like a grinding slog of hard labour: 'it's tough at the top', as they say. But it's not as tough at the top as it is for the rest of us. A classic series of illness and health studies in the UK civil service found the most senior people to have the *lowest* levels of stress-related illness.[71]

Jobs referred to as 'entry level' imply an opportunity to ascend to higher levels. But it's hard to ascend if there are no routes upwards, or if those routes are reserved for others. It's hard to shine in your job if your mental 'bandwidth' is congested with money worries, it's hard to work well if your work makes you unwell, and it's hard to keep a winning attitude if your job makes you feel like a loser.

EIGHT

For richer or poorer

Feeling at home

For Dean, social mobility had been an escape, an escape achieved in the face of considerable odds: overcoming a shaky start at school, managing to concentrate on his A-levels despite the severe stresses of his home life, and seizing an unlikely opportunity to get a job in publishing. But in his thirties he found himself going back to the home town he'd been so desperate to leave.

Dean was only 'going home' temporarily. He'd been diagnosed with arthritis in his hip, needed an operation and someone to look after him as he recovered. But having driven from London to the childhood home he'd been so desperate and lucky to escape, he says, 'I sat there in the car, thinking "I've failed". I felt really down.' Dean's new life had taken long hard work to establish, but this temporary setback made him realise that compared to those born in more privileged circumstances, life for people like him 'is often much more unstable. It's a longer drop if things go wrong.'

This sensation of precariousness is common among the upwardly mobile. Jane, despite having (at the time I interviewed her) a middle-class occupation and an address in a middle-class area, told me, 'I know I'll never ever truly belong to the tribe I've been taken into' (remarkably similar to Stephen's feeling of being an honorary member rather than full member of his new class, liable to get 'kicked out'). To become a full member of the other tribe, Jane suggests, cannot be achieved in your own lifetime: 'I know that it's not actually me that benefits from it, it's probably my kids.... I'm the fish coming out of the sea, I've had to do the painful metamorphosis.... I don't know who the fuck I am, but my kids will.' The feeling of never really leaving our background behind is very common. When the *British Social Attitudes* survey asked people in 'managerial and professional' occupations to describe themselves, almost half said they were 'working class'.[1]

My interviewees did not say they had somehow failed by not becoming middle class (or, for those who were middle class to begin with, not becoming upper-middle class). Jane, for example, was very clear she didn't want to be accepted into the middle class if this meant renouncing the working class: 'University was my escape, but I'm more firmly rooted than I realised ... working-class values are the ones that drive me.' Wanting to have access to the sorts of education and career usually apportioned to people of a higher social class did not mean wanting to lose access to the people and culture in which they were brought up (but that is, unfortunately, sometimes the result; Maria told me about trying to 'spot people like me' among the other parents at her child's school, but 'I've yet to spot someone').

Others felt they had become a different class to the person they were, but not quite the same class as the people they met in their working lives. Charlotte Dring, for example, says, 'Cleethorpes and Grimsby will always be my home, I'm incredibly proud of where I come from', but 'I don't really fit as much back home now. Sometimes I feel that quite strongly.' However, Charlotte is generally upbeat, and sees benefits in being an incomer: 'the people who've always lived here' she says of her professional London world, 'are disadvantaged to not know what life is like outside.'

The term 'social *mobility*' can imply a desire to leave one social class and join another, but on the whole, my interviewees wanted to pursue aspirations not normally offered to someone from their social class, rather than be admitted to another class. In terms of their careers, they were overwhelmingly successful in pursuing 'ideas above their station' (which is what initially brought them to my attention). A number of them, however, especially the younger ones, have been markedly less successful in pursuing another aspiration: that of becoming a homeowner.

The proportion of the UK population who own their own home rose sharply in the post-war building boom and again in the 1980s as council tenants took advantage of the Right to Buy policy. During the 21st century, however, this progress has gone into reverse. In just 10 years (2006/07 to 2016/17) the proportion of 35- to 44-year-olds in England who were owner-occupiers dropped from under three-quarters to just over half. The English (with the UK as a whole not far behind) are now nearing the tipping point at which having your own home in your late thirties and early forties is the exception rather than the rule for families in the middle of the income spectrum.[2]

The overheated UK housing market doesn't just affect *whether* you can afford a home, but also *where*, largely because recent increases in housing costs have not been uniform across the country. Between January 2005 and December 2017, the average cost of homes in London rose more than twice as fast as in the UK as a whole (and four times as fast as in Wales). The average house in London now costs more than twice as much as the UK average and almost four times as much as in North East England.

As a result, London has become increasingly unaffordable: by October 2017, the average London home was selling at almost 15 times the average income (that's 15 times the average *London* income, which is substantially higher than the UK average), but mortgage lenders will typically only approve mortgages up to four-and-a-half times annual income.[3]

Nor is renting a possibility for many people, in a city where rents in the late 2010s rose almost four times faster than earnings, so that by 2016, for someone with an average income, it had become 'impossible to rent a one, two or three bed property within the recommended limits [of affordability] across the whole of the capital'.[4]

More than a third (37%) of Londoners say they 'might have to leave my local area in the future because the cost of housing is too high,'[5] and the net flow of graduates to London from other parts of the UK has slowed to a trickle; by the mid-2010s it was just over a tenth of what it had been in the late 1990s.[6] However, as the capital's affordability declines, the share of career opportunities located there increases: the differing rates of economic development can be seen in the construction cranes in operation on London's skyline, which outnumber all the cranes in the rest of the UK combined.[7]

The shock of the Brexit vote caused house prices to fall slightly – by 0.7% in the year to March 2018[8] – but there is no consensus among experts about whether Brexit itself will make 'a home to call our own' a more realistic prospect for more people.[9] On the one hand, the economic shock may reduce house prices substantially (and in the process put large numbers of people who only recently got onto 'the property ladder' into negative equity). On the other hand, an economic shock of that kind could also be expected to reduce incomes (and the supply of builders, many of whom come from other EU countries), making the average person no more able to afford those cheaper homes. Also, the UK housing market has recently responded to falling demand more by reducing the number of properties sold rather than by reducing prices, and it should be remembered that most new 'affordable homes' are built as a result of local authorities making it a condition of planning permission for more expensive housing developments,[10] developments which are less likely to happen in an economic downturn. More meaningful projections, however, will be impossible until the long-term Brexit situation (that is, after any transition period) becomes clearer.

In the meantime, we are experiencing a phenomenon previously observed in the US, where rising housing costs stopped workers from 'moving to opportunity' and instead forced them to move *from* opportunity[11] (In parts of the US, this problem even affects very well-paid professionals. In 2016 Kate Downing, a local councillor in Palo Alto, California, had to resign her position because she – a lawyer married to a programmer – could no longer afford to live in the 'Silicon Valley' town.[12])

As the Social Mobility Commission said at the end of 2017, 'London and its hinterland are increasingly looking like a different country from the rest of Britain'.[13] That country is effectively imposing tough immigration restrictions on who can live there and how long they can stay. In 2016 Dean was one of those whose visa expired: he found himself priced out of London – this time permanently – and heading back to the West Midlands.

Work versus wealth

The Sunday Times Rich List has a smattering of UK-born self-made billionaires (Mark Dixon was placed 147th on the 2018 ranking). When he died in 2016, Gerald Grosvenor was the second-richest UK-born billionaire, beaten only by Galen Weston, UK-born but holding Canadian citizenship, who was two places – and US$3.5 billion – further up the ranking. Grosvenor's advice for aspiring entrepreneurs – based on his own experience – was 'have an ancestor who was a very close friend of William the Conqueror'. Gerald Grosvenor was not a self-made man; he was better known as the 6th Duke of Westminster.

The Duke's life is an illustration of how our lives can be constrained by the circumstances of our birth, even for those who were born phenomenally rich. 'Given the choice, I would rather not have been born wealthy', he told an interviewer, 'I'd rather be Joe Bloggs.' As a young man he had aspired to a career as a footballer (with good prospects of succeeding: he was offered a trial, as a centre-forward, by Fulham FC), but he was persuaded from football by his father and later persuaded from pursuing another aspiration – to be a soldier – by his feelings of obligation to his ancestors and successors: 'I never think of giving it up', he said, 'It doesn't belong to me.' The Duke, locked in his gilded cage by his own sense of duty, later suffered breakdown and depression.[14] Shortly after his death, however, the Duke caused a scandal for having avoided his duties – specifically 'death duties' – when his estate was revealed to have been passed on to his son largely intact, having been placed in trusts to dodge inheritance tax.[15]

The Duchy of Westminster is an archaic institution, but its fortunes illustrate a phenomenon that is not just alive and well but actually resurgent in the UK: people from ordinary backgrounds who sweat their way against the odds into high-paying careers are finding themselves outpaced by those from rich backgrounds who are merely sitting back and enjoying the benefits of inherited advantage. Since the mid-1970s, the value of old wealth has grown much faster than people's earnings. In the mid-2010s (the latest period for which data is available), the value of assets grew more than twice as fast as incomes.[16] And while the value of assets has grown two-and-a-half times faster than the overall economy in the last four decades, the value of taxes paid on wealth has not.[17] An individual's chances of prosperity are decreasingly influenced by their own efforts, and increasingly by their ancestry. As Paul Johnson, Director of the Institute for Fiscal Studies put it, 'Inheritance is increasingly contributing to life wealth which in turn has consequences for social mobility ... inheritance is probably the most crucial factor in determining a person's overall wealth since Victorian times.'[18]

The Dukes of Westminster have benefited from substantial amounts of inherited wealth, specifically from wealth in the form of land. The so-called 'property ladder' has become – for those who are already on it – more like an escalator, elevating the wealth of the wealthy regardless of whether they put in any effort. This is partly because the value of land has risen, but also because so has the rental income generated by land. In the year ending March 2016, for example, landlords could expect an average return of 13.6%, approximately 10 times the average returns from a bank of building society savings account in the same period.[19] The money that can be made from housing has meant that lenders are keen to supply buyers with more money to pump into the market, and concomitantly less keen to invest in budding businesses. Our fixation on old assets is causing us to neglect future opportunity.

For those who are not already owners of land or homeowners, the property market feels more like trying to climb up the down-escalator. The rising rents that help property owners become wealthier also hinder tenants from saving towards a home of their own (not helped by any student loan repayments). Between the 1970s and mid-2010s, the proportion of incomes spent on rent more than tripled, to 36%,[20] and the monthly amount being saved towards a deposit by a typical renter fell to zero.[21] Anyone who *does* manage to put aside any savings is unlikely to be in their own home anytime soon: for a family with a 'low-to-middle income', saving the deposit for an average 'starter home', which would have taken three years in 1997, would now take twenty.[22]

For a growing number of people, getting on the 'housing ladder' is impossible without help from parents,[23] and so many aspiring homebuyers have turned to this source of finance that the 'Bank of Mum and Dad' is now the UK's ninth-largest lender in the market. This has pumped more money into the housing market, inflating prices further, which in turn prompts some to approach more distant relatives, such as grandparents. The number of first-time buyers using money from the 'Bank of Gran and Grandad' has quadrupled in just five years.[24] Homeownership is increasingly financed not by salaries (even relatively high salaries aren't high enough), but by drawing on the equity of previous generations of homeowners.

Not everyone, however, has the option to get substantial sums of money from relatives. It is unlikely to be an option for anyone whose parents are not homeowners. It is increasingly not an option for those whose parents are homeowners in cheaper parts of the UK. As Maria tells me, she was initially surprised when, in her late twenties, people who'd been her peers at university were getting their own homes. But she soon realised the difference between herself and them: 'they may have similar educations and jobs', she says, 'but the difference is that they had inherited wealth.'

Anti-aspiration policies

Politicians who make speeches about enabling more of us to achieve our aspirations, and especially our aspirations of homeownership, are frequently those whose policies achieve the opposite.

An example is the Help to Buy scheme, which provides money and loans on preferential terms to aspiring homebuyers.[25] 'Help to Buy' only helps those who already have access to substantial amounts of money. The scheme's typical beneficiary has a household income roughly double that of the typical household, including large numbers with incomes over £100,000.[26] To make matters worse, it is paid for by the taxpayer and has the effect of increasing housing costs still further for the rest of us (anything that increases demand without increasing supply will tend to inflate prices). Another inflationary force in the housing market has been the pension reforms which, since 2015, have led to the withdrawal of billions of pounds from personal pension plans,[27] much of which was invested in buying housing (but not so much in building new housing) because bricks and mortar are widely seen as a high-return, low-risk investment: one in six 55- to 64-year-olds now owns a second property.[28]

Alongside policies that increased the cost of homes by boosting demand, others increased costs by suppressing the supply of new homes. These include reforms to social housing introduced by the Thatcher government. Although the best-known aspect of these – giving the Right to Buy to council tenants – increased homeownership, reduced wealth inequality and created greater social mixing,[29] other aspects did the opposite. Local authorities' borrowing to invest in housing was capped (a cap recently raised – but not removed – and only in a limited number of areas)[30] and they were allowed to spend only a small fraction of income from sales of social housing for building replacements.[31] As a consequence, the number of homes built by local authorities fell from over 100,000 a year throughout the 1970s to less than 3,000 in 2016-17, having hit a low in 2004/05 when just 130 new local authority dwellings were completed.[32]

Policies that increase the wealth of the wealthy at everyone else's expense are not confined to matters of housing. Our taxation system, too, has moved in favour of the wealthy, who now pay 20% tax or less on capital gains (except those arising from any increase in value of second homes, which are taxed at 28%), whereas taxes on work *start* at 20% and rise to 45% (plus National Insurance).[33]

Some recently introduced policies are pushing in a more progressive direction, albeit in a limited way. More money has been made available for building at least some 'affordable homes'.[34] Measures to tackle tax evasion and avoidance have risen up policy-makers' agenda, driven by public reaction to high-profile tax-dodging scandals – and the government's need for revenue – including measures enacted in 2017 to remove some of the tax advantages previously enjoyed by landlords.[35] (Other types of tax-dodging require international cooperation to fully address, such as the tax havens in which an estimated 30-40% of the wealth of the UK's richest 0.1% is held.[36])

The development of 'auto-enrolment' pensions under both Labour and Coalition governments has also made a substantial contribution to mitigating wealth inequality, by increasing the number of employees who were enrolled in workplace pension schemes from less than half in 2012 to more than two-thirds in 2016 (and rising).[37]

Looking to the future, there are encouraging signs of a growing awareness among policy-makers that middle-income voters now find their aspirations – and especially their aspirations toward homeownership – frustrated by being on the wrong side of the wealth divide. The 2017 General Election result, in which the Conservative Party unexpectedly lost its majority, made this frustration plain, especially when analysis of election data showed that 'the entirety of the swing from the Conservatives to Labour was attributable to people who rent rather than own their home'.[38] Until recently, politicians routinely appeared to assume the electorate is entirely made up of homeowners. (David Cameron illustrated this when, being interviewed about burglary, he promised, 'that homeowners and small shopkeepers who use reasonable force to defend themselves or their properties will not be prosecuted', implying either that renters should use persuasion alone to fend off violent intruders, or that they weren't electorally important enough for Cameron to have remembered their existence.[39]). Now, by contrast, politicians are starting to propose policies that improve the rights of tenants[40] or reduce the tax advantages enjoyed by owners of second homes.[41] Other positive signs include talk of a 'northern powerhouse' and other initiatives to reduce the wealth inequalities arising from regional economic disparities.

Many of the above proposals are still undeveloped or of limited impact, which raises the question of why more politicians aren't courting the majority of voters (57%) who say 'more should be done to reduce wealth inequality'.[42] There are a number of answers to that question. First, politicians know that people who stand to lose from a change of policy are more likely to vote against a policy than the potential beneficiaries are to vote for it. Second, the wealthy have many more resources to deploy in opposing policies they don't like. Third, the wealthy are more adept at the protocols of political engagement. And fourth, non-wealthy people are less likely to vote, partly due to disillusionment, but also due to practical constraints (for example, in any given year, renters are six times more likely than homeowners to move house, so the average renter has had less time to register to vote[43]). The results of this unequal distribution of political power include wealthy homeowners' ability to block the building of new homes, through 'NIMBY' activism at a local level or by opposing any relaxation of a national planning system that experts regard as 'extraordinarily rigid by world standards'.[44]

The wealthy are not the only ones opposing policies that could give us a fairer chance to attain our aspirations. The people who stand to benefit from such policies often oppose them too. For example, inheritance tax, which is the most pro-social mobility tax because it is levied only on the wealthiest 5 or 6% of estates and affects only unearned windfalls rather than earned income,[45] is unpopular with voters across the political spectrum.[46]

Majority opposition to policies that would benefit the majority partly happens because such measures are misunderstood (the average member of the public estimates the proportion of estates affected by inheritance tax at 4 to 8 times the actual figure[47]) and partly due to how they are implemented.[48] But the wealthy have also been able to persuade large numbers to oppose inheritance tax because their representatives are good at 'winning hearts and minds'. They deploy the emotionally powerful language of 'home', 'family' and 'children'. Their opponents, meanwhile, use dry statistics and abstract notions of 'progressiveness', rather than properly developing their own emotionally resonant message of inheritance tax as something that funds opportunities for all of us – most obviously through education – rather than just for the wealthy.

Opponents of inheritance tax (and other pro-social mobility measures) are also good at winning hearts and minds by being downright misleading. A change in inheritance tax introduced by George Osborne in 2015, which made millionaires up to £140,000 better off, was promoted as something to 'lift everyone *except* millionaires out of inheritance tax'.[49] Similarly, a change to Income Tax, described in 2012 by Nick Clegg as 'freeing the lowest-paid from income tax altogether and cutting income tax for millions of ordinary workers',[50] actually resulted in the highest-income households enjoying tax cuts six times larger than those for middle-income families, and the lowest-paid getting little or nothing[51] (in fact, the lowest-paid suffered a net cost if the spending cuts that funded the tax cut are accounted for). In this way, those of us with middling or modest wealth find ourselves scandalised by headlines about the about the unfair advantages of the tax-dodging Dukes, but give our consent at the ballot box for the continuation of those advantages.

Pairing up or marrying down

When Jane became the only girl from her school year group to go to university, Mum and Dad were understandably proud. They were also, says Jane, quite hopeful, not only that she would have a chance to broaden her horizons and career prospects, but also that she would have a chance to meet a Mr Darcy.[52] And sure enough, in her second year, Jane started 'going out' with Trevor, the son of a banker. It didn't work out, but then Jane met someone else, and this time struck it even luckier. She met Patrick, to whom she is now married. Patrick is someone I aspire to be more like – one of the most principled and kind people I've ever met. He is also a former car mechanic, whose dad and brother had criminal records. 'Trevor gave me opportunities I'd never dreamed of', says Jane 'paid for me to go round America. But I have to say Patrick was more "familiar", could understand what had happened to me, which Trevor didn't.'

Among my interviewees, some now have partners whose background is considerably 'posher' than their own. David Lammy is married to the artist daughter of a professor, and Barbara Stocking to a public school-educated doctor, for example. But in most cases, their partners' backgrounds are similar to their own. Jackie Doyle-Price, for example, is the daughter of a builder and now her partner is a former builder. This is typical in society as a whole, and becoming more typical: women born between 1976 and 1981 are less than half as likely to have married someone from a higher social class as women born in 1958.[53]

Sociologists refer to our tendency to form romantic relationships with people from similar social, ethnic or religious backgrounds by the resolutely unromantic-sounding term 'assortative mating'. It suppresses the social mobility of succeeding generations, by concentrating resources (and therefore life chances) in a small number of families. These resources include not only wealth but also access to non-financial resources such as well-educated and well-connected aunts, uncles and family friends, which have been shown to 'multiply the effects of having highly educated parents (or mitigate the effects of less-educated parents) on children's chances'.[54]

For a clue as to *why* we tend to choose romantic partners whose backgrounds are similar to our own, I consulted a guide to 'the best "flirting zones"' devised by the anthropologist Kate Fox. According to Fox, the best places in Britain[55] for successful flirting are those that pass what she calls the 'SAS test': 'S' for 'sociable places' (that is, where it is acceptable to strike up conversation with strangers), 'A' for alcohol and 'S' for 'shared interests'.[56]

To assess the relative merits of various 'sociable spaces', Fox turns first to bars and pubs. Licensed premises allow some degree of social mixing, but some are effectively reserved for the wealthy by the prices they charge (as I once discovered when invited to the birthday party of a friend of a friend: it turned out to be in the bar of a very smart London hotel. I and five others could, by pooling funds, just about afford the hotel's cheapest bottle of wine, so we asked for six glasses to go with it – to the disdain of the *sommelier* – and eked it out for as long as possible before sneaking off to a pub.) In other cases the ambience of a place can be just as effective a way to tell you you're not the sort of clientele they want.

Bars and pubs are good for what was referred to in my youth as 'getting off' with people, but statistics show they aren't such a good place to meet a long-term partner (and are becoming less popular with younger generations, whose leisure preferences are becoming healthier). Higher education institutions have a better record of fostering lasting relationships. One in five graduates 'meet the loves of their life on campus', with numerous other couples being introduced post-graduation by friends they met as students.[57] The expansion of higher education therefore has the potential to create more assortative mating, as we saw in the

1960s, when the number of students entering higher education and the number of people marrying someone from a different background both increased dramatically. But after the 1990s the number of students in higher education increased even more sharply and the number of cross-class marriages stayed flat.[58] The explanation for this may partly lie in the segregation of privileged and non-privileged students into different institutions, courses and social circles, as shown in a previous chapter. (It is notable that Barbara was introduced to her husband by the same school friends who encouraged her to go to Cambridge.)

Beyond licensed premises and institutions of higher education, it is unclear whether social spaces will become more or less segregated. On the one hand, social classes are increasingly being divided into separate spaces, with the elites especially driving an 'intensification of class geographies'.[59] On the other, couples increasingly don't conduct their first flirtations in a geographical location at all. An estimated one in five relationships are now estimated to begin online.[60] What little relevant research has so far been done into this suggests it is helping break down class boundaries,[61] although there are now a growing number of 'exclusive' online dating services such as Toffee ('the world's first dating app for people who were privately educated').

Another element of Kate Fox's formula for fruitful flirting, 'shared interests', presents challenges to cross-class courtship due to the prevalent preference of the privileged for expensive leisure activities such as skiing and sailing. Also, my interviewees' accounts of their relationships suggest 'shared interests' have to be accompanied by something deeper. A number of my interviewees said the most important thing they had in common with their partner was 'values', which they frequently saw as being products of their class background, referring to what academics might call 'kinship'. Often, my interviewees said they appreciated their partner's ability to understand their experiences, in contrast to people in their working and social lives who didn't. Tom Stocks, the actor – whose partner, like him, is from a former mill town in the North West – says, 'you don't have to go to an effort just to be with them … you know where they're coming from.'

Couples who do overcome class divides are likely to experience discouragement from friends and families. A friend of mine – a privately educated North London woman – is in a happy, long-term relationship with a man who works as a bricklayer; her relatives know about the relationship, but it hasn't stopped some of them trying to introduce her to the occasional 'nice boy' who would make a 'better' match. Almost everyone likes the *idea* of commoners marrying princes – no one begrudges Cinderella – but some families aren't so keen on their own little prince (or princess) marrying a scullery maid. As a contributor to a Mumsnet discussion of 'Did you marry "beneath" you?' said (repeated here verbatim) 'my parents always taught us that all honest jobs, done well, are worthwhile, be that a cleaner or ceo of a multinational. as long as its an honest job, there's no difference. having said that, i dont think i would want my kids to have partners working menial jobs'.[62]

Snobbery about 'menial jobs' aside, parents have a growing financial incentive to stop their offspring 'marrying down'. The increasing importance of family wealth to chances of homeownership means wealthy families have an interest in their progeny finding a partner whose family won't diminish the couple's ability to pay for the deposit on a 'suitable' home. But resistance doesn't always come from the higher-status family. The families of people who are 'marrying up' frequently fear being humiliated before their 'betters' as a result of their lack of financial resources or cultural polish. Stuart Alford describes having had upper-middle-class girlfriends as a student, with whom his lower-middle-class mother 'felt uncomfortable'. Stuart's parents, he says, had 'a sense that society is quite stratified; that you stay within your strata.' More recently, however, Stuart has married outside his stratum. His wife Sylvia is a judge with an aristocratic ancestry. Stuart thinks this has become less of an issue than it was in the days when his girlfriends made his mum uncomfortable. So what has changed?

Partly what changed is that Stuart became more acceptable in elite society by effectively serving a long probationary period. As he says, by the time of his wedding, 'I was a barrister, knew how to speak, how to hold a knife and fork.' He was helped in this process – as were so many of my interviewees – by 'posh friends' who built on the training he received in the protocols of privilege from his sixth form girlfriend.

But also, Stuart thinks social snobbery is diminishing in society as a whole. 'Twenty years ago', he says, 'with my wife's friends, I wouldn't hide my background but I would try to steer conversation away from it. Now it has flipped. To some extent it is my wife's background that's a bit embarrassing. Society has moved.... In the early to mid '80s the establishment, institutions, professions were still very much the dominant force, and they were still extremely dominated by private school mindsets. Those institutions have become less important. Our society has become much more fragmented.' Part of the elite's increased tolerance for 'lower-class' culture, Stuart suggests, may be a result of wider social liberalism brought about by 'greater mixing of cultures and nationalities'.

Ferdinand Mount – a writer, erstwhile Conservative political adviser, baronet and cousin of David Cameron – agrees that 'this sort of snobbery' is waning, 'except perhaps among a tiny cluster of dinosaurs.'[63] (In the next chapter, however, we'll see evidence of it being buried rather than dead.) But Mount also suggests that snobbery based on culture has given way to snobbery based on economics, or as Stuart says, background has become less important, but 'money is more important'.

Buying chances

The idea that each of us has a soul mate, a perfect partner out there somewhere meant only for us, is, of course, guff.[64] But if you *did* have a perfect soul mate, and if they happened to have been born into different social or economic class to you, you're unlikely to end up with them. There isn't an actual prohibition against you having a relationship with them, it's just that – as the previous section showed – the odds are stacked against it. You're not likely to meet them, you're not likely to have much in common with them, and you're not likely to get much encouragement from friends and family.

The same applies to most of the other factors that determine the chances of attaining our aspirations. There is no actual prohibition, but the odds are stacked against it. Those from non-privileged backgrounds aren't debarred from having parents able to give them a good level of 'school-readiness', but they're less likely to have such parents. They're not disallowed from being taught by the most qualified teachers, but such teachers are less likely to be found in their schools. They're not forbidden from choosing careers that are not 'class-appropriate', but they're less likely to become aware of such careers and the means of entering them. And so on.

It is noticeable that a large proportion of the people featured as case studies in this book experienced social mobility as a result of something that happened *in spite of* the odds: unlikely friendships and unusual encounters. This isn't to say they didn't display extraordinary ability or dedication – they did – but rather that they were able to fully realise their potential as a result of some against-the-odds circumstance not granted to others who may have been just as able and dedicated. To paraphrase Karl Marx, 'we make our own history, but not in circumstances of our own choosing'.[65]

The most privileged – against whom the rest of us must compete if our aspirations happen to lie in an area they dominate – play with the dice loaded in their favour. They also get to roll the dice more often. Left university unable to find a graduate-level job in a squeezed labour market? Roll again by paying for a postgraduate degree. Done an internship that didn't lead to a job? Roll again by asking your family to fund your living costs while you do another one, or pay the set-up costs for a business, and if that fails, for another one.

For the most privileged, it's easy to become accustomed to the idea that having the funds to 'have another go' is normal. (A friend of mine recently had an insight into this outlook. Having withdrawn her application to study for a Master's degree due to being unable to secure a bursary, a wealthier acquaintance quizzically asked why she didn't just get her parents to pay for it.) To people who're privileged enough to think it's normal to have access to a substantial 'opportunity fund' of family wealth, it doesn't seem unreasonable to design career opportunities that can only be accessed with such an opportunity fund. What was once an advantage (a postgraduate degree, experience as an unpaid intern or of overseas volunteering) becomes an expectation.

For the worst-off, the odds are sometimes stacked against their being able to play the game at all, because they are priced out of aspirations the rest of us take for granted. People with no family wealth, or no family – such as those who are estranged from their families, or who were brought up in local authority care – may be locked out of opportunities by being unable to scrape together enough money to attend interviews (for jobs or educational institutions) outside their region.

But the elite, whose advantage over the rest of us was shrinking until the late 1970s, now see their advantage growing again. Between 2006-12 the amount of wealth held by the average UK household fell by 2.5%, but the wealth of 'the 1%' increased by 8.4% (having stagnated or fallen in other comparable countries).[66] More money to pay for themselves or their children to have another roll of the dice, and another, and another, until they roll a six. For the rest of us, we have limited chances to realise our aspirations, and greater chances that – having run out of options – we give up on our dreams.

NINE

Does social mobility matter?

Business, public services and the economy: out of touch and out-performed

In 1585, southwest of Greenland, three ships were caught in a gale. The mainmast of the lead ship, the *Gabriel*, was cracked and the top of the foremast torn off in the screaming winds. One of the ships went down. Men drowned. The gale lasted more than a week. The crew of one of the two remaining vessels mutinied, refused to continue the voyage, and sailed home to London, where they would claim to have seen the *Gabriel* sink. But the remaining ship carried on, north-west, towards the unmapped Arctic.

The captain in charge of the expedition, Martin Frobisher, had been hired by the Cathay Company to sail in search of the North-West Passage, which the company hoped would create a trading route to China via Canada's north coast. Having endured the loss of a further five men in a dispute with an Inuit tribe, Frobisher did discover a passage leading north-west. He returned to London and was commissioned for a second voyage. A great step forward.

Well, not quite. Frobisher wasn't the first to find that route. He wasn't even the first non-Inuit to find it. Fishermen were there before him. (As one historian of Arctic exploration put it, they 'stepped aside long enough to let the gentlemen discover the land, and then went back to fishing.'[1]) Those fishermen could have saved Frobisher the arduous journey. They could also have told him the passage he'd found wasn't a passage at all,

202

but a 140-mile-long inlet (now called Frobisher Bay) that does not lead to China. Frobisher Bay is a dead end, which had sent sailors to their deaths and the Cathay Company into bankruptcy.

Frobisher's voyage is just one episode in a long history of financial and humanitarian disasters that could have been averted if the 'establishment' had been open to people from 'the lower orders'. But the contributions of common seamen and fishermen 'were thought by the upper classes not quite appropriate to the developing purposes of science'.[2]

Almost half a millennium later, things have changed. But some things haven't changed as much as we might like to think. In 2005, after repeated safety warnings from workers in a BP refinery were ignored, a leak killed 15 and injured 500, blasted in the explosion or burned as a result of the air having caught fire.[3] Five years later, BP experienced another leak, another explosion, another environmental catastrophe, and another 11 men dead. This new disaster, on the Deepwater Horizon offshore drilling rig, also cost the company tens of billions of dollars.

The HR expert Norman Pickavance cites the incidents at BP as examples of a 'boardroom bubble', especially prevalent in the US (where BP's disasters took place) and the UK (where it is headquartered), in which senior managers lack understanding of their workforce, their customers, and the opportunities and risks facing their organisation. Partly, boardroom bubbles are the result of recruiting senior managers from an international elite rather than developing the talent of existing employees with hands-on knowledge of their business.[4]

Many businesses and other organisations do little to open opportunities to a more socially representative group of people as a result of the 'status quo bias' we encountered in previous chapters (overestimating the value of what we already have and underestimating that of what we could have). Making the necessary adjustments to access the potential of social diversity is seen as a chore, just as learning how to use computers rather than card-filing systems was once seen as 'more trouble than it's worth'.

Some of the more enlightened companies, such as the global accountancy firm KPMG, are now recognising that 'a broader spectrum of views ... makes good business sense'.[5]

Senior management teams whose members come from diverse backgrounds are less prone to 'groupthink', more likely to take an analytical, evidence-based approach, more innovative, and more profitable.[6] Investment portfolios managed by professionals from non-privileged backgrounds perform significantly better than the portfolios managed by their colleagues.[7]

However, the performance-enhancing effect of the fund managers from poorer backgrounds is limited in the UK by there not being many of them. Financial services companies are effectively turning away talent, and therefore turning away profits. This phenomenon is not confined to 'the City'. The UK's scientific research industry is another important pillar of our economy,[8] but Katherine Mathieson, chief executive of the British Science Association, says barriers to non-privileged people's entry to scientific careers are 'extreme'.[9] Scientific institutions may no longer think that the contributions of non-privileged classes are 'not quite appropriate to the developing purposes of science', but they still reject those contributions.

The consequences of turning away talent on a (literally) industrial scale have recently been hinted at by a long-term research project in the US, a country with an even worse social mobility problem than the UK. The project compared students' test scores with the jobs those students later went into, and found that 'low-income students who are among the very best math students – those who score in the top 5 percent of all third graders – are no more likely to become inventors than below-average math students from affluent families'.[10] The researchers who analysed the data concluded 'there are many "lost Einsteins" – people who would have had high-impact inventions had they become inventors'.[11] By suppressing opportunity for individuals, we are suppressing progress for humanity.

When capable people from ordinary backgrounds are prevented from becoming investment managers or scientists – or executives or policy-makers – those jobs are taken by mediocre people from privileged backgrounds. This dumbing-down is expensive. One assessment suggested the UK's poor levels of social mobility could cost up to £140 billion a year by 2050.[12] Sir Mark Boleat, of the City of London Corporation, thinks it isn't just a lost opportunity, but a threat. Unless employers begin 'casting the net wider in the search for talent', says Boleat, the UK's 'long-term economic sustainability is left vulnerable'.[13]

Politics in a bubble: not on the same page, not on the same story

In the autumn of 2015, at a meeting in London with the head of a think tank, I asked a question, and the reaction I got made it instantly clear that it was a particularly stupid one. We were discussing plans for a project, and I'd asked how those plans would be affected if the UK voted to leave to EU, referring to the referendum that was to take place six months later. With a look of surprised disdain, he told me that was clearly 'not going to happen' and returned to what he was saying.

In retrospect, my question hadn't been so stupid, but neither was his reaction. All the evidence he'd seen – the analysis in broadsheet newspapers and periodicals, the financial markets – clearly indicated 'Remain' would win by a substantial margin. Perhaps more importantly, he, as an Oxbridge-educated member of the establishment, would have intuitively 'known' Remain would win because everyone he knew would have thought leaving the EU a spectacularly bad idea. Across wide swathes of London, Leave voters were nowhere to be seen. (The evening before the Brexit vote I cycled home from a meeting, a half-hour journey from Highgate to Tottenham, and made a mental note of the number of 'Leave' or 'Remain' posters in the windows of houses I passed on the way. Remain won, forty-nil.)

But another member of the establishment, Paul Monekosso Cleal, wasn't so sure Remain was going to win. By 2015 he was a partner in a major accountancy firm and a member of the government's Social Mobility Commission. Unlike the man from the think tank, Paul wasn't surrounded by people who thought leaving the EU was a spectacularly bad idea. His boyhood friend, for example, in Paul's native Croydon, told him that – other than Paul himself – he 'didn't know anyone who was voting Remain'.

In the days following the 'shock' Brexit vote, many of the newspapers ran opinion pieces about listening to people from outside the metropolitan elite. In the vast majority of cases, these articles were written by members of the metropolitan elite.

Typical headlines included 'we need to start listening to each other', 'we have to step out of our echo chambers and listen' and 'politicians should listen to real people, says Camilla Tominey'.[14] The referendum result might have prompted newspaper editors to let their usual columnists have the week off, and give space to journalists from Basingstoke or Bedford (which voted for Brexit in similar proportions to the UK as a whole), based on day-to-day experience of actually living there. But they didn't. The Brexit vote was a wake-up call for metropolitan elite, but they soon went back to sleep. It gave them an inkling that their assessment of the outside world contained flaws, but it didn't show them the scale of their misconception, the scale of the differences between themselves and their compatriots, the scale of the mutual incomprehension.

One of the misconceptions common among the metropolitan elite was that Leave voters had cast their votes with more emotion than consideration, and were now regretting their decision. Deborah Mattinson, of the opinion research agency BritainThinks, says 'movers and shakers' have repeatedly asked her for data demonstrating the extent to which Leavers 'were now obviously regretting their folly'. Mattinson has had to tell them that no such data exists, and Leave voters are overwhelmingly feeling positive about their decision.[15] Another elite misconception is that Leave voters are 'poor people'. *Spectator* readers (a demographic with average investable assets, 'excluding home', of £925,000[16]) were told that Brexiteers were 'the poor ... council-estate dwellers, Sun readers ... a second peasants' revolt'.[17] This is untrue. Most Leave voters were middle-class, with middling levels of income and education.[18]

It's easy to see why the elite like to think of Leave voters as either having suffered some form of temporary insanity in June 2016, or being in some way alien, the 'others' in the periphery of one's vision, from those estates on the edge of town one sometimes sees on the news. But the unattractive truth is that Leave voters were just ordinary people. The elite are 'the others', living an unrepresentative reality that can cause them to regard ordinary people as odd.[19] The former Conservative Cabinet minister Stephen Crabb, for example, was regarded by some of his party's grandees as exotic – 'a fascinating fellow' –

because 'his mother brought up three sons in a council house'[20] (despite almost one in three households being council tenants when Crabb was a boy[21]). The former government adviser Sam Freedman who, like four-fifths of his colleagues,[22] was privately educated, recalls realising he was the odd one, saying, 'I had literally no conception of the [ordinary] world.... It wasn't until I started working in education that I realised this other world existed'.[23]

The limited world view of those who dominated the Remain campaign also prevented them from realising the level of public animosity toward their fellow members of the establishment. I'd had an insight into this during another referendum campaign. Sitting on the steps of Glasgow's Tenement House museum, I spoke to a woman who'd arrived, like me, shortly before opening time. We talked about the independence referendum that would take place the following week. She'd initially been inclined to vote 'No' to independence, but 'since the banks have been saying "vote No", I'm leaning towards "Yes"'. In Scotland, the 'No' campaign's endorsement by prominent members of the corporate elite was one of the 'Yes' campaign's biggest vote-winners. Just over a year later, a former corporate chief executive was appointed as chair of the 'Britain Stronger in Europe' campaign.

Alan Milburn, former Chair of the Social Mobility Commission, also thinks antagonism towards the 'establishment' was part of the reason the Remain campaign lost the referendum. That antagonism, he says, is driven by a widespread perception that the establishment has failed to deliver the 'post-war promise' of social mobility. People get angry, says Milburn, when they don't get the rewards they've worked for or when others appear to get rewards they haven't worked for (referring to public perceptions of bankers, immigrants and benefit claimants).[24] There is strong evidence supporting Milburn's point of view: workers who felt themselves to be slipping down the social hierarchy were very likely to have voted Leave.[25] When asked to choose between two statements about Britain today ('Everyone has a fair chance to go as far as their talent and their hard work will take them' and 'Where you end up in society is mainly determined by your background'), those who held the latter view outnumbered those who held the former, 48% to 32%. The view that life chances are mainly determined by background is especially pronounced in emerging generations: among 18- to 24-year-olds, they outnumber those who think 'everyone has a fair chance' by more than two to one.[26]

Public discontent at not having a fair chance to attain aspirations is exacerbated by a feeling of not having their views fairly represented. Interviews conducted shortly after the Brexit vote by John Harris – a journalist who spends most of his time outside the metropolitan bubble – suggested a widespread dissatisfaction at having 'had no say' in the so-called 'national conversation'.[27] Large proportions of the public see a picture of the UK being painted by politicians, the media and other members of the establishment that doesn't look much like the country they live in.

The establishment reaches flawed conclusions about the public's experiences, views and priorities, partly because members of the establishment disproportionately don't come from similar backgrounds to the average member of the public. But this is only part of the explanation. Across large swathes of the establishment the most-privileged are overrepresented, but are not in the majority. What is also happening is people from non-elite backgrounds having to adapt their thinking in order to be accepted into the establishment or into elite educational institutions or workplaces (as the former ministerial adviser Sam Freedman says, they encounter a 'strong social incentive to shift their views'[28]). There are numerous examples throughout this book of upwardly mobile people undergoing a process of adaptation, self-censoring their own culture, opinions and experiences and replacing them with those with which others are comfortable. The result of this is that the 'dominant values of politics and the media', as the former Cabinet minister John Denham says, become dominated by 'only one strand, one set of values'.[29]

The sense of having had one's world view ignored is something that the most committed advocates of Brexit shared with large numbers of Leave voters. People such as Jacob Rees-Mogg, John Redwood and Daniel Hannan were widely seen – and treated – as oddities within Westminster before the referendum. This allowed them to portray themselves as having common ground with the common people, when all they really had in common was a sense of being marginalised. Their vision of a post-Brexit UK is even more centralised on London's financial industry than is currently the case, and their free trade ethos (removing regulations that protect consumers, workers and the environment[30]) is opposed by a large majority of the public.[31] The pro-Europeans had a better understanding of what the average voter needed, but little understanding of what they were feeling.

When the establishment exists in a bubble, it has – as the newsreader Jon Snow says of the media establishment – 'little awareness, contact, or connection with those not of the elite'.[32] Tony Blair provided an example of this when he resisted proposals he thought would 'hit average earners' and refused to believe an adviser, Ed Balls, who pointed out that average earnings were only a third of the amount Blair had assumed.[33] This compromises the competence and perceived legitimacy of the establishment. It results in policies being introduced that meet the needs of a version of the UK in which most of us do not live. And when ordinary members of the public – and their views – are kept out of the establishment bubble, they are pushed toward fractious post-truth populism: people who feel they lack control over their own lives are, as psychological experiments have shown, more likely to turn to conspiracy theories.[34]

Dissenting without differing

I met a lot of people while researching this book, and went to a variety of places. In one weekend alone I racked up more miles of train travel than the average Brit does in an entire year. My marathon weekend on the rails included a return trip from London to Glasgow – and nothing else. You might have expected 'more miles of train travel than the average Brit does in an entire year' to have involved more mileage than that, but the 800 miles I travelled that weekend easily beats the average person's annual total of 558 miles.[35] Three-quarters of us won't take a train trip this month, and more than four in ten won't take a single train trip this year.

Frequent train travel is a minority activity in the UK, but you wouldn't get that impression from the blanket media coverage of rail fare rises every December (when new fares are announced) and January (when they take effect). In contrast, you'll read and hear very little about increases in bus fares, despite the average person using buses twice as often as trains, and the percentage increases in bus fares often being much larger (in 2017-18 they were *four times* larger).[36] This is because the sort of people who set the political and media agenda are the sort of people who use trains: they are likely to be in the highest income group and likely to live in London or its commuter belt. They wrongly assume they're normal.

The disproportionate coverage given to rail fares isn't entirely due to the usual suspects among the 'establishment'. The press releases and briefings that prompt journalists to run stories about 'angry commuters' are mostly coordinated by transport campaign groups and the opposition Labour Party,[37] whose most recent manifesto mentioned railways almost three times as often as buses and gave far more space to the idea of nationalising railways than to nationalising water supply[38] (which would affect everyone, and is supported by a larger proportion of the public).[39]

The tendency of the Labour Party to give disproportionate attention to matters that affect the few more than the many may be related to the unrepresentativeness of its representatives. The party was formed to represent the interests of working people, but by 2015 only 7% of its MPs had a background in manual work (but even this scant proportion dwarfs that of Conservative Party MPs, of whom approximately 1% are former manual workers[40]). The two main political parties have a disproportionate number of MPs (and especially advisers) from backgrounds that are not just middle class but upper-middle class or above. As the representativeness of party personnel has declined, so has the proportion of the population who feel 'strongly aligned' to one of the major parties: since the 1960s, the proportion has fallen from one-in-two to one-in-eight.[41]

This could be regarded as an opportunity for 'insurgent' parties on the left or right to appeal to voters who wish to be represented by people like themselves. However, the right-wing UKIP, while currently led by former salesman Gerard Batten, is considerably influenced by the former public schoolboy Nigel Farage. On the left, the Green Party's sole MP, Caroline Lucas, was privately educated, as was the founder and chair of Momentum, Jon Lansman. (The Scottish National Party, SNP, is an honourable exception: its proportion of privately educated MPs is approximately reflective of the wider Scottish population.[42])

Political parties' grassroots members – who have a varying influence on the parties' policies and priorities, depending on the party – are also disproportionately drawn from privileged groups. Almost nine out of ten Conservative and Liberal Democrat members are classified as 'middle class' (compared to just over half of the wider population), and even in Labour, traditionally seen as a working-class party, more than three-quarters of its members are in middle-class occupations.[43] Among the 'insurgent' parties – the Greens, SNP and UKIP – the higher social classes are also overrepresented, at 80%, 72% and 66% respectively.[44] The unrepresentativeness of party activists is reflected in the issues they focus on: anti-social behaviour, for example, is frequently mentioned to canvassers 'on the doorstep' in Labour-voting neighbourhoods, but isn't discussed nearly as often in local party meetings attended by activists who are less likely to live in those neighbourhoods.

There is a widely-held (if not conclusively evidenced[45]) belief that the unrepresentativeness of our political parties are causing increasing numbers of people – especially young people – to turn instead towards 'single-issue' politics. But single-issue groups can also be disproportionately privileged in their leadership, membership and outlook. People who identify as working class can find involvement with, for example, environmental organisations to be an alienating experience. The agro-ecology activist Nicole Vosper is one example. In 2016 she blogged about how she and her background were patronised, romanticised and marginalised by fellow activists: 'If I hadn't had such solid self-esteem', she wrote, 'I would have abandoned all these movements years ago'.[46] But you don't have to be working class to find yourself socially out-classed in environmental organisations. The chief executives of both Greenpeace UK and Friends of the Earth (England, Wales and Northern

Ireland) are both privately educated, and my own experience of environmental campaigning suggests a grassroots movement largely drawn from society's higher strata: to my knowledge, I know three aristocrats, and met all of them, separately, through environmental campaigns.

This problem extends beyond the environmental movement. Even campaigns and debates that focus on issues affecting 'the lower classes' can be dominated by people from privileged backgrounds. Roger Harding, a working-class boy who got into the University of Oxford and now runs RECLAIM (a charity working to 'support and amplify the voices of working-class young people'), says, 'when it comes to Britain's working class, we too often find the job of representing our reality has gone to some sharp-elbowed middle (or even upper) class dude who seems to think we can't speak (or write, or organise) for ourselves'. Harding recalls receiving 'a lecture about understanding Britain's working class from somebody who had more spent on a half a year's worth of their schooling than my family lived on for a year'.[47] Maria Solomon had a similar experience at university, where she was put off joining the Labour Club by 'middle-class people talking about the working class but not interested in listening to an actual member of the working class.'

When the voices of people who have a personal stake in an issue are drowned out by those who don't, the effectiveness of the opposition – both in Parliament and outside of it – is reduced. It is less able to hold the establishment to account and less able to ensure that the country as a whole is properly represented in our democracy.

In addition to being 'crowded out' of grassroots activism by privileged people, the non-privileged face barriers to participation that often go unnoticed by others. Some of these barriers are practical, such as the tendency for such organisations' meetings to be held in university cities at times and places that fit middle-class working patterns. Other barriers are cultural, like the protocols of activism ('participating in debates, writing letters and emails and chairing and participating in meetings'[48]) being things that privileged people are more likely to have been 'trained' for, as part of their education or work.

Confidence is another issue. Not just the fear of making a fool of yourself, but the lack of social confidence drummed into you as a result of a lifetime, and sometimes generations, in low-status jobs where you're expected to 'do as you're told' rather than speak up for yourself. Kay (not her real name) – a working-class single mum who participated in a user-led project addressing unsatisfactory experiences of Jobcentre Plus – described her anxiety about the assertive aspects of activism: 'It's harder when you've always been told that you're wrong and bad', says Kay. 'Maybe if you're from a more privileged background you already in your head believe that you are right and the world is wrong. But we had to build confidence. And it's taken years, of working cooperatively, of learning, of feeling equal within our group, of having citizen's juries where all these important people came in and they had to actually listen to us. Now we might have the confidence.... But it's taken a long time'.[49]

Another barrier to non-privileged people's participation in single-issue campaigns is the stories campaigners tell about why their issue is important: they are mainly compelling to people like themselves. Again, environmentalism is an example. An internet search for images associated with the UK's main environmental groups produces (other than logos and people holding banners) pictures of landscapes and animals. For substantial numbers of privileged people, these images have an emotional power derived from their association with identity and ritual: childhood whale watching and tropical gap-year trips serve as both pilgrimages and coming-of-age ceremonies. Destroying tiger habitat is therefore an act of desecration. If you feel that way, it is hard to comprehend how anyone else could feel differently, how they could feel that the tiger isn't a sacred symbol of divine nature and its welfare isn't much of a priority. This becomes more of a problem when other people's priorities aren't taken into account by – as the campaigner Polly Billington puts it – 'those who would have the nerve to tell people already struggling to pay their bills that paying a bit extra to save the polar bear is worth it'.[50] Because environmentalists could all too easily be portrayed as having their head in the cloud forests, it was easy for their opponents to cast themselves as the champions of ordinary people, 'freeing the poor from the cost of environmentalism',[51] and for environmental problems – the rapidly approaching consequences of which will hit the poorest the hardest – to fall off the political agenda. In 2000, polling showed that 17% of people thought 'pollution/environment' was one of the 'most important issues facing Britain today'; by 2018 it was down to 8%.[52]

Some have begun to see the problem. In 2016 Ruth Davis, former Political Director at Greenpeace, wrote that the environmental movement and progressive political movements had lost touch with the emotional power of 'family, home, work and country that is central to most people's lives', and allowed ordinary voters to associate environmentalism with faraway places like the Arctic rather than the more tangible environmental problems that damage ordinary people's health and happiness.[53] Environmental groups have now begun to address this, by increasing their focus on issues such as urban air pollution, which is an immediate, relatable health problem for many non-privileged people.

In other campaigning organisations, moves are now being made to recruit a more socially representative mix of staff and activists. Oxfam is an example, having recently set up a trainee scheme for this purpose. One of its former participants – now working as a campaigner at Save the Children – says such schemes are necessary because 'the dismal absence of diversity often results in campaigns targeted at the same old audience, with the same old strategy and the same old tactics'.[54] The trainee scheme is attempting to remove some of the barriers that usually face non-privileged people who aspire to a career in a campaigning organisation, by being open to non-graduates, requiring no specific experience or qualifications except – as the scheme's manager, Alex Foxbatt tells me – 'compassion for people in need, and enthusiasm'. Oxfam has also changed the application procedure, including reducing the weight given to interview performance. Participants are paid just above the Living Wage and get a structured learning programme in which they are rotated around different teams in the organisation. Foxbatt is keen to point out that the scheme is still subject to teething troubles – such as the cultural misunderstandings between participants and other staff – 'I'm not sure we're yet fully equipped', she says, but 'we're getting better.'

Against social mobility: knowing one's place

I've lost count of the times I've taken part in protests against social mobility. To be fair, I was young at the time and lots of other people were doing it. To be more specific, I've sung along to the hymn by Cecil Frances Alexander called 'All things bright and beautiful', including the verse – now disappearing from most hymnbooks – that celebrates hereditary privilege: 'The rich man in his castle, The poor man at his gate, God made them, high or lowly, And ordered their estate.' The idea that God put you where you are, and it's best for everyone if you stay there, was widely accepted in previous centuries. In Thomas Hardy's 1895 novel *Jude the obscure*, the ambition of Jude, a stonemason, to study at 'Christminster' (a fictionalised version of Oxford), is dismissed by a college master who tells him 'you will have a much better chance of success in life by remaining in your own sphere'.[55]

Those ideas have now been buried. But they're not dead. We occasionally see them exhume themselves, especially in moments of unguarded emotion. In 2011 an unsuccessful *X-Factor* contestant, feeling publicly humiliated, called one of the show's judges, Tulisa Contostavlos, 'a scumbag from Camden'. Contostavlos shot back: 'I am really proud of what I have achieved',[56] but her achievements weren't being insulted, her origins were. The anthropologist Kate Fox reports similar sentiments being expressed by the possessors of hereditary wealth who – when suitably provoked – described nouveau riche Mercedes drivers as 'rich trash'.[57]

Sometimes, opposition to opportunity is revealed in implication rather than emotion. Even in 2016, in the land of the meritocratic 'American Dream', David Azerrad, of the influential (and appropriately named) Heritage Foundation, warned wealthy readers of *National Affairs* magazine that the pursuit of 'equality of life chances' would 'strip away their inherited advantages'.[58]

People like Azerrad are in a minority. Most defenders of hereditary privilege have learned to make their views sound less feudal by couching them in scientific-sounding language. In

2009, the former Chief Inspector of Schools, Chris Woodhead, told *The Guardian* that children's 'genes are likely to be better if their parents are teachers, academics, lawyers' and that there was little benefit in a full secondary education for some other children: 'Why do we think that we can make him brighter than God made him?'[59] (Note the echoes of 'God made them high or lowly'.)

The idea that our life chances are determined by the quality of our genes arouses strong emotions. It prompts memories of Nazi eugenics. But it is dangerous to pretend genes don't play any role in how humans or other organisms develop (in the Soviet Union of the 1930s, millions died because food crops proved unable to transcend their genetic codes in ways that Stalin's pseudo-scientists believed they should.[60]) And there *is* evidence of a genetic component to life chances. Geneticists use 'twin studies', which compare differences between identical twins (who have the same genetic make-up) and fraternal twins (whose genes differ) to allow them to discriminate between the effect of upbringing and the effect of genes. In one twin study, which used data on GCSE scores, the effect of genetic factors was found to be 'substantial'[61] (however, a larger, more recent, study found that although some attributes – such as height – are mostly determined by genes, less than a fifth of our educational attainment can be explained by genetic factors[62]).

Evidence of a genetic *component* in life chances doesn't mean 'genes are likely to be better' among the children of the professional classes, or that sons of billionaires become billionaires themselves because they have what Donald Trump calls 'the winning gene'.[63] There is no winning gene, just like there is no winning move in 'rock-paper-scissors'. There are slight *differences* between social classes' abilities (the average person from one of the higher social classes will have marginally higher scores in individual reasoning tests, while those from lower social classes tend to score better on skills associated with good teamwork)[64] but there is far greater variation within social classes – and within families – than between them. One of the authors of the study that showed a genetic influence on educational performance, Robert Plomin, says he is himself an example of genetic attributes being dispersed across social classes, being a boy from an under-privileged family in inner-city Chicago who happened to have a 'lucky combination of genes'.[65]

A lucky combination of genes, however, is not enough to attain our aspirations. Even before we are born, as we saw in Chapter 2, our mothers' physical and mental health can alter the working of our genes and affect our later physical and academic development. After birth, children's 'natural ability' (as unreliably measured by IQ scores) can be dramatically changed by their being made to feel more intelligent by teachers. Nor do opportunities to improve or impair our development end in childhood, as the cognitive neuroscientist Sarah-Jayne Blakemore found out. Professor Blakemore had initially studied schizophrenia, and wondered why every one of the hundreds of patients she examined had begun experiencing symptoms at around the same point in their lives, just after adolescence. Blakemore began shifting the focus of her research towards brain development, and discovered that the structure and working of our brains is 'in flux' – able to be shaped by external forces – well into adulthood and especially in adolescence. Blakemore found 'non-verbal reasoning' skills can be trained which, she says, tell us something about the notion of 'innate ability': 'there is no evidence for that whatsoever'.[66]

Whether or not a 'lucky combination of genes' leads to academic or career success appears to depend on the circumstances in which individuals are raised. Studies of children who were adopted suggest being brought up in a family with greater resources can add between 12 and 18 points to their IQ scores.[67] As one academic reviewer put it, 'richer families help their children to eliminate the effect of their defective genes and to enhance their productive genes',[68] or to put it another way, we can make them brighter than God made them.

Being made brighter, however, isn't a guarantee that we'll achieve our aspirations. Research shows 'brightness' is a becoming less important in determining chances of entry to 'top jobs', and family background is becoming more important. The 'professions', having become more socially mixed during the 20th century, have more recently moved in the opposite direction. To quote the researchers who discovered this, the 'average professional has become "nicer" in terms of their family income, but "dimmer"[69] as measured by their performance on childhood tests.'[70]

Against social mobility: an excuse for inequality

Prior to writing this book, I visited a former colleague, a committed social justice campaigner, someone frequently willing to do something about issues that others are merely willing to say something about. I mentioned my interest in social mobility to him, prompting the response 'I hate social mobility!'

My former colleague is not alone in seeing social mobility – or rather, the growing political interest in social mobility – as a threat to social justice. This view is perhaps best expressed by Danny Dorling, Professor of Human Geography and an authority on economic inequality. 'The idea of social mobility', he writes, 'is cherished in unequal countries as an excuse for inequality.'[71] Statements from some politicians on the political right suggest Dorling is correct. The Conservative MP John Hayes, for example, says 'inequality is the inevitable consequence of a free economy in a free society. The tensions to which this gives rise are both mitigated and ameliorated by social mobility.'[72]

There is also a widespread suspicion that talking about improving social mobility is seen as an alternative to acting to reduce poverty. Again, evidence suggests these suspicions are substantiated. The Social Mobility and Child Poverty Commission set up under the coalition government was renamed the Social Mobility Commission by its succeeding Conservative government, taking away the Commission's responsibility to consider poverty. Anti-poverty campaigners, such as Imran Hussain (formerly of the Child Poverty Action Group, now at Action for Children), point out that although some of the high-profile policies to increase social mobility may allow some people to escape poverty, they are nowhere near sufficient to address the sheer *scale* of poverty. 'If there are 3.9 million children in poverty', Hussain tells me, 'that isn't going to be solved by focusing on whether some of them can get into big law firms or Oxbridge. The number of people entering Oxbridge are piddling little figures compared with the number of children in poverty.' A few 'poor but talented' individuals may benefit from such initiatives, says Hussain, but 'what about average kids who aren't necessarily "talented"? You can't expect them all to be talented: don't they deserve a decent life?'

David Lammy makes a similar point, that giving chances to 'the brightest among the poor' is little use to the vast majority of us who don't think of ourselves as 'poor' and who aren't prodigiously talented. We still deserve a decent life. Those of us who aren't amazingly ambitious also deserve such decency: 'Not all of us *want* to be an MP or a lawyer or an accountant', says David 'What's wrong with being a nurse who doesn't want to be a matron? What's wrong with being a plumber?'

David is right. The idea that a person's worth is measured solely by the scale of their ambitions (in the narrow sense of career ambitions) sucks the joy and humanity out of life. As the writer David Brooks says, 'meritocracy subtly encourages an instrumental ethos in which each occasion – a party, a dinner – and each acquaintance becomes an opportunity to advance your status and professional life.'[73]

Those who idealise meritocracy don't just stand accused of labelling anyone who can't or won't climb the career ladder as defective, but also of applying that label to whole social classes. As Wanda Wyporska – my successor as Director of The Equality Trust – says, '"Social mobility" really says to me that being working class isn't something to be proud of, you need to move up the ladder.'[74] (The working classes aren't the only ones accused of being defective. Steve Siebold, author of how-to-get-rich books quoted in Chapter 6, believes the mindset of the middle class – as opposed to what he calls the 'world class' – is afflicted with a 'disease' and a 'missing ingredient'.[75])

I agree with pretty much all of the above. The fact that millions of people in the UK – the majority of them in working households – are unable to afford a standard of living their average compatriot regards as socially acceptable does not become acceptable just because a few of them get the opportunity to become more prosperous. Especially if that opportunity comes at the cost of having a career rather than a life, or of renouncing the culture in which they were raised.

But I disagree with the conclusion that social justice is advanced by denouncing social mobility.

For one thing, attacking 'social mobility' (which is widely understood to mean 'the opportunity to pursue "ideas above your station"') will just alienate the majority of the public. Jackie Doyle-Price is a case in point: her childhood experience of Sheffield City Council's efforts to prevent her family buying their own home was instrumental in Jackie becoming a member of the Conservative Party she now represents as an MP. Aspiration is now deeply rooted in British values. It's tempting to think of these ideas as invasive species, introduced into the UK by Margaret Thatcher from free market economists in Chicago and Vienna, but they were here long before Thatcher entered Downing Street. Their growth was nurtured by the same 'widespread feeling ... that hereditary elites had failed'[76] (and therefore upwardly mobile people must take their place) that helped bring Attlee's Labour government to power in 1945. They were also fed by the new post-war industries and expanded public sector that created increasing numbers of professional and higher-skilled jobs, giving the possibility – and later the expectation – of social mobility to millions.

One of the reasons the critics of social mobility tend to alienate the wider public is that they and the public have trouble understanding each other, partly as a result of moving in different social circles. Criticising aspirations to 'social status and material wealth'[77] may sound reasonable to someone for whom a decent level of status and wealth is assured, but for those with no such assurance, status and wealth (aka dignity and security) don't seem like unreasonable aspirations. For a number of the socially mobile people I interviewed, a desire to escape disrespect and poverty and their consequences (from family discord to debt and drinking problems) was a substantial motivator. Others among my interviewees did speak of having been motivated by something other than escaping poverty and disrespect, but these motivations weren't shallow materialistic one-upmanship either. Even for Mark – the wealthiest of my interviewees by a long way – his motivation is 'not about making money. Being successful is about ability to overcome challenges. Money is trivial. In the beginning it is money because you want security.' Rozina is another example; she sent me an email after our interview saying she had quit her well-paid and secure job to go freelance, leaving her 'happier and poorer than I've ever been.'

Mark and Rozina's motivations could be described as a desire to choose what sort of life they lived. This was referred to, unprompted, again and again. David talked about the 'ability to achieve your dreams', Barbara about the freedom to do 'the things that excite you', Paul about the 'opportunity to do what I want to do'. A number of people described it as something deeper: not just the ability to do what you want to do, but also the freedom to be who you want to be. Stuart Alford talked about 'getting into a place where I felt comfortable with who I was' and Maria about 'allowing people to be, to find their own place in life'. That idea, of a free life versus a constrained life, is important. We are, as a society, more and more comfortable with the idea that our aspirations should not be constrained by our gender; we ought to become more comfortable with the idea that our aspirations should not be constrained by our social or economic background, too.

As usual, my sister sums it up much better than I could: 'to me it's about everybody should have choice, about not having a proscribed life.'

Against social mobility: the individual and the collective

In 2012 Nick Clegg, the-then Deputy Prime Minister, made a speech in which he said it was 'a myth to suggest that reducing inequality will promote social mobility'.[78] It wasn't the first time Clegg had made a similar point: A year earlier, he presented the government's Strategy for Social Mobility to Parliament, in a report that cited academic studies critical of the supposed link between inequality and social mobility. But there was a problem. Of the two studies listed, one wasn't really an 'academic study' at all, but rather a pamphlet published by a right-of-centre think tank, and the other – by Professor Gary Solon – didn't appear to say what Clegg's strategy document said it said. Shortly after the Strategy for Social Mobility was published, my colleague at The Equality Trust (the economist Hector Gutierrez Rufrancos) emailed Professor Solon to ask for clarification, and was told that, as he had thought, Solon's research actually came to the opposite conclusion to that claimed by Clegg, as did many other studies on the same topic.

Our requests to discuss this matter with the Deputy Prime Minister's office were not successful. But my former colleague's enquiry meant by the time Clegg repeated his claim at the conference in 2012, we were in a position to suggest to a journalist that it might be a good idea to talk to Professor Solon, resulting in something of an embarrassment to the Deputy Prime Minister.[79]

As Nick Clegg found out, there *is* good reason to believe reducing inequality (and reducing poverty) would improve the UK's rates of social mobility. This appears to present an opportunity for those who want to reduce inequality: to make common cause with those who want to improve social mobility and thus build a larger consensus for action.

However, this opportunity may not be as good as it first appears. The *type* of social mobility the government's Strategy for Social Mobility was aiming to create wasn't necessarily the sort that happened in the post-war years, in which large numbers of people got better jobs than their parents had had without large numbers of people getting worse jobs than those of their parents. Instead, the government was clear that its 'focus is on relative social mobility'[80] (in which the number of good jobs doesn't necessarily increase, but everyone is given a more equal chance of getting them).

The promotion of relative social mobility raises a number of objections. First, it is difficult to achieve, because privileged families will put in considerable effort to oppose any measures that come at their own children's expense. And second, increasing relative social mobility doesn't necessarily reduce the numbers of people in poverty; it just gives more people an opportunity to leave poverty (at the expense of others being given a greater opportunity to enter it).

Christine Blower, former General Secretary of the National Union of Teachers (NUT), thinks the political preference for individual meritocracy rather than shared prosperity is part of a wider trend. 'The meaning of aspiration shifted', Blower says, from collective improvement to 'individual success, achieved through competition'.[81] The writer Owen Jones advocates a 'total redefinition of aspiration' to mean 'improving people's communities and bettering the conditions of the working class as a whole, rather than simply lifting individuals up the ladder.'[82] Others, like the higher education specialist Dr Graeme Atherton, propose broadening the definition of social mobility beyond 'a narrow obsession with economic mobility' to include 'progression in well-being across the spectrum of dimensions including health, work–life balance, self-actualisation at work, environmental quality, life satisfaction as well as changes in income and occupational status.'[83]

Owen Jones is right. There is a need to improve the lives of the working class as a whole (and everyone else) by improving the resources and esteem given to institutions from which we all benefit, such as the NHS and schools. Collective aspirations are widely held and insufficiently acknowledged, as are Atherton's non-economic aspirations.

But we do not need a 'total redefinition of aspiration' that rejects any role for individual aspiration. Just as attacking the idea of aspiration would alienate people, so would attacking the idea of *individual* aspiration.

As mentioned in the opening chapter of this book, the proportion of the public who think 'fairness is about getting what you deserve' outnumber those who think 'fairness is about equality' by more than two-to-one[84] (although the current degree of *in*equality is seen as excessive by a majority). Most people have both individual as well as collective aspirations, and don't take kindly to being told their cherished aspirations are reprehensible. Individual aspiration is now embedded in our national psyche. The post-war political and economic changes that created collective upward social mobility gave unprecedented numbers of people a career and standard of living that afforded them a degree of individual self-esteem, allowing it to become a source of pride and identity alongside their communal identity as part of a neighbourhood or congregation.[85] In particular, the welfare state reduced reliance on the safety net provided by community solidarity, and reduced the fear that over-ambitious aspirations could result in impoverishment. This resulted in the working class (and lower-middle class) putting increasing value on individual aspiration, as the newly prosperous upper-middle class had done a century before, creating – as the historian Donna Loftus writes – a set of values based on 'self-reliance and personal achievement as opposed to privilege and inheritance'.[86]

Neglecting individual social mobility makes it harder to achieve collective aspirations, by discouraging people from non-privileged backgrounds from gaining entry to roles that could give them the power and influence to achieve advances for others from similar backgrounds. This book contains numerous examples of people who were given opportunities, encouragement and coaching by mentors and sponsors from similar backgrounds to themselves. Individuals who 'get to the top' are also better able to build the structures that will allow collective improvement in the living standards, education and careers of people from non-privileged backgrounds, because they are likely to have a better understanding of the needs of people from those backgrounds. Keir Hardie is an example of this process: his parents – a servant and a carpenter – made sure their son had sufficient education to become a journalist and later an MP and founding father of the Labour Party, a party whose post-war reforms created probably the biggest ever collective improvement in working-class living standards.[87]

Opposing individual social mobility and aspiration also undermines society's ability to tackle discrimination on the grounds of disability, gender, ethnicity, sexuality and other characteristics. The progress that has been made in opening up high-profile careers and other opportunities to individuals from diverse groups is good, but unless efforts are made – and are seen to be made – to open up opportunities to individuals from lower socioeconomic backgrounds, it is likely to foster resentment towards groups who are perceived as specially favoured.

Despite attempts by some – such as Nick Clegg – to suggest we have to choose between individual and collective aspirations,[88] we do not. The preceding chapters of this book are a demonstration that the policies needed to facilitate individual social mobility are largely the same as those to reduce poverty and inequality. To give children the best chances of achieving individual social mobility, we must ensure that their families have decent, reliable homes, and incomes; that their teachers are well trained and well resourced (including with the resource of time). We must allow them to mix with children from different backgrounds, rather than selecting and segregating the most privileged. We must tackle the tendency of education to disdain working-class culture and thus alienate and discombobulate some pupils. We must give everyone a chance to get a full insight into the range of career options available, rather than just those that are 'class-appropriate'. We must dismantle the financial, cultural and social obstacles preventing access to experiences in work or education. And we must adopt an industrial strategy that prioritises the creation of good-quality jobs.

The people whose stories of social mobility are told in this book had mixed opinions about whether the promotion of individual social mobility should be a political priority, but there was considerable anger when I mentioned some of the arguments against it – such as that 'the social mobility agenda assumes we're stuck with a hierarchical society'.[89] I was told we are stuck with a hierarchical society (which is very probably true. Anthropologists regard 'a system of social status' as being universal to human society[90]) and that allowing some individuals to achieve their aspirations shouldn't have to wait until everyone has the opportunity to do so. Dean sums up that anger: 'middle-class people expect working-class people to wait – for socialism or whatever – why should we wait?'

10

Conclusion: Barriers and opportunities

An opportunity society?

I began writing this book with little idea how difficult it would be to persuade interviewees to tell their stories. I was warned that people may be unwilling to open up to a stranger about their personal lives and – sometimes painful – experiences. But I actually found it easier than expected. Often, I left these meetings with the impression they'd been *relieved* to talk about it, to 'let it all out'.

It was also easier than expected to *find* people to interview. Not because there were lots of people who had experienced what sociologists call 'long-range social mobility' to choose from, but because in many cases they were so rare within their professions as to be remarkable. Searching the 'trade press' of elite professions (such as *The Barrister* magazine) for phrases such as 'the son of a…' or 'the daughter of a…' produced results. Being 'the son of a shipwright' or 'the daughter of a postman' was unusual enough in those professions to be considered newsworthy.

The adventures and endurances of my interviewees' journeys, and the fact they met so few others from similar backgrounds along the way, are a more compelling answer to the first question posed at the beginning of this book – how far the UK is from being an 'opportunity society' – than any amount of hard data.

The hard data, however, point in the same direction. Using a financial measure of social mobility, we have low rates compared with other countries and with other periods in our own recent history (although policy changes in the first decade of this century increased financial mobility in the lower reaches of the income spectrum). If we use an occupational measure of social mobility, we see that we and our children are now more likely to fall down the social scale than rise up. Levels of social mobility in the UK are not, as some believe, 'non-existent' or 'worse than they have ever been', but they are inadequate to our notions of fairness – and our country's ability to function – in the 21st century.

Turning from the traditional measures of social mobility to the criteria that form the focus of this book (the chances we, or our children, have of attaining the aspirations that most of us hold, and of living a life determined more by our effort and choices than by our background), the picture remains poor. We are less likely to find a job that matches our qualifications than our counterparts in comparable countries; we are decreasingly likely to have 'a home to call our own' (either owned or with secure tenancy); and are increasingly finding ourselves putting plans to start a family on indefinite hold. The odds of attaining these aspirations are heavily weighted in favour of the privileged, and successive generations are, accordingly, more likely to think their prospects are determined more by their background than by themselves.

The immediate future is also pessimistic (don't worry, this chapter becomes more hopeful later). Brexit is likely to reduce the UK's ability to persuade employers to create good-quality jobs and to reduce the financial and political capital available to the government, both of which will be necessary to drive through the necessary measures to allow a significantly increased proportion of our population to develop and pursue their aspirations. Whether Brexit will cause house prices to fall enough to make 'a home to call our own' a more realistic prospect for more people is, as we have seen, as yet unknown.

The second question raised at the beginning of this book was whether social mobility is desirable and whether it should be a priority of policy-makers. The answer to that question depends on what is meant by 'social mobility': If social mobility means opportunities that are only available to those who are prepared to 'leave to achieve', by renouncing the people, place and culture into which they were born, then no, it is not desirable.

If it means 'meritocracy' (in Michael Young's original meaning of the word, in which all but the few whose talents are deemed valuable and who are willing to sacrifice anything and anyone for their career are regarded as worthless), then it is not desirable. But if social mobility means our lives and opportunities should be unconstrained by the expectations placed on the social or economic class into which we were born, then yes, it should be pursued as an objective of policy. Individual opportunity is not – as ideologues on both left and right would have us believe – incompatible with pursuing collective social progress for all our children. The two are inseparable.

The other question posed in this book's opening chapter – what barriers stand in the way of an opportunity society and how to remove those barriers – requires a longer answer.

My theory when I began researching this book was that by identifying the routes some individuals used to successfully pursue their aspirations, I could recommend ways to expand the number of such routes. On many occasions, that idea spectacularly failed to work. The life stories of many of my interviewees hinged on anomalous situations, chance encounters and the idiosyncrasies of the individuals themselves. But some themes did emerge.

One theme is that the establishment's ability to create opportunities for people from non-elite backgrounds is compromised by their own backgrounds, and not just because they balk at initiatives that erode the advantages enjoyed by their own families: there is some genuine commitment to widening opportunity. Unfortunately, commitment is not enough. The privileged, who dominate large swathes of the establishment, are constrained in their ability to take action because they lack the lived experience of the barriers and opportunities faced by ordinary people. As the psychologist Tom Gilovich says, 'when you're running or bicycling into the wind, you're very aware of it. You just can't wait till the course turns around and you've got the wind at your back. When that happens you feel great. But then you forget about it very quickly – you're just not aware of wind at your back'.[1] People from privileged backgrounds didn't notice their parents paying for their after-school activities, or paying their rent at university, or allowing them to live at home during an unpaid internship; they didn't think it unusual that their family's dinner table conversations provided insights into the protocols of professional life. They didn't notice because it wasn't remarkable: their friends were having the same experience. Even where the privileged no longer dominate the establishment in numerical terms, they dominate how it thinks, because their forebears shaped its culture and their non-privileged colleagues have learned to self-censor any insights that are inconsistent with received wisdom. As a result, the ladders to opportunity tend to be designed by people who've never had to climb one.

A second theme is the tendency of people who've never had to climb a ladder to believe that ladders are made of rungs. They forget the other components of ladders, the side rails that keep the whole ladder together. Far too often, people attempting to pursue their aspirations find that their experience on one rung of the ladder of opportunity does not adequately prepare them to climb the subsequent rungs, and sometimes (as we have seen) it actively hinders them. If the government is serious about creating an opportunity society, there has to be a Cabinet-level minister with responsibility for an overarching strategy for expanding the opportunities for people to pursue their aspirations, making sure the various agencies see themselves as rungs in the ladder rather than ladders in themselves.

The following sections each focus on barriers to opportunity that featured more prominently in the experiences of people who have had to climb a ladder – my interviewees – than in established discussions of opportunity.

Hostile environment

Quarter-past seven on a Friday morning. I'm in the corner shop, buying milk for breakfast. One of my neighbours is ahead of me in the queue, there to top up his Oyster card with enough money for the bus to work that he catches from the stop across the road. He has the Oyster card ready in his hand, tapping it nervously against this thigh. The queue is longer than he'd anticipated. The bus is almost due. When it's his turn, he asks how much credit is on the card, is told £1.10, and hands over

40p to top it up, just as the bus arrives. Dodging through the traffic, he gets across the road just in time.

Topping his Oyster credit up to £1.50 gave my neighbour precisely enough to get the bus to work that morning. To catch a bus home he'd have had to put another £1.50 on his card. Paying such small amounts so frequently is a huge hassle – you don't do it if you can afford not to. (My Oyster card is topped up automatically from my bank account, which I can be fairly confident has enough money to cover it, so I don't have to worry about where the next £1.50 is coming from, and don't have to spend so much time queuing.)

People like my neighbour are not rare. Large numbers of people have incomes so low or so insecure that they spend a large proportion of their time and mental bandwidth on micro-managing their cash flow on transport expenses, food, rent and everything else. They find themselves constantly harassed by a swarm of responsibilities, any one of which, if neglected, could become an even worse problem.

Feelings of harassed vulnerability don't just arise from tight budgets. For a large proportion of the population, minor mistakes of the sort we all make, especially if we're tired or stressed, can mean being sacked by an employer or sanctioned by the Department for Work and Pensions. This constant harassment is toxic to the pursuit of aspirations. It stops people making plans by forcing them to be reactive. It prevents us and our children from investing in our long-term prosperity. It preoccupies us, making it harder to be an attentive parent or partner. As history shows, people scale down their aspirations and their entrepreneurialism when they feel vulnerable.

In contrast, the households in which my interviewees grew up typically had incomes and housing tenures that provided enough security in which to develop and pursue their aspirations. It's hard to reach for the stars when you're clinging to what you have.

People with little security also tend to have little esteem, and this too is toxic to the development of aspirations. As we saw in Chapter 3, our minds (and even our abilities) adapt to how we are seen by others. If employers expect us to wait around just in case they want us to work today, we learn our time isn't worth much. If landlords can evict us on a whim, we learn that our home is worth less than their convenience. If our neighbourhoods are dilapidated, plagued by crime and anti-social behaviour, we learn that we live somewhere unimportant. If we are constantly treated like we're worthless, we start to believe it, and we pass those beliefs on to our children.

Sometimes the belittling of the non-elite classes is overt: the hostility some of my interviewees experienced from people who resented their 'getting above themselves' or the middle-class people accused of having a 'missing ingredient' by self-described members of the 'world class'. Sometimes the belittling is more subtle, such as the implicit assumption among some middle-class teachers that working-class children should try to suppress any signs of their 'inferior' origins. People who grew up amid constant implications of inferiority, if they later find themselves in elite-dominated schools, universities, workplaces and social situations, are put on the back foot, attempting – as they have been trained to do since childhood – to conform to others' ways rather than expecting others to conform to theirs.

Living in this hostile environment takes its toll on our health, increasing the risk of heart problems, hypertension, diabetes, skin conditions, asthma, arthritis, depression and anxiety, all of which are more common in people from non-privileged backgrounds. Inadequate food and accommodation can leave us struggling to concentrate at school or work and struggling to fight off infections. Alongside our financial, cultural and social resources, our health and wellbeing (and that of our family members) is a strong determinant of opportunity. Poor health in childhood is correlated to lower pay in adulthood.[2] There are numerous examples in this book of my interviewees' careers being disrupted by their own health problems or those of their relatives. In most cases, these were temporary setbacks or near-misses rather than fatal blows, but there are countless others – such as the one in twelve young people in the UK who act as carers – who weren't so lucky and whose careers never progressed far enough to catch the attention of someone writing a book like this. Those from privileged backgrounds are less likely to experience ill health (health differences between different income groups are substantial, and widening[3]) and are more likely to be able to pay for a solution. Mental health treatment, for example, can be accessed *much* more quickly if you can pay for private treatment,[4] insurance or savings can cover any unexpected loss of income, and private social care can look after the needs of incapacitated relatives. Health is a form of capital.

Insecurity, humiliation and hostility are not just something that affects 'the poor'. Rising costs and weak incomes mean more and more middle-income families find themselves unable to afford 'a minimum, socially acceptable quality of life'. The safety net of social security, which most of us will need at some point – and more of us will need as economic changes accelerate and respond to political changes such as Brexit – is becoming less effective and more punitive. An increasing proportion of middle-income households lack security of housing tenure. Growing numbers are working excessive hours and enduring long commutes. The *Financial Times* warns that, 'shifts in pensions, housing and employment have transferred more risk and instability on to the shoulders of young people'.[5]

The hostile environment harms us all. It even harms the wealthy, who find themselves in an arms race to give their child the 'best start in life' and whose children's lives consequently resemble a boot camp. But as any physicist – or my neighbour – can tell you, the pressure is greatest at the bottom of the pile.

Segregation

The North Downs Golf Club is situated amid the leafy lanes of Surrey, between the village of Woldingham and the M25. If a drop of rain falls on the club's 18-hole course and finds its way into a nearby stream, it will be carried north, into the Thames and through central London, past civil servants on Millbank and politicians in the Houses of Parliament, past actors in the National Theatre and barristers in Temple Gardens, past financiers in the old financial district of the 'Square Mile' and in the new one in Docklands.

Or perhaps not. The North Downs Golf Course lies on a watershed that separates the drainage basins of two river systems. A second raindrop, perhaps pushed by a slight rise or a fall in the wind, perhaps landing a centimetre further south, will be carried a different way, up through Dartford to join the Thames downstream from London, by a scrapyard in an industrial park.

Like raindrops on the North Downs Golf Course, we, too, can find the course of our lives determined by which side of a line we find ourselves on. Someone in South East England can expect to get a better-paid job than someone in the North East, Wales or Scotland, to become wealthier and to live longer. But not everyone in the South East. The differences *within* regions are wider. Two children growing up next door to each other can find themselves in different school catchment areas, with very different chances of getting good exam results, and different odds of becoming one of the civil servants on Millbank or one of the politicians in Parliament, or actors or barristers or financiers.

Separating children into different streams that flow towards different opportunities is most obvious in the segregation between private and state schools, and between grammar schools and secondary moderns (or their post-modern equivalents), but also happens when children are assigned to different schools, streams and sets in the comprehensive system. Outside school, our children are segregated by different neighbourhoods, out-of-school activities and the social circles of their families. All these processes are influenced by the child's social and economic background.

Once segregated, our children are taught – consciously and unconsciously – in ways that are 'appropriate' to their background, pushed or nudged towards appropriate aspirations by people like the teacher who encouraged David Lammy to become a firefighter rather than a barrister. More subtly, children get the message about which careers are appropriate for someone like themselves – and an idea of the route towards those careers – by observing their family, friends and neighbours, and the adults who were their predecessors at school.

Once in a stream, it becomes harder to swim against the flow. As we have seen, teachers subconsciously mark down and under-predict the performance of pupils who have been classified into lower sets, even where the quality of their work is the same, and children adjust their own self-esteem, and choices (and IQ) accordingly. Employers' tendency to restrict their recruitment efforts to universities that disproportionately serve privileged students, and progression pathways to those employees who have entered through graduate schemes, also shuts off opportunities.

My interviewees' pursuit of their aspirations were frequently made more difficult by being segregated along class lines (like Joanne, forced to spend long hours travelling across Glasgow because the school serving her housing estate didn't offer the subjects needed to apply to a medical school). But the boosts they received were very often the result of social mixing and 'posh friends' – Alvin making the acquaintance of the boy who encouraged him to apply for a place at the London Oratory School, Barbara's friends whose upper-middle-class parents helped her to apply to Cambridge, Stuart Alford being inducted into the protocols of upper-middle-class life by his privately educated girlfriend, and Rozina learning 'manners, confidence and chutzpah' from her fellow medical students. Social mixing is how we become aware of the existence of opportunities beyond the experience of our friends and families, how we come to regard different people as being like ourselves, and their aspirations as therefore being relevant to people like ourselves, and how we demystify the process of achieving those aspirations.

Segregation between economic and social classes has mutated over the decades. The secondary modern system has gone from most areas of the country, but has often been replaced by 'selection through streaming'[6] or through the affordability of homes in the catchment area. And segregation between those in the middle and those at the top of the financial scale appears to be worsening, as elites increasingly inhabit their own inaccessible spaces rather than sharing their lives, aspirations and opportunities with the rest of us.

Toll roads on the route to opportunity

Until the late 18th century, social mobility was all but illegal for most of the population of Ireland. The Catholic majority were barred from owning land, getting an education or entering the professions. Half a century later, the legacy remained strong. Ireland was still largely in the hands of English landlords and the population still desperately poor, with 3 million people entirely dependent for food on a single crop, potatoes. The potato blight of the 1840s – during which time the landowners continued to export food out of Ireland – led, famously, to famine.[7]

One of the million or so Irish who fled the country in the aftermath of the Great Famine was Patrick Kennedy, from Dunganstown, County Wexford. He and his descendants became Americans and pulled opportunity out of tragedy. Patrick's grandson Joe became one of the richest men in Boston, and Joe's son, Jack, became 35th President of the United States.[8]

Others weren't so lucky. Sailing to America came at a cost. A number of charitable American citizens paid for ships to be sent for those who couldn't afford to pay, but places were limited and starvation doesn't wait. They were buried in mass graves.

Sometimes the route to opportunity is a toll road.

In the UK in the 21st century, famine has gone, but hunger hasn't, and some of the opportunities apparently available to anyone still turn out, on closer inspection, to have costs some of us are unable to meet. Children are excluded from certain schools by the cost of the uniform; aspiring actors find that drama schools charge an audition fee; jobseekers' lack of expensive travel experience counts against them in interviews; families trying to get on the housing ladder can't save enough to qualify for the 'Help to Buy' scheme.

For those from affluent backgrounds, such costs are small enough to go unnoticed. Unfortunately, such people disproportionately have decision-making power (in government, education institutions, employers and elsewhere), with the result that the means of accessing opportunities frequently contain an implicit assumption that everyone has a family who can pay.

Unnoticed by the elite, the amount that families are assumed to be willing and able to pay has crept up. Large numbers of parents have now become accustomed to spending large amounts on, for example, meeting the shortfall between students' maintenance loans and their actual living costs, so their offspring don't have to resort to a term-time part-time job and therefore miss out on CV-enhancing extra-curricular activities. Others are now paying for deposits so their children can rent a flat (as a sort of 'bridging' grant to cover the gap created by salaries being paid in arrears). Among the very privileged, some *extremely* expensive opportunities such as the six-figure cost of business school, is now considered to be just 'one of the endless costs of raising children'.[9] The more the costs grow, the more likely it is that low- and even middle-income families will be left behind, or financially broken, by the spending arms race. Numerous careers require those who wish to enter or remain in the industry to make a big upfront investment in their own qualifications and experience, with no guarantee of work at the end of the process. Many of us can't afford to take such a risk, go for safer options, and give up on our dreams.

This problem hits people whose families have little or no wealth the hardest, and especially those who, for example, were brought up in care or are estranged from their parents. (In other cases, however, opportunities are cut off because you *do* have a family – especially dependent children or others who require care.)

There are attempts to make the routes to opportunity toll-free (or at least less costly). The Education Maintenance Allowance, for example, was rolled out from 2004-07 to help 16- to 18-year-olds from low- and middle-income households pay for transport and other costs of attending school or college (and resulted in improved rates of participation, retention and academic performance[10]) but was abolished for English students following a change of government in 2010. Other initiatives, including initiatives to support parents in helping their children become 'school-ready', have also been cut back.

Heroes and heroines

Hundreds of organisations and projects are now working to widen opportunity in the UK, from government agencies such as the Social Mobility Commission to informal groups of people in places of work or education. One example, Hands-On!, is a small charity supporting children who show aptitude for manual occupations but lack family experience of such careers. Working mainly with independent schools, it allows pupils from privileged backgrounds an insight into hands-on roles in construction, agriculture and cleaning.

Hands-On! is, of course, fictional. Privileged parents may like the idea of their cleaner's child having the chance to enter the 'elite professions', but they don't like the concomitant idea of their own child working as a cleaner.

Despite the paucity of projects encouraging downward social mobility, many people are working energetically and effectively to give those from non-privileged backgrounds a fairer chance of developing and pursuing 'ideas above their station'. Against the hostile environment, segregation and toll roads stands a resistance force.

The most obvious heroes and heroines of the resistance are the individuals themselves, those who are interviewed in this book and others like them who refused to be told their aspirations were unrealistic or inappropriate, or who grew up as misfits and, like Auden's oddball organisms, chose to make an evolutionary virtue of it and 'emigrate to unsettled niches'.[11]

Behind them are huge numbers of family members, including the UK's low-educated parents who, since the mid-1970s, have collectively doubled the amount of time they devote to educational activities with their children. Untold numbers of parents, including those of some of my interviewees, put in heroic efforts to shield their children from the insecurity, shortages and everyday humiliations they faced themselves, so their children could grow up feeling enough security and optimism for their aspirations and self-belief to develop; in many cases at a heavy cost to these parents' own long-term health.

In addition to help received from family members – or for some, in the absence of such help – are other people who acted as inspiration, mentors and guides – the fairy godmothers of the Cinderella story. Often these were people who had themselves successfully pursued 'ideas above their station' and followed Jack Lemmon's credo to 'send the elevator back down', including teachers who helped children overcome their initial lack of school-readiness, bought toiletries for children whose families were in financial difficulties, or participated in sponsored North Sea swims to pay for students to attend university open days.

There are also people in government, charities, campaigning organisations, research institutions and social enterprises who go beyond the call of duty to create policies and practices that promote opportunity:

- tax credits created by the last Labour Government that families overwhelmingly spent on giving their children a strong start in life;
- the Pupil Premium introduced by the coalition government to help schools reduce the educational disadvantages faced by children from low-income backgrounds;
- research schools and opportunity areas created by the Conservatives;
- education charities like the Education Endowment Foundation, Education Policy Institute, Challenge Partners and Ambition School Leadership;
- projects to help children and young people develop and pursue 'ideas above their station' run by The Brilliant Club, The Sutton Trust, the Social Mobility Foundation or the Access Project;
- organisations like The Challenge that allow young people to pursue extra-curricular activities in socially mixed groups;
- universities and employers who are starting to adjust their entry requirements to reflect a candidate's promise rather than their privilege;
- trades unions working to tackle to the hostile environment that many workers (and consequently their children) have to endure;
- the Social Mobility Pledge and the 'social mobility champions' now helping workplaces and universities become more user-friendly for people from non-privileged backgrounds;
- support for aspiring entrepreneurs provided by The Prince's Trust and Young Enterprise;
- researchers at the Learning and Work Institute, Higher Education Policy Institute and think tanks across the political spectrum;
- campaigners at the Child Poverty Action Group and Action for Children whose work is helping children grow up in an environment that is more hospitable; and
- organisations like The Bridge Group, the Social Mobility Commission and members of the All-Party Parliamentary Group on Social Mobility, pursuing a broader mission to open up opportunity.

Progress is hard-won, and sometimes an uphill struggle. For example, a typical child from a disadvantaged background is now educationally 19 months behind their peers, a gap that has narrowed by just two months in nine years. It is estimated that at current rates of progress it will take 50 years to close the gap completely, and the most-disadvantaged are actually falling *further* behind.[12] Similarly, individuals from non-elite backgrounds have become more likely to enter higher education in the last few decades, but so have the most-privileged, who remain much more likely to enter the most prestigious universities.[13] The heroes and heroines of this book have not succeeded in evening the odds, but are having an impact; they have become more experienced and more effective, and have already given many of us enough strength and support to overcome the odds.

The scarcity of the objects of aspiration

Londoners have a reputation for unfriendliness, and a recent experience of mine suggests the reputation is deserved. Waiting for a bus in Sheffield, I soon found myself chatting with other passengers who, when the bus arrived, appeared unconcerned about the order in which people got on and therefore got a seat. The next day, in London, my tube journey was a very different experience. No one spoke. Commuters competed for position on the platform, to be nearest the train door when it arrived, so they could leap inside and pounce on any available seat.

But this is an unfair comparison. My tube journey took place at 8.30am, whereas my bus ride in Sheffield was in the mid-afternoon. The tube carriage was packed, the bus mostly empty. What I'd experienced wasn't a result of cultural differences between London and Sheffield – not entirely, anyway – but a demonstration that people are more relaxed about someone else getting a seat when they know they'll get one too.

When opportunities are in short supply, we are more likely to shove someone else aside to get them, especially when the opportunities are something more important than the chance to have a nice sit-down for a couple of stops.

One of the opportunities currently in short supply is the opportunity to get 'a job I love'. We are now better educated, better equipped and better prepared to compete in the jobs market than we have ever been, but the supply of jobs that require highly educated people isn't keeping up. Recent governments have succeeded in increasing the proportion of us who have jobs rather than the proportion of us who have *good* jobs.

The scarcity of jobs with good pay, security and prospects of progression is especially pronounced outside the major cities, forcing many to choose between career opportunities and the opportunity to remain where they feel they belong. (The privileged tend to misinterpret this different aspiration as a lack of aspiration.)

The opportunity to fulfil another aspiration held by the majority, for 'a home to call my own', is also in short supply. The proportion who become homeowners, having increased during the 20th century, went into reverse a few years into the 21st, as homebuilding rates declined and landlords bought a larger proportion of the housing stock.

As competition for the objects of our aspirations becomes more intense, the privileged have a greater incentive to ensure that their children get what they want at the expense of the rest of us. Up until approximately 1980, the ability of the rich to outbid the rest of us for the goods and services that enhance our life chances was falling. The proportion of the UK's wealth held by the top 1% had been declining since the early decades of the 20th century. But since then, the wealth of the wealthy has grown at a faster rate than that of the rest of us. Opportunity is being impoverished by scarcity, but it is also being impoverished by wealth.

The following sections are about how the barriers to opportunity can be broken down, and also about the how the supply of opportunity can be built up.

Creating an environment hospitable to aspiration

In 2010, I went to a party conference fringe meeting on how to make the UK 'the most family-friendly country in Europe'. It turned out to be mostly about promoting marriage. The audience was invited to ask questions. I asked a question, referring to evidence that the most effective way to improve children's life chances is to improve their families' income by, for example, increasing social security payments for low-paid parents. One of the panellists rewarded me with an icy stare and said any evidence of a link between family incomes and children's wellbeing was just 'anecdotal' (which, as you can see in Chapter 2, it isn't). She also said she'd met people who'd been 'inspired' by parents who worked long hours to make ends meet on low incomes (which is anecdotal).

Alongside supporting marriage, another proposal to improve children's life chances that has grown in popularity in political circles is to teach children to develop a mindset that is more resilient, assertive and has a greater sense of agency. Mindset interventions are already widely used in schools, but have been the subject of academic scepticism. Some of the interventions appear to be based more on intuition than evidence, and indications of the effectiveness of others is mixed.

Criticisms of attempts to improve children's mindset are valid. But mental attitude *is* important. For many of my interviewees, at various stages of their life, it was decisive. Any interventions that can be demonstrated to be effective should be implemented, to help repair the psychological damage that the hostile environment has already produced and (due to Utopia existing only in fiction) will continue to produce, and to counterbalance the self-confidence that privilege instils in the privileged.

Fostering a more positive mindset, however, will be akin to pushing water uphill unless the hostile environment is itself addressed. If we live with chronic insecurity, stress, powerlessness and humiliation, our mindset is likely to become one of fear, timidity, resignation and despair.

Any serious strategy to give children (and adults) sufficient security in which to develop and pursue their aspirations must address family incomes. Measures such as the introduction of the National Minimum Wage (NMW) under the last Labour government and above-inflation increases in NMW levels under both Labour and Conservative chancellors have helped, as has the adoption of the Living Wage by some employers.

Raising the minimum level of hourly pay, however, still leaves many of us with insufficient or insecure incomes, especially if we have to work part time or incomes are unreliable as a result of self-employment or unpredictable working hours. Even for full-time workers, the level at which the Living Wage is set assumes some social security top-ups. Social security has to be made fit for the 21st century, not just to improve the life chances of low- and middle-income families, but also to allow us all to cope with the not-at-all-distant future. The turbulence of Brexit and other, unforeseeable, economic shocks, combined with the fact a large proportion of middle-income households don't have adequate savings to withstand even moderate shocks, means large numbers are going to need a social security system capable of rapid-response financial support at a level adequate to allow us to retrain and look for the next opportunity without compromising our ability to do so by making us feel hounded. This would also allow entrepreneurs to ride out the dips in income that characterise self-employment without excessive fear of poverty.

Creating a 21st-century social security system will be less expensive than many think. Much of the necessary changes are matters of approach rather than budget, and there are potential sources of income to match the expenditure, such as the corporations who would benefit from a social security system that allows workers to adapt and to modernise their skills. This doesn't require high corporate taxes: asking companies to contribute an extra per cent or two (and tackling tax-dodging) would still leave the UK with the lowest corporation tax in the G7.

Besides secure incomes, we need secure homes – places of restorative refuge rather than stress and illness. Landlords should therefore be obliged to ensure that their properties meet good minimum standards of safety, security, health and prompt repair, and local authorities given the necessary duties and resources to register and inspect them.[14] Tenants' rights should be strengthened to bring them into line with standards found elsewhere in Europe (including by abolishing 'no-fault evictions'). Some landlords may struggle to meet these obligations but frankly, anyone unable to provide safe, secure, healthy, promptly repaired and dependable homes is unfit to be a landlord and should sell up to make more homes available for aspiring owner-occupiers: we can help create a nation of homeowners by treating renters with respect.

The uncomfortably high debt-to-income ratio of UK households, and the stress and insecurity it causes, also needs addressing. This requires that families who find themselves in debt – for example, as a result of being in employment that doesn't guarantee a stable income – should, as The Children's Society suggests, be given a 'breathing space', in which enforcement, interest and other charges are frozen until they have had chance to make a realistic repayment plan.[15]

Developing and pursuing (our own and our children's) aspirations also takes time as well as money. This requires employers to address the culture of long and unpredictable working hours that damage both wellbeing and productivity. Despite some employers' fear of innovation, reforming working hours is effective. When the clothing chain Gap improved employee scheduling practices in a randomly chosen group of 28 of their US stores, the consequent improvement in workers' wellbeing had a large enough knock-on effect on sales to earn Gap an extra US$2.9 million from just 28 stores in 35 weeks. As one of the store managers said, they had fallen into the habit of using short-notice scheduling 'as a safety net to handle business and workload – but we learned we really didn't need it'.[16]

The prevalence of excessive and erratic working hours – and the demotivating treatment of workers, lack of staff development and other contributors to the UK's productivity problem – arise from a widespread failure to invest in management skills. The Chartered Management Institute estimate up to *four-fifths* of UK managers are 'accidental managers', without the training and/or aptitude for the job,[17] probably working long hours in an attempt to cope, presenting this as a sign of 'commitment' and thereby setting a bad example to their teams, creating a cycle of inefficiency, exhaustion, fractiousness and demotivation. The UK's unusually laissez-faire attitude to training its managers is a relic of the days when a manager's background was assumed to qualify them for the role (as one management expert sarcastically put it to me, 'a chap knows how to manage the chaps'). In todays' post-feudal world, however, employers should invest in management competence.

All the above measures are about creating enough stability to nurture aspiration. They are also about treating each other with respect. The Rosenthal experiment summarised in Chapter 3 is an illustration of how increased esteem produces increased performance. This implies that all our educators, employers and government agencies (and anyone else who interacts with humans) should ask themselves whether their policies, practices, relationships and language are those of mutual respect.

Respect includes respecting each other's identity and background rather than, for example, requiring teachers to stop speaking in their native accents (thereby depriving children of a role model who sounds like them). It includes respecting those who do not wish to enter higher education, a professional occupation or management (and employers taking steps to ensure that management is not the only route of progression). And it includes ceasing to imply that everyone from non-elite backgrounds should aspire to social mobility.

Desegregation

In April 1968, the Shadow Secretary of State for Defence made a speech opposing treating people with respect. Specifically, Enoch Powell was arguing that employers and landlords should be legally allowed to practise racial discrimination.

Fifty years after what became known as the 'Rivers of Blood' speech, a poll was commissioned by the think tank British Future to assess whether attitudes had changed. Most respondents (whether or not they were themselves members of minority ethnic groups) said racial prejudice had declined. When asked why this had happened, the most popular answers were 'Children mixing at school with kids from other ethnic/ religious backgrounds' and 'Workplace contact with people from other ethnic/religious backgrounds'.[18]

If we want to break down the demotivating disrespect experienced by members of 'lower' social and economic classes, and allow them to meet the 'posh friends' who so often played a major role in my interviewees' stories, desegregating our educational institutions and workplaces is a good place to start.

Private schools, which are very effective in segregating children along lines of social and economic background, should no longer be subsidised through charitable status or the 'assisted places' scheme still available to senior military officers.[19] (It is sometimes argued that ending private schools' taxpayer subsidies would make them even more exclusive to the really-rich, by pricing out the merely-rich, but the really-rich already send their offspring to a different class of private schools to the merely-rich anyway.) Policy-makers and school leaders should also act on the overwhelming evidence that selective schools, setting and streaming have a negative impact on social mobility.[20] 'Selection by postcode', whereby wealthy families monopolise certain state schools by buying properties in their catchment areas must also be addressed: Schools should be required to ensure that their intake is at least approximately reflective of the population of the surrounding local authority (for example, by having non-contiguous catchment areas – in some cases, a whole housing estate can be served by a single school bus).

Higher education institutions – and employers – can and should be desegregated by strengthening the 'contextualised recruitment' practices already in use at some institutions to help recruiters see candidates' potential rather than their privilege. But those practices need to be applied in more sophisticated ways than is often the case, and due consideration given to the fact that privileged students have an advantage over those from middling families as well as their (larger) advantage over those from the least-privileged backgrounds. Contextualised recruitment –and the reporting of recruitment data – also needs to be applied in sufficient detail, so that, for example, higher education institutions are required to disclose *course-by-course* data to avoid universities claiming to have 'widened participation' while the most prestigious courses remain monopolised by the privileged. Recruitment decisions based solely on (contextualised) performance data have such a reliably better success rate in predicting candidates' future performance than decisions based on interviews and personal statements that it is difficult to make an argument for retaining the latter. As has often been pointed out, contextualised recruitment techniques result in larger numbers of people from non-elite backgrounds entering elite institutions and careers, and such people are more likely to struggle culturally and financially in such environments, but the solution lies in making the environment less hostile rather than assuming the fault lies with the individual.

Some employers are already recognising that graduate or 'fast-track' schemes are restricting the ability of talented people to 'rise up from the factory floor', like Zhou Qunfei did (Ms Zhou being the woman whose company made the screen of your smartphone).[21] Others who wish to avoid wasting talent should follow their lead, by creating and supporting more progression pathways, making the protocols of progression clearer, and removing the disadvantages suffered by employees with little family experience of workplace politics.

NCS, the National Citizen Service (which exists to promote social cohesion, social mobility and social engagement[22]) is already rising to the challenge of desegregating extra-curricular activities. But it has huge untapped potential to have a similar effect on young people's career opportunities and friendships as National Service did for an earlier generation (or at least the male half of it). This would involve NCS having stronger relationships with schools and local authorities to allow it to reach more participants, making it more intensive and long-lasting, and integrating its work with that of an expanded careers support and work experience service (of which more later). Other CV-enhancing extra-curricular opportunities available through public and semi-public institutions (including universities' societies, sports clubs and student union officer roles) should also be required to report data on the backgrounds of participants and whether these reflect the backgrounds of the wider population.

Desegregation of education, work and leisure opportunities, however, will be undermined unless we tackle the growing segregation of the neighbourhoods in which we live. As we saw in Chapter 3, children with a wider range of neighbours have a wider range of opportunities. It is also the case that neighbourhoods that include people with high levels of 'social and cultural capital' are more successful in persuading local authorities and management companies to improve services and tackle disrepair and anti-social behaviour. Local authorities should promote social diversity in new housing developments by integrating housing for social rent with housing for private sale (possibly through private sector partnerships), considering the existing social mix when assessing planning applications, and ensuring shared amenities and mixed participation in resident representation bodies. (This is not to suggest that anyone should be put under pressure to move away, which tends to break up social bonds and the networks through which people hear of job opportunities, but rather that new building should be mixed-tenure.)

But there are instances in which social mixing isn't always helpful, as the Scottish Government's former Head of Higher Education Lucy Hunter-Blackburn encountered at the Oxford open day in which she felt 'awkward and scruffy and excluded' among the crowds of public schoolboys.[23] In such situations, the incomer finds him or herself constantly outside their comfort zone, and while spending time outside your comfort zone should be encouraged (for example, by ending universities' baffling practice of asking students to pair themselves up with – usually socially-similar – friends for group work), we all need to spend some time *inside* our comfort zone. We all need a 'home room', a space to retreat, recuperate, reflect and regroup, and to spend at least some time with people who understand us. Hunter-Blackburn suggests separate open days for private schools. I would add that elite workplaces and educational institutions should follow the lead of some companies who already have 'social mobility champions', responsible for advocating ways in which organisations can better met the needs of the non-privileged, and also for creating spaces in which they can meet and support each other.

Wider horizons

As any project manager can tell you, a substantial proportion of total project time is spent on the initial objective setting, scoping and planning. But some projects expected to last for decades are routinely begun with just a few hours of upfront discussion.

In my own case, the total time I spent receiving advice and guidance for the project I'll call 'my career' amounted to a couple of hours (if that) by the time I left university.

My interviewees' experiences suggest I'm not unusual. They learned about career options from chance events and random encounters. They and others reported 'stumbling' into jobs, sometimes via expensive cul-de-sacs and sometimes into long careers that in retrospect they'd rather not have had. Countless others never find their way into careers that match their aptitude rather than their background. Under successive governments, the provision of careers advice and guidance has been, as a former Universities Minister said, 'one of our worst policy failures'.[24]

We should invest in providing every one of our children with a guaranteed, high-quality careers support service. It should begin in primary school, but its key element should not be delivered by or within schools (partly because teachers already have too much on their plates). Once a term, pupils from across each local authority – or group of local authorities in densely populated areas – should go to day-long discovery days that each focus on a different sector or career type (for example, professions, STEM [Science, Technology, Engineering, and Maths], public and emergency services or the voluntary sector), ideally held in a mixture of higher education institutions and workplaces, giving an idea of what's *really* involved in different jobs – for example, that barristers don't spend most of their time arguing in court – and allow hands-on experiences and encounters with potential role models. Holding these at local authority level reduces the risk that children are nudged towards class-appropriate or 'realistic' careers, because pupils from a range of schools – and therefore from a range of backgrounds – will be present. (It will also allow some of their teachers a day for professional development, marking or lesson preparation.)

Once pupils enter secondary school, the 'discovery' elements can be supplemented with information on, for example, salary ranges, demand for such roles, locations of relevant employers, necessary qualifications and experience, along with familiarisation with higher and vocational education. (Charities like the Social Mobility Foundation and The Sutton Trust already do great work in this area, and are well placed to help design and deliver such initiatives, but our children's careers shouldn't be constrained with what can be provided with charitable funding.) Back at school (with local authority support), young people should be guaranteed regular personalised discussions with a qualified careers advice worker, aimed at identifying suitable work experience and/or mentors as well as discussing the academic or vocational routes to careers. The individual's careers file should follow them through school, so that opportunities in which they express an interest are followed up and reviewed.

Careers provision should also include experience-based training in business skills, such as that currently offered in some schools by Young Enterprise, which supports young people to set up and run small short-term businesses. This isn't because entrepreneurship is something everyone should aspire to (it isn't, and anyone wanting to set up a business would be well advised to spend some time 'learning the trade' in someone else's business first). It is because the skills such initiatives teach, including opportunity-spotting, negotiation, teamwork, problem-solving and financial capability – as well as a sense of agency – are necessary in almost all walks of life, including in not-for-profit sectors. It would allow all children an insight into the protocols of workplace life, rather than restricting this opportunity to those who can learn it at their professional parents' dinner tables.

Project managers can also tell you that although the initial plan is important, it isn't the final plan. Adjustments are made in response to developments and re-thinks. And again, the project management of our careers often fails to heed the lesson. The directions of our careers are heavily influenced by circumstances that applied in our childhood and ill-informed decisions we made as teenagers.[25] Finding ourselves stuck in a current that flows towards an unsuitable career often begins by being allocated to either 'academic' or 'vocational' routes. As proposed in Chapter 5, some of this unhelpful segregation can be broken down by ending the distinction between 'degrees' and 'degree apprenticeships', and making the former more like the latter. A similar principle should be applied to lower-level qualifications, so that, for example, when students are choosing subjects to study at 16, they are routinely offered a combination of A-levels (or, in Scotland, Highers) and advanced-level apprenticeships, rather than choosing *between* 'academic' and 'vocational' routes. Unless the distinction between academic and vocational is broken down, vocational routes will continue to suffer the neglect that comes from being outside policy-makers' personal experience).

As the world of work changes, and changes at an accelerating pace, and as our circumstances, aspirations and abilities develop, we are all more likely require career re-planning and re-training. Some attempts are being made to find ways to support this process, such as the introduction of the Apprenticeship Levy (although that initiative clearly needs some work, not least to avoid employers concentrating the spending of their allowance on already-senior staff, and the absence of provision for the self-employed). We also need something similar to the careers support service mentioned above, adapted for adults and replacing the current patchwork of underfunded services. This should provide insights into career opportunities, guidance on training and the financing of training, and — for those whose new direction is towards entrepreneurialism —a route to help with creating business plans and (if business plans are assessed to be robust) sources of finance. Such services should be linked with the bodies responsible for local industrial strategy, so that aspiring entrepreneurs are able to work in symbiosis with the strategic approach of the former.

Demolishing toll booths

Writing this book took two years — ample time to meet people socially and be asked 'so what do you do?' A large proportion of them, having been told the subject of the book, offer policy suggestions. Easily the most popular of these is the abolition of tuition fees for higher education.

I usually respond to this with some of the points made in Chapter 5, or Karl Marx's observation that abolishing fees without drastically reforming admissions practices would constitute a huge subsidy for the education of an already disproportionately privileged group at the expense of everyone else. (In 1875, Marx's *Critique of the Gotha programme* described free higher education as 'defraying the cost of education of the upper classes from the general tax receipts.') I try to do so diplomatically, but rarely make myself popular.

Some of the issues around tuition fees do need to be addressed, including the restrictions and repayment terms on loans for part-time students, interest rates, and the worryingly widespread misapprehension that loans must be paid back regardless of income.

A more pressing priority, however, are costs that prevent some students taking up their places in higher education institutions, impair their ability to fully participate in higher education, or cause them to drop out, rather than those whose financial implications come after graduation. To widen participation in higher education, the most urgent change that should be made to student finance is that loans or grants for living expenses should actually be enough to cover the cost of living (and the cost of any necessary academic materials).

Beyond higher education, there is a long list of other priorities. These include the improved social security provision, expansion of the National Citizen Service and the careers support service mentioned in previous sections, but there are numerous other examples: reversing cuts to pre-school provision; increasing Pupil Premium payments; restoring the Education Maintenance Allowance; and funding for schools to send pupils to university or apprenticeship open days and interviews (including the cost of travel, accommodation or audition fees).

While some of the financial barriers to opportunity can be tackled by employers (such as offering advances on salaries to allow new recruits to pay landlords' deposits and rent-in-advance), it is impossible to remove all the conceivable tolls on the road to opportunity. So people should be enabled to pay the tolls they do encounter. A more supportive social security system would help, by offering people what the *Financial Times* calls, 'a base level of security that enables them to be confident and take risks'.[26] But some costs require a larger outlay: a car for travelling to work in areas public transport doesn't reach or tools of the trade, for example. Various versions of a 'citizen's opportunity fund' to cover such costs have already been tried or proposed. The Child Trust Fund, in which the government invested £250 on behalf of each child born after 1 September 2002 (until the scheme was discontinued in 2011), produced a lump sum when the child turned 18.[27] It wasn't perfect (flaws included its vulnerability to the vagaries of the markets, demonstrated when, five years after the scheme was launched, the financial crisis caused the value of investments to crash and not recover for another six years), but we won't begin to see the benefits until late in 2020. Another model, which spreads the risk, is the 'Citizen's Inheritance' proposed by the Resolution Foundation's Intergenerational Commission and the similar 'Citizens' Wealth Fund', proposed by the Institute for Public Policy Research, which would create a one-off payment of £10,000 to all 25-year-olds, to help them put a deposit on a home, invest in their education or set up a business.[28]

Such schemes raise big questions. One obvious question, about whether the recipients would spend the money most effectively, could be answered by linking them to the careers support service, so recipients have a good understanding of how they could most effectively spend (or save) all or part of their payment before they receive it. But there are other questions, of how to pay for a substantial payment to a large number of people, and how to reduce the probability that already-affluent families will use it – as they have with the 'Help to Buy' scheme – to bid-up house prices for the rest of us. Those question will be answered in the next section.

A bigger pie

The above proposals can give ourselves and our children a fairer chance to develop and pursue our aspirations. But it is mathematically impossible to give the average citizen of the UK a better chance of actually *attaining* their aspirations unless the supply of the objects of their aspiration (notably homes and good jobs) increases relative to the population.

Creating a more hospitable, desegregated and affordable environment would itself increase the number of employment opportunities (by tapping into previously unmet demand for skilled workers or, for example, by increasing the number of people who set up businesses) and possibly homes (especially if those businesses being set up are building firms). But not by anything like the amount needed. The rapid increases in homeownership in the 1950s and 1980s were the result of government interventions, as was much of the post-war boom in the number of high-quality jobs. A proactive state is a consistent feature of economies that have recently succeeded in making significant improvements to the quality and quantity of jobs and housing.[29]

Happily, the UK government has recently begun to think more seriously about how to attract, retain and support jobs and businesses, after decades in which anything beyond lowering corporation tax, 'deregulation' and promoting financial services was out of step with free market fashions. But any industrial strategy is unlikely to produce high-quality jobs – those with good pay, security, esteem and prospects – unless such jobs are made one of the main objectives of the strategy. It has to be said that Brexit may significantly reduce our room for manoeuvre in this area. Having an urgent need to secure trade deals would put us in a weak negotiating position compared to any potential partner who isn't as desperate (that is, pretty much anyone), and mean we have to forgo some of our objectives. But, Brexit allowing, there are some features of an industrial strategy that would make it more likely to attract, retain and support high-quality jobs.

Some efforts have recently been made to shift the economy towards a higher value model, but not nearly enough. To compete on the basis of high quality rather than low cost, and to avoid being left behind in the race for the new opportunities created as the third industrial revolution is superseded by the fourth, requires the UK to adopt as proactive and ambitious a strategy as its competitors.

International evidence strongly suggests that industrial strategies have more success when they give an active role to the state and public sector.[30] This should include a dedicated body to work with experts and with employers' and employees' representatives. Such a body should be responsible for identifying areas of potential growth, and have influence over the planning of infrastructure necessary to take advantage of these opportunities. Reform of our corporate governance regime is also necessary to tackle short-termist and wealth-extracting tendencies encouraged by current arrangements and foster more forward-looking, sustainable, wealth-creating practices.[31]

Any industrial strategy should have a strong focus on spreading prosperity around the country, so opportunity isn't restricted to people who are willing to 'leave to achieve'. This requires local or regional government to have the powers and resources to form taskforces for regional economic development with business groups, universities and colleges, and other experts, to identify where their region's potential competitive advantages lie and how to make the most of them.[32]

Local government is also key to increasing the supply of homes. In the 20th century, local authorities built tens of thousands of homes each year, but their ability to borrow to invest in housing is now legally restricted, and they are disallowed from spending all but a fraction of the receipts from Right to Buy sales of social housing on new homes. These restrictions must be removed, and investment made, to unleash local authorities to once again become large-scale homebuilders. (The democratic accountability of local authorities also makes them more likely to consider what sort of housing is most needed rather than most profitable: a wide choice of one-bedroom flats is no help to a family of four.)

But boosting the supply of homes isn't enough to make homes as affordable as they should be. There is a need to reduce the upward pressure on costs created by forces other than people wanting to buy themselves a home. This includes scrapping the so-called 'Help to Buy' scheme that subsidises already-wealthy buyers and inflates prices for everyone else. It also includes reducing the buying power of landlords relative to that of aspiring owner-occupiers (some tax changes have already been introduced for this purpose, and appear to have had a moderating effect on the market).

The scarcity of both high-quality jobs and affordable homes, however, is related to a subtler, underlying feature of our economy: the growing power of wealth relative to earned income. To create an economy that favours future opportunities rather than past privilege, it is necessary to change our tax system to reflect the needs of the 21st century rather than the values of the feudal era. In addition to shifting Corporation Tax rates towards those of other G7 economies and tackling corporate tax-avoidance (which would also help budding businesses compete on a less-unlevel playing field), we must also reverse the trend, which has taken place over the last half-century or so, to shift the taxation regime in favour of those with family wealth and very high incomes at the expense of others.

The majority of the public believes that the richest do – and should – contribute a larger proportion of their incomes to the public purse than the poorest, whereas in reality the opposite is true.[33] The government should move the tax regime towards the progressive model that the public favours. For example, property taxes should be reformed, towards land value and away from the current Council Tax model, which hasn't kept up with changes in the property market for almost 30 years, and has therefore effectively handed a subsidy to those who have gained most from the windfalls of house price rises at everyone else's expense. The richest 5 or 6% of families in the UK – to whom inheritance tax changes have gifted up to £140,000 each in the last few years – must once again make a fair contribution (which would also act as a counterbalance against the risk of an 'opportunity fund' being used by its wealthiest recipients to bid up house prices).

Reforming inheritance tax is necessary to rebalance our economy towards work and aspiration rather than wealth and speculation, but it won't be easy. Across the developed world, progressive property and inheritance taxes have been in retreat, driven by a relentless campaign to mislead 'ordinary families' into thinking that reducing such taxes is in their own interest. But opposition has also been driven by a distaste for inheritance tax *in principle*. As discussed in Chapter 8, it would help if inheritance tax were replaced by a windfall tax, levied not on the giver but on the receiver. A windfall tax would give each of us a lifetime's tax-free allowance up to a level that all but the most-privileged would regard as more than enough to provide financial security (for example, enough to buy an average-priced house outright), after which the inheritor still gets to keep the majority of any receipts over that amount (say, 55%). Steps should also be taken to tackle the trusts and loopholes that allowed the likes of the Dukes of Westminster to avoid paying their share.

Altering the balance of taxation in favour of aspiration – and investing so that opportunities don't require wealth – won't be easy, but it is necessary if all of our children are to have a chance to pursue the opportunities that the most-privileged take for granted.

Hope, and a story of hope

It is traditional for books about economic or social issues to end with suggestions for ways in which the issue can be addressed. It is also traditional for those suggestions to be ignored.

Often, such suggestions are ignored because they cost money. But most of the proposals above require changes in approach rather than amount, and others don't cost as much as you may think (for example, restoring decent levels of social security for working-age families is more affordable than most people imagine, because most people hugely overestimate the proportion of 'welfare' spending that goes to this group). However, some proposals, such as an 'opportunity fund' and a fit-for-purpose careers service, do have significant costs attached. Some of the costs can be met by asset sales, such as the government's stake in RBS, and others by reversing some of the tax advantages that have increasingly been enjoyed by those who live on inherited wealth. Brexit will reduce the amount of available money by reducing growth, but will leave us damaged rather than helpless. We were damaged by the Second World War (to an extent that dwarfs Brexit) but we raised a greater edifice – the NHS and the other pillars of the reasonably decent society in which we now live – above the rubble. Too often in the recent past, we as a country have chosen to shrink back rather than go forward – choosing austerity rather than investment or protesting problems rather than proposing improvements. These *are* choices. We need a political vision that has a 'growth mindset'.

Beyond the challenges of costs and mindsets, the prospects of a policy programme to address the aspiration crisis look good. There is growing recognition that unfulfilled aspirations are causing our economy, society and democracy to become increasingly dysfunctional. However, as policy responses to climate change have shown, getting a problem acknowledged isn't the same as getting it solved.

Just because the voting public think that opportunities are unfairly distributed doesn't mean they're thinking about it when they're in the voting booth and therefore creating electoral pressure for change. In the case of unmet aspirations, however, voters apparently *are* taking their resentment into the polling station. Voters who'd expected the chance of a home of their own as 'part of the deal' in return for being good scholars and willing workers, deprived the government of a majority in the 'rise of the renters' at the 2017 General Election.[34] Large numbers of people don't forget their unmet aspirations because their everyday reality is of life in put on hold by the insecurity of a short-term tenancy, a job that feels like an indefinite stop-gap, and without the financial groundedness to start a family.

Another issue that can prevent policy solutions being implemented is that the electorate often dislike the solution even more than they dislike the problem: the NIMBY tendency to think more homes should be built somewhere, just 'not in my back yard'. According to the *British Social Attitudes* survey, however, by 2017 a majority of us supported more homebuilding in our local area, compared to only 28% seven years earlier. Families' own experiences of unmet housing aspirations – and some excellent campaigning by Shelter and their allies – has changed minds.[35]

Policy-makers' ability to act is also increased by the growing proportion of the electorally important families of 'Middle Britain' who are finding themselves unable to get the jobs, homes and financial security they had come to expect. Middle-income families don't experience the hostile-to-aspiration environment anything like as harshly as those at the bottom of the economic and social scale, but now experience it harshly enough to act on it. Nor is 'middle Britain' the only politically important constituency now concerned about opportunity. Numerous businesses, concerned that potential recruits are being locked out of their workforces, depriving them of both talent and goodwill, are now becoming more engaged with the issue, signing up to the Social Mobility Pledge, competing to score highly in the Social Mobility Employer Index, and declaring it a major issue.[36]

As the risks to politicians of developing and championing a policy programme to open up opportunities are declining, the risks of *not* doing so are growing. Most voters see little positive vision (as opposed to critiques of other parties' thinking) in the current political landscape, little to identify with or become enthused by. More worryingly, segregated opportunities create conditions in which politics and politicians are viewed as at best irrelevant and at worst illegitimate.

A political narrative based on creating more opportunities to attain our aspirations *does* have the potential to present a positive vision, and one with potential appeal to a far wider range of voters than the jargonistic and politically divisive language of 'social mobility'. The key themes of such a narrative – a job that is rewarding (in all senses of the word), a home to call one's own, family, and underlying themes of security, respect, belonging and a life determined by yourself rather than your background – refer to things many of us feel we have lost or are at risk of losing; things that lie at the root of the widespread disenchantment with current politics that populists and extremists have very effectively exploited.

Popular politics currently finds itself without the broad (if not total) consensus of consent that allowed our country to pursue national aspirations post-1945 and post-1979. To move forward from the retro tribalism of left and right and the emerging animosities of populism against metropolitan liberalism, a consensus of consent has to be built on the shared values that underpin the popular appeal of both 'opportunity' and 'equality': work, home, family, security, respect, belonging and reward.

It won't be easy, because public perceptions of the establishment as being made up of people with alien backgrounds, experiences, outlooks and values means any proposals or narratives will be subject to suspicion (which is another reason to urgently address – and be seen to address – the representativeness of the establishment).

It won't be made any easier by the inevitable resistance of those who fear the loss of their advantages if others are allowed to compete more fairly and won't be entirely pacified by the promise that opportunities will become more numerous as well as more fairly distributed. There will be the usual attempts to misrepresent and frustrate. It will require politicians to demonstrate resilience. It will also require a strong story, and for each of the policies necessary to build an opportunity society to be promoted with reference to that story, a story we can not only all believe in, but also participate in.

The story has to be about all of us, regardless of our class. The beneficiaries of policies to increase opportunity are not just 'the poor' (despite politicians' habit of inadvertently suggesting otherwise). Those who wish to create a fairer distribution of opportunity must make it clear that the objective is to benefit everyone who was not born into exceptional privilege (and some of them, too, who are locked by expectation into class-appropriate lives that make them miserable). Unless that happens, the defenders of privilege will find it easy to mobilise the majority by suggesting 'the poor' will benefit at the expense of the middle. Hardly anyone – including people we might regard as poor – thinks of themselves as 'the poor', so promoting a policy by saying it will help 'the poor' might make privileged people feel better about their own selfless pursuit of social justice, but it is counterproductive. The pressure that allowed national and local politicians to replace selective schools (a system in which the poorest were the biggest losers) came as a result of *middle-income* families realising that their own children were also more likely to find themselves in secondary moderns than grammar schools.

The story has to be a national one. It requires a national project, involving all government departments, all educators, all employers, all of us. A national project enables the unleashing of pride, as was the case when the UK faced down fascism, or implemented the Beveridge report. Unleashing pride and belonging will be necessary to foster a more positive mindset, to counter the insidious messages that people from non-elite backgrounds are 'different' and not really up to the best education or careers. It is unapologetically a *national* pride, not just because most of the UK's citizens value their national identity (either as British, English, Scottish, Welsh or Northern Irish), but also as a basis for acknowledging that everyone in the UK deserves opportunities on an equal basis, regardless of which of the UK's nations, regions or neighbourhoods they are from.

The inclusive national pride that such a project requires (and creates) also helps overcome the idea that we have to choose between helping the individual to achieve their aspirations and helping everyone. Despite the polarised debate among politically aligned commentators, most of the public do not believe that collective wellbeing and individual flourishing are incompatible,[37] and they are right. There is synergy rather than conflict between these two goals. In the 2012 Olympics, athletes won medals as individuals, and also as part of Team GB. In the 2018 World Cup, the leadership style of Gareth Southgate propelled England to expectation-defying progress by creating a strong camaraderie, and allowed Harry Kane to achieve individual glory as the tournament's leading goal scorer. As anyone who watched those two events is aware, the individual does well when the team does well. We achieve our aspirations together, as Team UK.

Notes

Chapter One: The world's great meritocracy

1   Christopher Snowdon (2016) 'The establishment by Owen Jones: A review', Institute of Economic Affairs blog, 8 September.
2   Margaret Thatcher, speech to Conservative Party rally in Cardiff, 16 April 1979.
3   John Major, speech to Conservative Party Conference, 11 October 1991.
4   Tony Blair, speech to Labour Party Conference, 1 October 1996.
5   Tony Blair, speech to Labour Party Conference, 28 September 2004.
6   Gordon Brown (2010) 'An age of aspiration can benefit everyone', *The Observer*, 3 January.
7   David Cameron, speech to Conservative Party Conference, 7 October 2015.
8   Theresa May (2016) 'Statement from the new Prime Minister Theresa May', 13 July.
9   Theresa May, 'Britain, the great meritocracy', Speech, 9 September 2016.
10 Michael Young (1958) *The rise of the meritocracy 1870-2033: An essay on education and society*, London: Thames & Hudson.
11 Neil O'Brien (2011) *Just deserts? Attitudes to fairness, poverty and welfare reform*, London: Policy Exchange, p 10.
12 ResearchBods and BritainThinks (2013) *(Ex)aspiration nation: A study on the aspirations and expectations of young people and their parents*, July.
13 James Slack, Jason Groves and Eleanor Harding (2016) 'March of the meritocrats: May loads new Cabinet with state educated Ministers on the most brutal day of top-level sacking in modern history', *Daily Mail*, 15 July.
14 Labour Cabinets tend to have smaller proportions of privately educated members than Conservative Cabinets, but a far higher proportion than is representative of the wider population (see also Chapter 9, this book).
15 The Sutton Trust (2016) 'Sutton Trust analysis shows big rise in state educated ministers', Press release, 14 July.
16 The only coverage I found was in Legal Cheek, an online news site for junior lawyers and law students. See Katie King (2016) 'Six judges have been appointed to the Court of Appeal and they're pretty much all Oxbridge-educated white men', Legal Cheek, 14 September.
17 Philip Kirby (2016) *Leading people 2016: The educational backgrounds of the UK professional elite*, London: The Sutton Trust, p 2.
18 Data cited in this section are the latest available at the time of writing (October 2018).
19 Ken Clarke (2014) 'My school days: Ken Clarke', *Nottingham Post*, 9 June.
20 Francis Green, Jake Anders, Morag Henderson and Golo Henseke (2017) *Who chooses private schooling in Britain and why?*, LLAKES Research Paper 62, Centre for

Research on Learning and Life Chances in Knowledge Economies and Societies (www.llakes.ac.uk).

[21] 'Hereditary peers removed', UK Parliament website.

[22] Rebecca Montacute and Tim Carr (2017) *Parliamentary privilege – The MPs 2017*, London: The Sutton Trust.

[23] David Leask (2016) 'Revealed: MSPs five times more likely to be privately educated than average Scot', *The Herald*, 7 June; Paul Cairney, Michael Keating and Alex Wilson (2016) 'Solving the problem of social background in the UK "political class": Do parties do things differently in Westminster, devolved and European elections?', *British Politics*, vol 11, issue 2, pp 142-63.

[24] Oliver Heath (2015) 'Policy representation, social representation and class voting in Britain', *British Journal of Political Science*, vol 45, p 182.

[25] Montacute and Carr (2017) op cit; Kirby (2016) op cit, p 25.

[26] Lee Elliot Major (2018) 'Stuck: Britain's social mobility problem', Presentation, University of Warwick, November.

[27] Elizabeth Rigby and Andrew Bounds (2014) 'Concerns over UK Conservatives' "posh" manifesto', *Financial Times*, 23 February.

[28] Social Mobility and Child Poverty Commission (2014) *Elitist Britain?*, London, p 12.

[29] Ten organisations including the Royal United Services Institute, whose Director-General is American. *Prospect* (2018) 'Think Tank Awards 2018: The full shortlist'. Author's own research on directors' education.

[30] Social Mobility and Child Poverty Commission (2014) op cit, p 10.

[31] Joe Mellor (2017) 'Dominated by "posh boys": Number of public school Army officer cadets jumped a fifth last year', *The London Economic*, 11 August.

[32] Sally Weale (2016) 'Privately educated elite continues to take top jobs, finds survey', *The Guardian*, 24 February.

[33] Georgia Snow (2015) 'Only 10% of actors are working class', *The Stage*, 6 May.

[34] Sam Friedman (2018) 'The class ceiling', Presentation, NatCen Social Research, London, 18 September.

[35] Orian Brook, David O'Brien and Mark Taylor (2018) *Panic! Social class, taste and inequalities in the creative industries*, p 14.

[36] Aaron Reeves, Sam Friedman, Charles Rahal and Magne Flemmen (2017) 'The decline and persistence of the old boy: Private schools and elite recruitment 1897 to 2016', *American Sociological Review*, 29 October.

[37] The Sutton Trust (2011) *Degrees of success: University chances by individual school*, London, p 34.

[38] Condé Nast (2017) '*Tatler* media pack 2017.'

[39] Adi Bloom (2018) '*Tatler* publishes state schools guide for "people like us"', *TES*, 2 January.

[40] English data: The Sutton Trust (2011) op cit; Scottish data, which refers to total higher education entry: Scottish Government (2016) *Initial destinations of senior phase school leavers*, Table 5; Welsh data: ITV (2016) 'Wales' top ten schools on The Sunday Times list'.

[41] Social Mobility and Child Poverty Commission (2014) op cit, p 35.

[42] Kurt Vonnegut (1979 [1989]) *Slaughterhouse-Five*, Boulder, CO: Paladin Press, p 11.

[43] Christopher Jencks and Laura Tach (2005) *Would equal opportunity mean more mobility?*, KSG Working Paper No RWP05-037, p 2.

[44] Boston Consulting Group (2017) *The state of social mobility in the UK*, London: The Sutton Trust, p 7.

Notes

45 Jo Blanden, Alissa Goodman, Paul Gregg and Stephen Machin (2002) *Changes in intergenerational mobility in Britain*, London: London School of Economics and Political Science, p 18.

46 The countries studied were Australia, Canada, Denmark, Finland, France, Germany, Italy, Norway, Spain, Sweden, the UK and USA. A short summary of Corak's findings can be found in Anna D'Addio (2007) *Intergenerational transmission of disadvantage: Mobility or immobility across generations?*, OECD Social, Employment and Migration Working Paper No 52, Paris: Organisation for Economic Co-operation and Development (OECD), pp 32-3.

47 OECD (Organisation for Economic Co-operation and Development) (2018) *A broken social elevator: How does the United Kingdom compare?*, Briefing Paper, Paris.

48 Tony Blair, speech to the Institute for Public Policy Research (IPPR) and Demos, Beveridge Hall, University of London, 2004.

49 Attributed to Geoffrey Crowther, former Editor of *The Economist*. Schumpeter (2011) 'The case against globaloney', *The Economist*, 20 April.

50 Lola Okolosie (2016) 'Social mobility doesn't exist – and grammar schools are part of the problem', *The Guardian*, 28 July. Okolosie does, in the same article, soften her stance a little to say, 'there will be outliers…. But…. Your family background is in fact most people's destiny.'

51 Jo Blanden (2013) 'Social mobility matters, and government can affect the mechanisms which promote it', LSE Politics and Policy blog, 4 November.

52 John Goldthorpe (2016) *Social class mobility in modern Britain: Changing structure, constant process*, Centre for Social Investigation (CSI) Briefing Paper 21, Oxford: Nuffield College.

53 Franz Buscha and Patrick Sturgis (2016) 'Declining social mobility? Evidence from five linked censuses in England and Wales 1971-2011', *British Journal of Sociology*, vol 79, issue 1, pp 154-82.

54 James Bartholomew (2015) 'The NHS is broken. What should replace it?', *Daily Telegraph*, 9 September.

55 James Bartholomew (2015) 'Britons are on the move upwards', *Daily Telegraph*, 16 June.

56 Paul Gregg, Lindsey Macmillan and Claudia Vittori (2016) 'Moving towards estimating sons' lifetime intergenerational economic mobility in the UK', *Oxford Bulletin of Economics and Statistics*, vol 79, issue 1, pp 79-100.

57 Gavin Kelly (2018) 'Where has income mobility been rising fastest? Britain', *Medium*, 5 July.

58 Lee Savage (2011) *Moving on up? Social mobility in the 1990s and 2000s*, London: Resolution Foundation; Danny Dorling (2014) 'Class segregation', in C. Lloyd, I. Shuttleworth and D.W. Wong (eds) *Social–spatial segregation: Concepts, processes and outcomes*, Bristol: Policy Press, pp 363-88.

59 Mike Savage (2016) *Social class in the 21st century*, London: Pelican, p 91.

60 Gregory Clark and Neal Cummins (2013) *Surnames and social mobility: England 1230-2012'*, LSE Economic History Working Papers No 181, November, London: London School of Economics and Political Science.

61 Danny Dorling (2015) *Inequality and the 1%*, London: Verso, pp 18-19.

62 Adam Corlett and Stephen Clarke (2017) *Living standards 2017: The past, present and possible future of UK incomes*, London: Resolution Foundation.

63 John Goldthorpe (2016) 'Social class mobility in modern Britain: Changing structure, constant process', *Journal of the British Academy*, vol 4, pp 94-5.

64 *Forbes* profile, accessed on 17 August 2018.

65 Civil Service Fast Stream website.

Chapter Two: Early years

1   Gaby Hinsliff (2015) 'Grammar schools are not the answer: The road to a better life starts at birth, not at 11', *The Guardian*, 15 October.

2   Some details on the 'Dutch Hunger Winter' can be found in L.H. Lumey, Aryeh Stein, Henry Kahn, Karin van der Pal-de Bruin, G.J. Blauw, Patricia Zybert and Ezra Susser (2007) 'Cohort profile: The Dutch Hunger Winter families study', *International Journal of Epidemiology*, vol 36, no 6, pp 1196-204. The phenomenon is more accessibly described in Nessa Carey (2012) 'Beyond DNA: Epigenetics', *Natural History*.

3   Richard Rothstein (2014) 'The urban poor shall inherit poverty', *The American Prospect*, 4 January.

4   Petra Persson and Maya Rossin-Slater (2016) *Family ruptures, stress, and the mental health of the next generation*, NBER Working Paper No 22229, Cambridge, MA: National Bureau of Economic Research (NBER).

5   YouGov and *The Times* (2016) 'Finance (£500) results', 7 June.

6   RSA (2018) 'Revealed: The seven new classes of worker in the modern British economy', Press release, 25 January.

7   Pregnant City Girl (2015) 'How to give your child a headstart in the womb! – Prenatal education', Blog, 12 September.

8   Sophie McBain (2012) 'Bringing up Einstein: Can money buy brains?', *Spears*, 10 April.

9   Alison Garnham, speaking at the All-Party Parliamentary Group (APPG) on Poverty and Child Poverty Action Group's (CPAG) parliamentary launch of *Improving children's life chances*, 16 November 2016.

10 *Hansard*, 18 December 2012, col 711.

11 Paul Gregg, Jane Waldfogel and Elizabeth Washbrook (2006) 'Family expenditures post-welfare reform in the UK: Are low income families with children starting to catch up?', *Labour Economics*, vol 13, no 6, pp 721-46.

12 Kitty Stewart (2016) 'Why we can't talk about life chances without talking about income', in J. Tucker (ed) *Improving children's life chances*, London: Child Poverty Action Group (CPAG), p 9.

13 Andre Hood, Agnes Norris Keiller and Tom Waters (2017) 'Significant cuts to two parts of the benefit system to be phased in from next week', Observation, London: Institute for Fiscal Studies, 30 March.

14 Joseph Rowntree Foundation (2008) *A Minimum Income Standard for Britain: What people think*, York.

15 Matt Padley (2017) *A Minimum Income Standard for London, 2017*, Loughborough: Loughborough University and Trust for London, p 4.

16 A village in Germany whose inhabitants, once every decade, stage a Passion Play, portraying the Easter story.

17 Jane Waldfogel and Elizabeth Washbrook (2010) *Low income and early cognitive development in the UK*, London: The Sutton Trust, p 45.

18 BBC News (1998) 'Stars back reading drive', 16 September.

19 Social Mobility Commission (2016) *State of the nation 2016: Social mobility in Great Britain*, London: The Stationery Office, p 22.

20 Damien Gayle (2018) 'More than 500 children's centres have closed in England since 2010', *The Guardian*, 20 February.

21 Social Mobility Commission (2016) op cit.

22 Becky Gulc and Kay Silversides (2016) *Parents' experiences of services and information in the early years*, London: Social Mobility and Child Poverty Commission, pp 12, 13, 18, 21.

23 Alison Gopnik, quoted in Katherine Reynolds Lewis (2016) 'Abandon parenting, and just be a parent', *The Atlantic*, 23 September.

24 Kate Zernicke (2011) 'Fast-tracking to kindergarten', *The New York Times*, 13 May.

25 Baroness Ruth Lister, speaking at the All-Party Parliamentary Group (APPG) on Poverty, Portcullis House, Westminster, London, 16 November 2016.

26 Igniter Media (2009) 'The marshmallow test' [video].

27 Yuichi Shoda, Walter Mischel and Philip Peake (1990) 'Predicting adolescent cognitive and self-regulatory competencies from preschool delay of gratification: Identifying diagnostic conditions', *Developmental Psychology*, vol 26, no 6, pp 978–86.

28 Jerry Useem (2016) 'Is grit overrated?', *The Atlantic*, May.

29 Heather Joshi (2014) *'Non-cognitive' skills: What are they and how can they be measured in the British cohort studies?*, CLS Working Paper 2014/6, London: Institute of Education, University of London.

30 DfE (Department for Education) (2016) *Educational excellence everywhere*, White Paper, London.

31 Dawood Rehman (2015) 'Meet 20 super women who are earning respect for Pakistan', *Daily Pakistan Global*, 16 September.

32 Yvonne Roberts (2009) *Grit: The skills for success and how they are grown*, London: The Young Foundation, p 14.

33 See de Vries and Rentfrow (2016) op cit; Joshi (2014) op cit.

34 Grover ('Russ') Whitehurst (2016) *More on soft skills: Time to flit the grit*, Brookings 'Evidence Speaks' series, 9 June.

35 Cinzia Rienzo, Heather Rolfe and David Wilkinson (2015) *Changing mindsets: Evaluation report and executive summary*, London: Education Endowment Foundation.

36 A selection of experiences can be found in a blog post by Anything Left Handed (2012) 'The effects of making a left-hander write right-handed'.

37 Tanya Altstatt Menchaca (2015) *Enhancing native student achievement: What works?*, Olympia, WA: The Evergreen State College.

38 Carol Dweck (2014) 'The power of believing that you can improve', TEDx, Norrkoping.

39 Gareth Cook (2018) 'The case for the self-driven child', *Scientific American*, 13 February.

40 Jane Wells, Jane Barlow and Sarah Stewart-Brown (2003) 'A systematic review of universal approaches to mental health promotion in schools', *Health Education*, vol 103, no 4, pp 197–220.

41 Neenah Ellis (2008) [radio] 'Survivors of the Great Depression tell their stories', *All Things Considered*, National Public Radio (NPR), 27 November.

42 Ulrike Malmendier and Stefan Nagel (2011) 'Depression babies: Do macroeconomic experiences affect risk taking?', *The Quarterly Journal of Economics*, vol 126, issue 1, pp 373–416.

43 Henrik Cronqvist, Stephan Siegel and Frank Yu (2015) 'Value versus growth investing: Why do different investors have different styles?', *Journal of Financial Economics*, vol 117, issue 2, pp 333–49.

44 Prime Minister's Office, 10 Downing Street and The Rt Hon Theresa May MP (2016) 'PM reaffirms commitment to bold programme of social reform', Press release, 1 September.

45 John Philpott: data provided to Robert Booth (2016) 'More than 7m Britons now in precarious employment', *The Guardian*, 28 November 2017.

46 Shelter (2016) 'One in three working families only one paycheque away from losing their home', Press release, 9 August.

47 Lindsay Judge and Daniel Tomlinson (2018) *Home improvements: Action to address the housing challenges faced by young people*, London: Resolution Foundation, p 12.

48 Dr David Webster, cited in John Owen (2018) 'I was sanctioned for going to a funeral', BBC News, 30 January.

49 The Children's Society (2017) *Understanding childhoods: Growing up in hard times*, London.

50 Francis Green (2016) 'Job insecurity is bad for our health', Centre for Research on Learning and Life Chances in Knowledge Economies and Societies (LLAKE) blog, 21 November.

51 Jessica McCrory Calarco (2018) 'Why rich kids are so good at the marshmallow test', *The Atlantic*, 1 June.

52 UCL (University College London) Institute of Education (2017) 'One in four girls is depressed at age 14, new study reveals', UCL News, 20 September.

53 BSA (British Sociological Association) (2016) 'Grit, governmentality and the erasure of inequality? The curious rise of character education policy', Conference, King's College London, 11 July.

54 Dr Angela Donkin, speaking at the All-Party Parliamentary Group (APPG) on Poverty, Portcullis House, Westminster, London, 16 November 2016, at the APPG on Poverty and CPAG parliamentary launch of *Improving children's life chances*.

55 Erin B. Godfrey, Carlos E. Santos and Esther Burson (2017) 'For better or worse? System-justifying beliefs in sixth-grade predict trajectories of self-esteem and behavior across early adolescence', *Child Development*, 19 June.

56 Fiona Bruce (2016) 'Improving life chances means strengthening family stability', *Huffington Post*, 23 May.

57 Paul Goodman (2016) 'The Social Justice Queen's speech 2) Through same-sex marriage to more marriage – to help raise life chances', *Conservative Home*, 10 May.

58 Andrew Cherlin, David Ribar and Suzumi Yasutakea (2016) 'Nonmarital first births, marriage, and income inequality', *American Sociological Review*, p 17.

59 Andrew Cherlin, quoted in Alexia Fernández Campbell (2016) 'Why are so many millennials having children out of wedlock?', *The Atlantic*, 18 July.

60 Sarah Green Carmichael (2015) 'The research is clear: Long hours backfire for people and for companies', *Harvard Business Review*, 19 August.

61 Emma Luxton (2016) 'Which European countries work the longest hours?', World Economic Forum, 1 June.

62 Paul Sellers (2018) 'What is the Working Time Directive that Boris and Gove are plotting to scrap?', TUC blog, 18 December; Michael Cowan (2018) 'Superheroes don't work 90-hour weeks', BBC Business, 17 January.

63 Figures from the Office for National Statistics, quoted by BBC News (2016) 'Two-hour daily commute "on rise among UK workers"', 18 November.

64 Working Families (2018) *2018 Modern Families Index*, London.

65 Adam Perkins (2015) *The welfare trait*, London: Palgrave Macmillan, p 130.

66 Adam Perkins (2016) 'The ugly truth about benefits CENSORED by a left wing hate mob', *Daily Mail*, 21 February.

67 Dr Kitty Stewart, 'The welfare trait: How state benefits affect personality', LSE lecture, London, 29 June 2016.

68 Jack Grove (2016) 'Welfare state critic savaged at LSE talk', *Times Higher Education*, 30 June.

69 Adam Perkins (2016) op cit.

70 John Hills (2015) *Good times, bad times: The welfare myth of them and us*, Bristol: Policy Press; OBR (Office for Budget Responsibility) (2017) *An OBR guide to welfare*

Notes

spending, London; Centre for Labour and Social Studies (2013) *Exposing the myths of welfare*, London, p 9.

[71] *Evening Standard* (2008) 'The "terrible legacy" of the children growing up in families who haven't worked for generations', 10 March.

[72] Tracy Shildrick, Robert MacDonald, Andy Furlong, Johann Roden and Robert Crow (2012) *Are 'cultures of worklessness' passed down the generations?*, York: Joseph Rowntree Foundation.

[73] Quoted in Jamie Dunkley (2009) 'Funds, friends and Clive Cowdery's resolve to help', *The Daily Telegraph*, 19 July.

[74] Jo Blanden, Emilia Del Bono, Sandra McNally and Birgitta Rabe (2016) 'Universal pre-school education: The case of public funding with private provision', *The Economic Journal*, vol 126, issue 592, May, p 684. The research focused on England only, although the authors point out that 'similar policies exist in Wales and Scotland' (p 682).

[75] Christelle Dumas and Arnaud Lefranc (2010) *Early schooling and later outcomes: Evidence from pre-school extension in France*, THEMA Working Paper No 2010-07, Université de Cergy-Pontoise, p 22.

[76] Tarjei Havnes and Magne Mogstad (2009) *No child left behind: Universal child care and children's long-run outcomes*, Discussion Papers No 582, May, Statistics Norway, Research Department.

[77] Katy Morton (2018) 'Early Years teacher trainees down for a third year', *Nursery World*, 1 December.

[78] Carolina Abecedarian Project (ABC) and Carolina Approach to Responsive Education (CARE).

[79] Jorge Garcia, James Heckman, Duncan Leaf and Maria Prados (2016) *The life-cycle benefits of an influential early childhood program*, HCEO Working Paper 2016-035, Chicago, IL: University of Chicago.

[80] ESRC (Economic and Social Research Council) (2012) 'Child poverty casts a long shadow over social mobility', Evidence Briefing, p 4.

[81] ESRC (Economic and Social Research Council) (2012) 'Employment key to social mobility', Evidence Briefing, p 3.

[82] Jo Faragher (2016) 'High earners more likely to work flexibly, says Working Families', *Personnel Today*, 5 October.

[83] Graham Allen (2011) *Early intervention: The next steps. An Independent Report to Her Majesty's Government*, London: HM Government, p 24.

[84] Graham Allen (2011) ibid, pp xiii, 14.

[85] Nicole Hair, Jamie Hanson, Barbara Wolfe and Seth Pollack (2015) 'Association of child poverty, brain development, and academic achievement', *JAMA Pediatrics*, vol 169, no 9, pp 822-9.

[86] Iain Duncan Smith, quoted in Paul Lewis and Sarah Boseley (2010) 'Iain Duncan Smith "distorted" research on childhood neglect and brain size', *The Guardian*, 9 April.

[87] Claire Crawford, Paul Johnson, Steve Machin and Anna Vignoles (2011) *Social mobility: A literature review*, London: Department for Business, Innovation and Skills, p 10.

[88] Bruce Perry, quoted in Lewis and Boseley (2010) op cit.

[89] Abigail McKnight (2015) *Downward mobility, opportunity hoarding and the 'glass floor'*, London: Social Mobility and Child Poverty Commission, p 36, table 12. ('High income families' are those in income quintile five, 'low income' in quintile one. 'High earners' at age 42 are those in income quintile five.)

90 Bénédicte de Boysson-Bardies (2001) *How language comes to children: From birth to two years*, Cambridge, MA: MIT Press, p 140.

91 ESRC (Economic and Social Research Council) (2012) 'Employment key to social mobility', Evidence Briefing; Rucker Johnson and C. Kirabo Jackson (2018) *Reducing inequality through dynamic complementarity: Evidence from Head Start and public school spending*, NBER Working Paper 23489, Cambridge, MA: National Bureau of Economic Research (NBER).

Chapter Three: School years

1   Both 'sets' and 'streams' are referred to in this chapter. 'Setting' is the practice of dividing pupils into different classes for specific subjects, based on assessments of their ability in that subject; 'streaming' means dividing pupils based on an overall assessment of their academic ability. As education experts have noted, 'research has consistently failed to find significant benefits of "ability" grouping' (Becky Francis, Louise Archer, Jeremy Hodgen, David Pepper, Becky Taylor and Mary-Claire Travers [2016] 'Exploring the relative lack of impact of research on "ability grouping" in England: A discourse analytic account', *Cambridge Journal of Education*, vol 47, issue 1, pp 1-17).

2   Claire Crawford, Lindsey Macmillan and Anna Vignoles (2015) *When and why do initially high attaining poor children fall behind?*, CASE (LSE) Social Policy in a Cold Climate Working Paper 20, London: London School of Economics and Political Science, p 19.

3   Nick Clegg, Rebecca Allen, Suella Fernandes, Sam Freedman and Stephen Kinnock (2017) *Commission on Inequality in Education*, London: Social Market Foundation, p 6.

4   Jon Andrews, Jo Hutchinson and David Robinson (2017) *Closing the gap? Trends in educational attainment and disadvantage*, London: Education Policy Institute.

5   Stephen Machin, quoted in Jess Staufenberg (2017) 'Education has "done nothing" to improve social mobility', *Schools Week*, 16 July.

6   ONS (Office for National Statistics) (2014) *How do childhood circumstances affect poverty and deprivation as an adult?*, Newport.

7   Andrews et al (2017) op cit, pp 18-20.

8   Miles Corak (2012) 'Social mobility and inequality in the UK and the US: How to slide down the Great Gatsby curve', Economics for Public Policy blog, 22 May.

9   Jo Blanden and Lindsey Macmillan (2014) *Education and intergenerational mobility: Help or hindrance?*, CASEPaper 179, London: London School of Economics and Political Science, p iii.

10 Yonat Zwebner, Anne-Laure Sellier, Nir Rosenfeld, Jacob Goldenberg and Ruth Mayo (2017) 'We look like our names: The manifestation of name stereotypes in facial appearance', *Journal of Personality and Social Psychology*, vol 112, no 4, April, pp 527-54.

11 Laura Clark (2005) '"Chav" names feared by teachers', *Daily Mail*, 23 September.

12 M.W. Kraus, J.W. Park and J.J.X. Tan (2017) 'Signs of social class: The experience of economic inequality in everyday life', *Perspectives on Psychological Science*, vol 12, pp 422-35.

13 King's College London (2013) *ASPIRES: Young people's science and career aspirations, age 10-14*, London: School of Education and Professional Studies, p 18.

14 Robert Rosenthal, quoted in Alix Spiegel (2012) [radio] 'Teachers' expectations can influence how students perform', *Health Shots*, National Public Radio (NPR), 17 September.

Notes

15 Tammy Campbell (2017) 'The relationship between stream placement and teachers' judgements of pupils: Evidence from the Millennium Cohort Study', *London Review of Education*, vol 15, no 3, November, pp 505-22 (18).

16 Mary-Claire Travers (2017) 'Streaming dampens the aspirations of white working-class boys', *Schools Week*, 2 July.

17 Anne-Laure Sellier (2017) 'Do you look like your name?', *The Conversation*, 22 March.

18 Val Gillies (2005) 'Raising the "meritocracy": Parenting and the individualization of social class', *Sociology*, vol 39, no 5, p 847.

19 Polly Toynbee (2011) [radio] 'The class ceiling' (Episode 1), BBC Radio 4, 1 September.

20 Carol Vincent (2016) 'At the school gate: Do parents make friends with those different to themselves?', Institute of Education blog, 10 September.

21 Andrea Ashworth (1998) *Once in a house on fire*, London: Picador, p 125.

22 Trisha Greenhalgh, Kieran Seyan and Petra Boynton (2004) '"Not a university type": Focus group study of social class, ethnic, and sex differences in school pupils' perceptions about medical school', *British Medical Journal*, vol 328, p 1541.

23 Marco Schmidt and Michael Tomasello (2012) 'Young children enforce social norms', *Current Directions in Psychological Science*, vol 21, issue 4, pp 232-6.

24 Paul Willis (1977) *Learning to labour: How working class kids get working class jobs*, Farnborough: Saxon House; Christine Griffin (1985) *Typical girls? Young women from school to the job market*, London: Routledge & Kegan Paul.

25 Iesha Small (2018) 'What middle class teachers need to know about their working class pupils in poverty', Blog, 13 May.

26 Tony Connor (1965) *Lodgers: Poems*, Oxford: Oxford University Press.

27 L. Richards, E. Garratt and A.F. Heath with L. Anderson and E. Altintaş (2016) *The childhood origins of social mobility: Socio-economic inequalities and changing opportunities*, London: Social Mobility Commission, p 6.

28 Set texts listed by the UK's largest examining board, AQA.

29 Richards et al (2016) op cit, p 64.

30 Lynsey Hanley (2016) *Respectable: The experience of class*, London: Allen Lane, p 50.

31 Lynsey Hanley (2010) [radio] 'Wall in the mind' (Episode 3), BBC Radio 4, 28 November.

32 W.H. Auden (1973) 'Unpredictable but providential', *The New Yorker*, 14 April.

33 Raj Chetty, John Friedman and Jonah Rockoff (2014) 'Measuring the impacts of teachers II: Teacher value-added and student outcomes in adulthood', *American Economic Review*, vol 104, no 9, September, pp 2633-79.

34 Ben Alcott (2017) 'Does teacher encouragement influence students' educational progress? A propensity-score matching analysis', *Research in Higher Education*, vol 58, issue 7, pp 773-804.

35 Education Endowment Foundation (2018) 'Metacognition and self-regulation', Briefing, 30 August.

36 Peter Sellen (2016) *Teacher workload and professional development in England's secondary schools: Insights from TALIS*, London: Education Policy Institute.

37 Education Support Partnership and YouGov (2017) *Mental health and wellbeing in the education profession, 2017 Final report*.

38 Forty-eight per cent of teachers in England have more than 10 years' experience, compared to an OECD average of 64% (Sellen, 2016, op cit, p 9).

39 NUT (National Union of Teachers) (2017) 'NUT/CPAG figures show government school funding proposals will hit schools with the poorest children hardest', Press release, 3 March.

[40] Allegra Pocinki and Richard Reeves (2017) 'Social skills matter, but how do we measure and grow them in the classroom?', Brookings Institution Social Mobility Memos, 2 June.

[41] Rebecca Allen, Emran Mian and Sam Sims (2016) *Social inequalities in access to teachers*, London: Social Market Foundation.

[42] Alcott (2017) op cit.

[43] Thatcher's parents were members of the '1%" by the time Margaret went to university. See Danny Dorling (2013) 'How social mobility got stuck', *New Statesman*, 16 May.

[44] OECD (Organisation for Economic Co-operation and Development) (2017) *PISA 2015 results (Volume III) Students' well-being*, Paris: OECD Publishing, p 51.

[45] Bank of Scotland (2016) 'Parents pay premium to get children into top Scottish state schools', Press release, 28 October.

[46] Andy Cook (2016) 'Whether we like it or not, school selection is happening, and usually by wealth', *Conservative Home*, 5 December.

[47] David Willetts (2016) 'Our education system is tilted against social mobility', Resolution Foundation blog, 12 September.

[48] Jon Andrews and Natalie Perera (2017) *Access to high performing schools in England*, London: Education Policy Institute, p 6. (Data apply to England only.)

[49] Carl Cullinane, Jude Hillary, Joana Andrade and Stephen McNamara (2017) *Selective comprehensives 2017: Admissions to high-attaining non-selective schools for disadvantaged pupils*, London: The Sutton Trust.

[50] Becky Francis and Merryn Hutchings (2013) *Parent power? Using money and information to boost children's chances of educational success*, London: The Sutton Trust, p 25.

[51] Miles Corak (2012) 'Social mobility and inequality in the UK and the US: How to slide down the Great Gatsby curve', Economics for Public Policy blog, 22 May.

[52] Jane Bird (2016) 'More pupils are told to "bring your own device" as school budget cuts bite', *Financial Times*, 4 May.

[53] NASUWT (2014) *The cost of education*.

[54] Andrew Sparrow (2018) 'Poorer pupils far more likely to be in failing schools, finds research', *The Guardian*, 21 August.

[55] Cook (2016) op cit.

[56] Graham Brady MP (1998) *Hansard*, col 495, 15 July.

[57] DES (Department of Education and Science) (1965) *Circular 10/65: The organisation of secondary education*, London: HMSO.

[58] Charles Moore (2016) 'Opposition to selective schools is the last taboo stopping poor, bright kids from excelling', *The Daily Telegraph*, 9 September.

[59] Figures on social mobility from John Goldthorpe (2016) 'Social class mobility in modern Britain: Changing structure, constant process', *Journal of the British Academy*, vol 4, pp 94–5. Figures on grammar schools are from Paul Bolton (2017) *Grammar school statistics*, House of Commons Library Briefing Paper 1398.

[60] Timo Hannay (2016) 'Poverty of opportunity?', SchoolDash, 2 August (www.schooldash.com/blog.html#20160802).

[61] Tak Wing Chan and Vikki Boliver (2013) 'The grandparents effect in social mobility', *American Sociological Review*, vol 78, issue 4, pp 662–78.

[62] Alan Little and John Westergard (1964), cited in David Kynaston (2015) *Modernity Britain*, London: Bloomsbury, p 219.

[63] Jess Staufenberg (2016) 'Consultation responses reveal widespread resistance to government selection plans', *Schools Week*, 12 December; Quotation from the Chief Inspector of Schools is from Ofsted (2016) 'Sir Michael Wilshaw's speech at the London Councils Education Summit', 5 September.

Notes

64 Karen Wespieser (2017) 'When I saw the opportunity to take the prime minister to task over grammar schools, I had to take it', *TES*, 22 May.

65 NAHT (National Association of Head Teachers) (2016) 'Four out of five heads and teachers oppose new grammar schools', Press release, 14 September.

66 Robert Frank (2017) *Success and luck: Good fortune and the myth of meritocracy*, Princeton, NJ: Princeton University Press.

67 Examples of accessible introductions to cognitive bias include George Lakoff (2004) *Don't think of an elephant*, White River Junction, VT: Chelsea Green; Drew Weston (2007) *The political brain*, New York: Public Affairs Books; and Daniel Kahneman (2011) *Thinking, fast and slow*, London: Penguin.

68 Simon Burgess, Claire Crawford and Lindsey Macmillan (2017) *Assessing the role of grammar schools in promoting social mobility*, UCL Department of Quantitative Social Science Working Paper No 17-09, May, London: University College London (UCL).

69 The Conservative Party (1979) *Conservative General Election manifesto 1979* (www.margaretthatcher.org/document/110858).

70 Michelle Brook (2014) 'What the hell am I doing here?', Quantumplations, Blog, 5 February.

71 See 'The funding gap: Financial and human capital in the state and private sector' (pp 10-14) in Anthony Seldon and Claudia Hupkau (2014) *Schools united: Ending the divide between independent and state*, London: Social Market Foundation.

72 Sally Power (2016) 'The state has helped poor pupils into private schools before – did it work?', *The Conversation*, 9 December.

73 Tim Brighouse, *Local authorities and the London Challenge* (www.londoncouncils.gov.uk/our-key-themes/children-and-young-people/education-and-school-places/lessons-london/tim-brighouse).

74 As is frequently the case, opponents of progressive policies pose as defenders of the 'middle class' when opposing measures that displease a minority who are far above the 'middle' of the income scale.

75 Margaret Morrissey, of ParentsOutloud, quoted in Steven Swinford and Peter Hutchison (2011) 'School lotteries hitting the middle class', *Daily Telegraph*, 25 February.

76 Marc Kidson and Emma Norris (2014) *Implementing the London Challenge*, York and London: Joseph Rowntree Foundation and Institute for Government.

77 David Willetts (2016) 'Our education system is tilted against social mobility', Resolution Foundation blog, 12 September.

78 Social Mobility Commission (2017) *Time for change: An assessment of government policies on social mobility 1997-2017*, London, p 36.

79 DfE (Department for Education) (2011) *Evaluation of Every Child a Reader (ECaR)*, London.

80 'Disadvantaged' includes children with a history of free school meal (FSM) eligibility, local authority care or with parents in the armed forces; see Education Funding Agency (2016) 'Pupil Premium 2015 to 2016: Conditions of grant'.

81 Chris Belfield, David Goll and Luke Sibieta (2018) *Socio-economic differences in total education spending in England: Middle class welfare no more*, London: Institute for Fiscal Studies Briefing Note BN242. (Note that IFS data refers to England only.)

82 Andreas Schleicher (2014) *Equity, excellence and inclusiveness in education: Policy lessons from around the world*, Paris: Organisation for Economic Co-operation and Development (OECD).

83 Charlotte Santry (2017) 'A third of headteachers using Pupil Premium to plug budget shortfalls', *TES*, 12 April.

84 UpRising (https://uprising.org.uk).

[85] Beckett Broh (2002) 'Linking extracurricular programming to academic achievement: Who benefits and why?', *Sociology of Education*, vol 75, no 1, January, p 86.

[86] Education Endowment Federation (2017) *Teaching and learning toolkit: Outdoor adventure learning*.

[87] Conversation with author, 13 June 2016.

[88] NASUWT (2014) op cit.

[89] The Sutton Trust (2014) *Extra-curricular inequality*, Research Brief, p 4.

[90] Conversation with author, 8 December 2016.

[91] Jackie Campbell, Victoria Bell, Sarah Armstrong, John Horton, Natasha Mansukhani, Hugh Matthews and Andy Pilkington (2009) *The impact of the Duke of Edinburgh's Award on young people. Final report*, Northampton: University of Northampton, p 25.

[92] Megan McArdle (2017) 'How Utah keeps the American dream alive', *Bloomberg View*, 28 March.

[93] Adi Bloom (2017) 'National Citizen Service increases chances of pupils going to university, UCAS figures suggest', *TES*, 1 May.

[94] Angus Holford (2012) *Take-up of free school meals: Price effects and peer effects*, Working paper 2012-12, Colchester: Institute for Social and Economic Research, University of Essex.

[95] Lorraine Dearden and Christine Farquharson (2017) *Free school meals for all primary pupils: Projections from a pilot*, 9 May, London: Institute for Fiscal Studies.

[96] Vicky Brown, Claire Crawford, Lorraine Dearden, Ellen Greaves, Sarah Kitchen, Colin Payne, Susan Purdon and Emily Tanner (2013) *Evaluation of the Free School Meals Pilot impact report*, DfE Research Report DFE-RR227, London: Department for Education.

[97] Shelter (2017a) 'The Living Home Standard' (www.shelter.org.uk/livinghomestandard).

[98] Shelter (2017b) 'The impact of bad housing.'

[99] Shelter (2017c) 'Bedroom tax: Are you affected?'.

[100] BBC News (2016) 'Libraries lose a quarter of staff as hundreds close', 29 March.

[101] Charles Desforges and Alberto Abouchaar (2003) *The impact of parental involvement, parental support and family education on pupil achievement and adjustment: A literature review*, London: Department for Education and Skills.

[102] National Institute of Adult Continuing Education (2013) *Family Learning Works: The inquiry into family learning in England and Wales*, p 9.

[103] Richards et al (2016) op cit, pp 26-7.

[104] David Torgerson, Carole Torgerson, Hannah Ainsworth, Hannah Buckley, Clare Heaps, Catherine Hewitt and Natasha Mitchell (2014) *Improving writing quality: Evaluation report and executive summary*, London: Education Endowment Foundation.

[105] Geraint Johnes (2018) 'GCSE results: Why bright, poor students fail to achieve top grades', *The Conversation*, 23 August.

[106] Raj Chetty, Nathaniel Hendren and Lawrence Katz (2016) 'The effects of exposure to better neighborhoods on children: New evidence from the Moving to Opportunity Project', *American Economic Review*, vol 106, no 4, p 1.

[107] Chetty et al (2016) ibid.

[108] The Children's Society (2017) *Understanding childhoods: Growing up in hard times*, London, Section 3.

[109] Patrick Sharkey and Bryan Graham (2013) *Mobility and the metropolis: How communities factor into economic mobility*, Philadelphia, PA: The Pew Charitable Trusts, pp 9-10.

[110] Local authorities currently have little choice but to work with private sector partners if they are to build significant numbers of homes, due to legal restrictions on their

ability to finance homebuilding introduced in the 1980s. Private developers are often allowed access to land and/or planning permission in return for which a proportion of the development will be for social rent or shared ownership (in Woodberrry Down, this proportion in 41%).

[111] Philip Glanville, Mayor of Hackney, in conversation with author, 1 August 2018.

[112] Danny Dorling (2014) 'Class segregation', in C. Lloyd, I. Shuttleworth and D.W. Wong (eds) *Social-spatial segregation: Concepts, processes and outcomes*, Bristol: Policy Press, p 363.

Chapter Four: Choosing a path

[1] Simon Burgess (2016) *Michelle Obama and an English school: The power of inspiration*, Bristol: Department of Economics, University of Bristol.

[2] Claudia Hammond (2016) 'Do big sporting events make us do more sport?', BBC Future, 5 August.

[3] BBC News (2016) 'Three jobs and still poor', 5 September.

[4] Angela John (2015) *The actors' crucible: Port Talbot and the making of Burton, Hopkins, Sheen and all the others*, Swansea: Parthian Books.

[5] Michelle Obama, quoted in Burgess (2016) op cit, p 2.

[6] Trisha Greenhalgh, Kieran Seyan and Petra Boynton (2004) '"Not a university type": Focus group study of social class, ethnic, and sex differences in school pupils' perceptions about medical school', *British Medical Journal*, vol 328, p 1541.

[7] Jessica Elgot (2016) 'Dancer, painter, soldier… Tottenham brothers on their way to the top', *The Guardian*, 28 May.

[8] James Dunn, Larrisa Brown and Ian Drury (2016) 'From Tottenham to Sandhurst: The extraordinary moment a cadet from a broken home on a tough north London estate – who only learned to read aged 12 – received the British Army's prestigious sword of honour', *Daily Mail*, 15 April.

[9] Elgot (2016) op cit.

[10] Mike Savage (2015) *Social class in the 21st century*, London: Pelican, p 180.

[11] Mark Brown (2018) 'Arts industry report asks: Where are all the working-class people?', *The Guardian*, 16 April.

[12] Lynne Truss, quoted in Joanne O'Connor (2016) 'Lynne Truss: My rescue cats inspired me to write two novels', *The Guardian*, 19 November.

[13] Nick Chambers (2017) 'If we're serious about improving social mobility, the issue must be addressed at primary level', *TES*, 8 August.

[14] Steven Neuberg and Mark Schaller (2016) 'An evolutionary threat-management approach to prejudices', *Current Opinion in Psychology*, vol 7, February, pp 1-5.

[15] Chris McManus, quoted in Martin Beckford (2008) 'Working classes "lack intelligence to be doctors", claims academic', *The Daily Telegraph*, 4 June.

[16] Michelle Obama, quoted in Burgess (2016) op cit, p 2.

[17] Hammond (2016) op cit.

[18] Sarah-Jane Leslie, Andrei Cimpian, Meredith Meyer and Edward Freeland (2015) 'Expectations of brilliance underlie gender distributions across academic disciplines', *Science*, vol 347, issue 6219, pp 262-5.

[19] Sarah Harris (2016) 'Death of ambition in poor white boys: Consumerism replacing aspiration to overcome their background, warns expert', *Daily Mail*, 23 June.

[20] Jane Lakey, Neil Smith, Anni Oskala and Sally McManus (2017) *Culture, sport and wellbeing: Findings from the Understanding Society survey*, London: NatCen Social Research, p 112; Claire Crawford, Paul Johnson, Steve Machin and Anna Vignoles (2011) *Social mobility: A literature review*, London: Department for Business, Innovation

& Skills, p 26; Education and Employers (2018) *Drawing the future: Exploring the career aspirations of primary school children from around the world* (www.educationandemployers. org/wp-content/uploads/2018/01/DrawingTheFuture.pdf).

[21] Education Endowment Foundation (2018) *Aspiration interventions*, Briefing Paper, 31 August.

[22] Angela Rayner, speaking at Fabian Women seminar 'Working Class Aspiration', Houses of Parliament, 3 July 2017.

[23] Jennifer DeWitt and Louise Archer (2017) 'Participation in informal science learning experiences: The rich get richer?', *International Journal of Science Education*, Part B, vol 7, issue 4, pp 356–73.

[24] APPG (All-Party Parliamentary Group) on Social Mobility (2016) *Access to Leading Professions Inquiry; Session Four: Access into the media and entertainment sectors.*

[25] Greenhalgh et al (2004) op cit.

[26] David Willetts (2016) 'Our education system is tilted against social mobility', Resolution Foundation blog, 12 September.

[27] Morag Henderson, Alice Sullivan, Jake Anders and Vanessa Moulton (2017) 'Social class, gender and ethnic differences in subjects taken at age 14', *The Curriculum Journal*, vol 29, issue 3.

[28] Teach First (2016) 'Teach primary school children about university or poorer pupils will miss out says report', Press release, 15 August.

[29] Katherine Mathieson, quoted in Elizabeth Gibney (2016) 'United Kingdom: The paths not taken' (in 'Is science only for the rich?', *Nature*, vol 537, 22 September, pp 466–70).

[30] APPG (All-Party Parliamentary Group) on Social Mobility (2017) *The class ceiling: Increasing access to the leading professions*, p 9.

[31] Sir Michael Wilshaw, speech at 'Ofsted: Where Next?' conference, Education Policy Institute, London, 25 November 2016.

[32] Louise Archer and Julie Moote (2016) *ASPIRES 2 Project Spotlight: Year 11 students' views of careers education and work experience*, London: King's College, p 2.

[33] Elnaz Kashefpakdel and Christian Percy (2016) *Career education that works: An economic analysis using the British Cohort Study*, Education and Employers (Online research summaries), 17 May.

[34] Eton College, 'Career education' (www.etoncollege.com/CareerEducation.aspx).

[35] Archer and Moote (2016) op cit, p 4.

[36] Michelle Brook (2014) 'What the hell am I doing here?', Quantumplations, Blog, 5 February.

[37] Amanda Spielman (2017) *HMCI's commentary: October 2017*, London: Ofsted.

[38] Louise Archer (2018) 'How GCSE Science is failing students – and society', *The Conversation*, 14 June.

[39] Jake Anders, Morag Henderson, Vanessa Moulton and Alice Sullivan (2018) 'The role of schools in explaining individuals' subject choices at age 14', *Oxford Review of Education*, vol 44, issue 1.

[40] CBI (2018) 'Half of young people do not feel prepared for world of work – CBI/ Accenture/Hays survey', Press release, 19 November.

[41] Helen Pidd (2016) 'London and south-east children far more likely to go to top universities', *The Guardian*, 5 December.

[42] The Careers and Enterprise Company (2016) *What works in careers and enterprise?*, p 6.

[43] Barbara is being modest. Her school friends were not the only reason she got into Cambridge; she had also shown unusually strong academic ability at school, which was necessary (but not sufficient) for her to be admitted.

Notes

44 Conversation with author, Norwich, 16 March 2017.

45 The Sutton Trust (2016) *Teachers' Oxbridge perceptions polling*, London.

46 The Sutton Trust (2016) ibid.

47 Greenhalgh et al (2004) op cit.

48 Justine Greening, 'UK social mobility: Lessons learnt from international development: Secretary of State for International Development Justine Greening's speech to the Centre for Social Justice', 16 February 2016.

49 Gøsta Esping-Andersen (2005) 'Social inheritance and equal opportunity policies', in S. Delorenzi, J. Reed and P. Robinson (eds) *Maintaining momentum: Promoting social mobility and life chances*, London: Institute for Public Policy Research, p 25.

50 Greening (2016) op cit.

51 Diane Reay, Gill Crozier and John Clayton (2009) '"Fitting in" or "standing out": Working-class students in UK higher education', *British Educational Research Journal*, April, pp 107-24.

52 Claire Crawford , Ellen Greaves and Wenchao Jin (2015) *An evaluation of the impact of the Social Mobility Foundation programmes on education outcomes*, London: Institute for Fiscal Studies.

53 Crawford et al (2011) op cit, p 27.

54 Graeme Atherton (2017) 'A global view: What England can learn from the rest of the world', in HEPI and Brightside (eds) *Where next for widening participation and fair access? New insights from leading thinkers*, p 57.

55 Lucy Hunter-Blackburn (2017) 'Widening access: A modest proposal', Adventures in Evidence blog, 5 August.

56 On the subject of financial barriers, you may have noticed I haven't mentioned tuition fees. Don't worry, I will, but not in this chapter.

57 Dawn Foster, speaking at 'National Debate: Class – An Unequal Nation?', National Theatre, London, 2 November 2017.

58 Study conducted by Theodore Sarbin, cited in Kahneman (2011) *Thinking, fast and slow*, London: Penguin, pp 222-3.

59 Richard DeVaul, Faith Jervey, James Chappell, Patricia Caver and Barbara Short (1987) 'Medical school performance of initially rejected students', *Journal of the American Medical Association*, vol 257, no 1, pp 47-5.

60 K. Allen, J. Quinn , S. Hollingworth and A. Rose (2013) 'Becoming employable students and "ideal" creative workers: Exclusion and inequality in higher education work placements', *British Journal of Sociology of Education*, vol 34, no 3, p 440.

61 Gillian Wyness (2016) 'Grade prediction system means the brightest, poorest students can miss out on top university places', Institute of Education blog, 8 December.

62 UCAS website, 'How to write a UCAS Undergraduate personal statement.'

63 Steven Jones (2012) *The personal statement: A fair way to assess university applicants?*, London: The Sutton Trust, p 12.

64 Sir Peter Lampl, quoted in David Batty (2018) 'Middle-class teenagers "play the system to get into top universities"', *The Guardian*, 12 August.

65 Laura McInerney (2017) 'Historians will laugh at us when they look back at our university application system', *The Guardian*, 19 September.

66 David Woolley (2017) 'Evaluation' in HEPI and Brightside (eds) *Where next for widening participation and fair access? New insights from leading thinkers*.

67 Household income data from Jonathan Cribb, Andrew Hood, Robert Joyce and Agnes Norris Keiller (2017) *Living standards, poverty and inequality in the UK: 2017*, London: Institute for Fiscal Studies. Data on 'widening participation' criteria from Office for Fair Access (2017) 'Target groups'.

68 Office for Fair Access, 'Admissions.'

69 Anne-Marie Canning, Susannah Hume, Lucy Makinson, Maija Koponen, Kim Hall and Clare Delargy (2018) *KCLxBIT project report 2015-2017*, London: Behavioural Insights Team and King's College, London.

70 Quoted in Camilla Turner (2017) 'Diversity drive at top universities is failing, as official figures reveal largest ever gap between state and private school students', *The Daily Telegraph*, 3 August.

71 Lee Elliot Major (2013) 'Evaluating widening participation', The Sutton Trust blog, 18 March.

72 Jim Dickinson (2017) 'Academic freedom is holding back fair access to the professions', Wonkhe, 15 March.

73 Jim Dickinson (2018) 'Manifesto idea #13: Jim Dickinson', in Paul Clarke and Dr Diana Beech, *Reaching the parts of society universities have missed: A manifesto for the new Director of Fair Access and Participation*, Brightside/HEPI, p 31.

74 Scottish Government (2016) *A blueprint for fairness: The final report of the Commission on Widening Access*, pp 14-16.

75 Nigel Farndale (2013) 'Is there a private school prejudice?', *The Daily Telegraph*, 28 January. Farndale was educated at Barnard Castle School, according to their 2013 sixth form prospectus (p 4).

76 Quoted in Daniel Sanderson (2017) 'More middle-class pupils are missing out on university places', *The Times*, 9 August.

77 UCAS (2017) Daily Clearing Analysis: POLAR, Analysis at 00:05 on Thursday 14 September 2017 (28 days after A-level results day), p 5.

78 Lee Eliot Major (2016) 'From Cheltenham to Durham', The Sutton Trust blog, 27 October.

79 Vikki Boliver, Stephen Gorard and Nadia Siddiqui (2018) 'A more radical approach to contextualised admissions', in HEPI and Brightside, op cit, p 23.

80 Caroline Horst (2017) 'Supporting young carers in schools', The Children's Society blog, 9 August.

81 Joan Wilson (2011) 'By scrapping the Education Maintenance Allowance the Coalition government risks losing their opportunity to target entrenched problems of social mobility and educational disadvantage among pupils from deprived backgrounds in England', LSE Politics and Policy blog, 21 February.

82 George Ryan (2018) 'Labour calls on government to bring back EMA', *TES*, 22 August.

83 David Phoenix (2017) 'Let's bridge the divide between academic and technical education', *Guardian Higher Education Network*, 18 July.

84 Helena Kennedy (1997) *Learning works: Widening participation in further education*, Coventry: Further Education Funding Council (FEFC).

85 Kirstine Hansen, Elizabeth Jones, Heather Joshi and David Budge (2010) *Millennium Cohort Study; Fourth Survey: A user's guide to initial findings*, London: Centre for Longitudinal Studies, p 10.

86 Andy Norman (2018) 'Are attitudes to apprenticeships changing?', Centre For Progressive Policy blog, 13 August.

87 Alison Wolf (2002) *Does education matter? Myths about education and economic growth*, London: Penguin.

88 Paul Offord (2017) 'Breaking: Apprenticeship pay survey exposes rise in proportion paid illegal wages', *FE Week*, 19 July; Ben Kinross (2018) 'Why I don't want my child to be an apprentice', *TES*, 3 June.

89 Paul Johnson (2017) 'Education needs a revolution, not just more cash', *The Times*, 21 July.

90 Lisa Vernon MBE (of Derby College) conversation with author, London, 30 October 2018.

91 Joe Dromey (2017) 'Learning lessons from LearnDirect', *Medium*, 14 August.

92 Graham Hastings-Evans (2017) 'It's not too late for those let down by school careers advice', *TES*, 20 August.

93 Will Hazell (2017) 'New "T-levels" to replace thousands of post-16 vocational qualifications', *TES*, 5 March.

94 Paul Johnson (2018) 'My son taught me a lesson about university', *Times*, 5 January.

95 Johnson (2017) ibid.

96 BAE Systems.

97 BBC News (2017) 'Vocational training shake-up "most ambitious since A-levels"', 5 March.

98 Social Mobility and Child Poverty Commission (2016) *Apprenticeships, young people, and social mobility* (http://dera.ioe.ac.uk/25920/1/Social_Mobility_and_Child_Poverty_Commission_Submission_on_Apprenticeships_final.pdf), p 5.

99 Julia Belgutay (2017) 'Apprenticeship starts down by 61% after levy introduction', *TES*, 12 October.

Chapter Five: Higher education, and other higher education

1 Diane Reay, Gill Crozier and John Clayton (2009) '"Strangers in paradise"? Working-class students in elite universities', *Sociology*, vol 43, no 6, December, pp 1103-15.

2 'Sloane Rangers' is a term that became fashionable in the 1980s to describe young, fashionable, upper-class or upper-middle-class people, typically found in London, and stereotypically in Chelsea's Sloane Square.

3 BBC Schools (2015) 'Deciding if university is right for your child' (www.bbc.co.uk/schools/parents/is_university_right_for_my_child/)

4 I notice, however, that my two best friends from those days are those most like me: both their dads worked in car factories.

5 Peter Matthews (2014) 'Making peace with Cambridge', Urban Policy and Practice blog, 14 June.

6 Sebastian Salek (2013) 'How much? Student society fees soar even as tuition fees bite', *The Independent*, 18 September.

7 Paired Peers Project (2013) *The Paired Peers Project Year 3 report: A degree generation*, Bristol: University of Bristol and University of the West of England.

8 Michael Donnelly and Sol Gamsu (2018) *Home and away: Social, ethnic and spatial inequalities in student mobility*, London and Bath: The Sutton Trust and University of Bath.

9 Bystander (2017) 'Inside Durham University's June Ball 2017', *Tatler*, 21 August.

10 Flic Burgess, quoted in Nicola Woolcock and Eleanor Doughty (2014) 'Students vote to keep "sexist" title for their president', *The Times*, 10 December.

11 YTS, the Youth Training Scheme, which provided basic vocational training from 1983 to 1989, and whose participants were evidently held in low regard by the Master of University College, Oxford.

12 Sam Friedman, Dave O'Brien and Daniel Laurison (2016) '"Like skydiving without a parachute": How class origin shapes occupational trajectories in British acting', *Sociology*, 28 February.

13 Beccy Earnshaw, quoted in Chris Havergal (2016) 'Students with regional accents "ridiculed and silenced"', *TES*, 25 July.

14 Joseph Heller (1955 [2010]) *Catch-22*, New York: Vintage, p 39.

15 Simon Horobin (2014) 'Battels and subfusc: The language of Oxford', Oxford Dictionaries blog, 15 October.

16 Rushanara Ali, speech to AccessHE conference, London, 20 September 2018.

17 Trendence Research (2018) 'Value for money: The student perspective', Research commissioned by the Office for Students.

18 Seeta Bhardwa (2018) 'High rent costs draining student maintenance loans, finds new research', Times Higher Education, 23 February.

19 Becky Kendall, Head of Student Enrichment at IntoUniversity, conversation with author, 20 September 2018.

20 Jake Butler (2017) 'Student money survey 2017 – Results', Save the Student (www.savethestudent.org/money/student-money-survey-2017.html).

21 University of Oxford (www.ox.ac.uk).

22 Jack Grove (2017) 'State pupils on same grades as private counterparts "get better degrees"', Times Higher Education, 28 March.

23 Paired Peers Project (2013) op cit, p 5.

24 Lindsay Paterson, cited in Daniel Sanderson (2018) 'Middle-class pupils banned from clearing', The Times, 8 August.

25 Raj Chetty (2017) 'Higher education and intergenerational mobility', Lecture given at CUNY Graduate Centre, 6 February.

26 The Economist (2017) 'Skipping class', 28 January (www.economist.com/united-states/2017/01/28/skipping-class).

27 Jack Britton, Lorraine Dearden, Neil Shephard and Anna Vignoles (2016) How English domiciled graduate earnings vary with gender, institution attended, subject and socio-economic background: Executive summary, London: Institute for Fiscal Studies, p 3.

28 Mike Savage (2015) Social class in the 21st century, London: Pelican, p 227.

29 Sarah Howls, Head of Access and Participation funding and programmes, Office for Students, Presentation at AccessHE conference, 21 September 2018.

30 Vikki Boliver (2017) 'Misplaced optimism: How higher education reproduces rather than reduces social inequality', British Journal of Sociology of Education, vol 38, issue 3, pp 423-32.

31 Rushanara Ali, Speech to AccessHE conference, 21 September 2018.

32 The Bridge Group (2017) Social mobility and university careers services, London, p 6.

33 High Fliers Research Limited (2018) The graduate market in 2018, London, pp 30-1.

34 Mike Savage (2015) op cit, p 223.

35 HESA (Higher Education Statistics Authority) (2018) Widening participation summary: UK Performance Indicators 2016/17, London.

36 DfE (Department for Education) (2017) Participation rates in higher education: Academic years 2006/2007-2015/2016 (Provisional), SFR47/2017, London, 28 September.

37 DfE (Department for Education) (2018) A guide to looked-after children statistics in England, March 2018, London, p 21.

38 Jack Britton (2017) 'The degrees that make you rich ... and the ones that don't', BBC News Online, 17 November.

39 Quoted in Richard Adams (2017) 'Oxford and Cambridge "need to improve access for disadvantaged students"', The Guardian, 29 June.

40 HESA (Higher Education Statistics Authority) (2018) op cit. All HESA figures refer to school leavers.

41 Paired Peers Project (2013) Key findings, Bristol: University of Bristol and University of the West of England.

42 Nick Hillman (2018) Differential tuition fees: Horses for courses?, HEPI.

43 Nick Hillman, speech at HEPI, Bridge Group seminar 'University tuition fees: What is a fair deal for students?', 19 September 2017.

Notes

44 The Bridge Group (2017) *Social mobility and university careers services*, London.

45 Universities UK (2016) *Working in partnership: Enabling social mobility in higher education: The final report of the Social Mobility Advisory Group*, London.

46 The Bridge Group (2017) op cit.

47 Angela Wright (2017) 'The fight over free speech at universities comes down to the question of the purpose of higher-ed', CBC News, 11 December.

48 Lynsey Hanley (2016) *Respectable: The experience of class*, London: Allen Lane, p 32.

49 K. Allen, J. Quinn, S. Hollingworth and A. Rose (2013) 'Becoming employable students and "ideal" creative workers: Exclusion and inequality in higher education work placements', *British Journal of Sociology of Education*, vol 34, no 3, pp 431-52.

50 Stephanie Lambert and Ian Herbert (2017) *Are 'employable' graduates 'work ready'?*, Loughborough: Loughborough University.

51 University of York (2018) 'York Strengths Programme for undergraduates' (www.york.ac.uk/students/work-volunteering-careers/skills/york-strengths/).

52 Simon Gaskell and Rebecca Lingwood (2017) 'Social capital: The new frontier in widening participation at universities', *Guardian Higher Education Network*, 2 October.

53 The Bridge Group (2017) op cit, p 8.

54 Ephemera (2013) *Giving notice to employability*.

55 Different policies apply in other parts of the UK. The Scottish government pays the tuition fees of Scottish students in full, Welsh students can apply for a grant covering just over half the cost, and fees have a lower cap in Northern Ireland.

56 Ghazala Azmat and Stefania Simion (2018) 'Analysing the distributional effects of higher education funding reforms in the UK', LSE Business Review, 12 March.

57 Paul Callanan (of Youth Fight for Jobs), quoted in the *Daily Mail* (2010) 'Burning with anger: London streets in flames again as 25,000 go on rampage in new student fees riot', 15 December.

58 HESA (Higher Education Statistics Authority) (2018) *Widening participation summary*, op cit.

59 Richard Murphy, Judith Scott-Clayton and Gill Wyness (2018) *The end of free college in England: Implications for quality, enrolments and equity*, London: Centre for Economic Performance, London School of Economics and Political Science.

60 HESA (Higher Education Statistics Authority) (2018) *Higher education student enrolments and qualifications obtained at higher education providers in the United Kingdom 2015/16*, London.

61 Mark Leach (2017) 'Is there really a record number of disadvantaged students in HE?', WonkHE, 20 November.

62 Claire Callender and Geoff Mason (2017) 'Does student loan debt deter higher education participation? New evidence from England', *Annals of the American Academy of Political and Social Science*, vol 671, issue 1, pp 20-48.

63 Nicola Sturgeon, Statement to the Scottish Parliament, 5 September 2017.

64 Scottish Government (2018) *Initial destinations of senior phase school leavers, No 2: 2018 edition*, Table 3, Edinburgh.

65 Lucy Hunter-Blackburn (2015) 'Inequality, the establishment and student funding', Rattle, 24 November.

66 Butler (2017) op cit.

67 Aftab Ali (2016) 'Students struggling to fill £3,000 finance gap a year as living cost sour, survey finds', *The Independent*, 20 July.

68 NUS (National Union of Students) (2018) *Class dismissed: Getting in and getting on in further and higher education. The Poverty Commission Report*, London.

69 Gordon Marsden MP (2017) 'Let's use education to inaugurate a new era of social mobility', LabourList, 26 September.

70 According to the Institute for Fiscal Studies; see Chris Belfield, Jack Britton and Laura van der Erve (2017) 'Labour's higher education proposals will cost £8bn per year, although increase the deficit by more. Graduates who earn most in future would benefit most', Institute for Fiscal Studies, Observation, 11 May.

71 Angela Rayner, speech at Fabian Women event on 'Working Class Aspiration', Westminster, 3 July 2017.

72 Sophie Laura Weymes-McElderry (2018) 'University of Cambridge to start offering apprenticeships', The Cambridge Student, 8 February.

73 BBC News (2018) 'Ex-player Mark Aizlewood and others guilty of football fraud', 5 February.

74 Nick Linford (2018) 'Invest in Ofsted to guarantee apprenticeship quality', FE Week, 5 October.

75 See www.young-enterprise.org.uk

76 The work was being led by UnLtd; see 'Developing and delivering an apprenticeship for entrepreneurs – get involved' (www.unltd.org.uk/blog/news/developing-and-delivering-an-apprenticeship-for-entrepreneurs-get-involved). Information on discontinuation given to author by telephone, 15 March 2018.

77 The Sutton Trust (2018) '#BetterApprenticeships' (www.suttontrust.com/2018-better-apprenticeships-campaign/).

78 Will Martin (2017) 'Call degree apprenticeships "career degrees", leading head urges', TES, 3 May.

Chapter Six: Into a job

1 Hazel Blears, quoted in James Kirkup (2008) 'Politicians have no experience of "real life" and put voters off, claims Hazel Blears', Telegraph, 5 November.

2 The Bach Commission on Access to Justice (2016) Interim report: The crisis in the justice system in England & Wales, London: Fabian Society.

3 Paired Peers Project (2017) Paired peers: Moving on up? Project report, Bristol: University of Bristol and University of the West of England.

4 Simon Baker (2017) 'Sharp increase in first-class degrees triggers standards debate', Times Higher Education, 20 July.

5 Vikki Boliver (2017) 'Misplaced optimism: How higher education reproduces rather than reduces social inequality', British Journal of Sociology of Education, 2 March.

6 APPG (All-Party Parliamentary Group) on Social Mobility (2017) The class ceiling: Increasing access to the leading professions, London, p 12.

7 APPG on Social Mobility (2017) ibid.

8 UCAS (2018) 'Postgraduate fees and funding' (www.ucas.com/postgraduate/postgraduate-fees-and-funding).

9 Joshua Stubbs and Paul Wakeling (2017) 'The hidden costs of applying for postgraduate study', Times Higher Education, 22 August.

10 Paul Wakeling and Daniel Laurison (2017) 'Are postgraduate qualifications the "new frontier of social mobility"?', British Journal of Sociology, 12 July.

11 Carys Roberts (2017) The inbetweeners: The new role of internships in the graduate labour market, London: Institute for Public Policy Research, p 3.

12 National Union of Journalists (2013) 'Cashback for interns' (www.nuj.org.uk/campaigns/cashback-for-interns/).

13 Rebecca Montacute (2018) 'Internships – Unpaid, unadvertised, unfair', Sutton Trust Research Brief, January, pp 2-3.

Notes

14 K. Allen, J. Quinn, S. Hollingworth and A. Rose (2013) 'Becoming employable students and "ideal" creative workers: Exclusion and inequality in higher education work placements', *British Journal of Sociology of Education*, vol 34, no 3, p 443.

15 Simon Horobin (2014) 'Battels and subfusc: The language of Oxford', Oxford Dictionaries blog, 15 October.

16 Conversation with author, 13 June 2016.

17 Allison Pearson (2011) 'David Cameron interview: I wanted to berate him but Dave won me over', *Daily Telegraph*, 22 April.

18 Social Mobility and Child Poverty Commission (2013) *Business and social mobility: A manifesto for change*, London, p 12.

19 Alec Shelbrooke MP (2016) 'Alec seeks to ban unpaid internships' (www.alecshelbrooke.co.uk/alec-seeks-ban-unpaid-internships/).

20 Megan Bramall, speaking to the All-Party Parliamentary Group on Social Mobility, 24 October 2016.

21 Young Legal Aid Lawyers (2018) *Social mobility in a time of austerity*. YLAL Social Mobility Report 2018.

22 Ben Chu (2016) 'How to tell if you're working in a "tournament" job – starting with whether you ever took an unpaid internship', *The Independent*, 1 November.

23 Joshua Ackerman, Christopher Nocera and John Bargh (2010) 'Incidental haptic sensations influence social judgments and decisions', *Science*, 25 June, pp 1712-15.

24 Quoted in Louise Ashley, Holly Birkett, Jo Duberley, Louise Higham, Etlyn Kenny, Joanne Moore and Anna Mountford-Zimdars (2016) *Socio-economic diversity in life sciences and investment banking*, London: Social Mobility Commission, July, p 89.

25 Robert de Vries and Jason Rentfrow (2016) *A winning personality: The effects of background on personality and earnings*, London: The Sutton Trust, p 11.

26 Gill Crozier, Diane Reay, John Clayton, Lori Colliander and Jan Grinstead (2008) 'Different strokes for different folks: Diverse students in diverse institutions – Experiences of higher education', *Research Papers in Education*, vol 23, issue 2, pp 167-77; Patty Norman (2016) 'Teacher attitudes and perceptions of low and high socioeconomic status students', PhD thesis, Utah State University.

27 CIPD (Chartered Institute of Personnel and Development) (2015) *A head for hiring: The behavioural science of recruitment and selection*, London, p 7.

28 Alexandra Kalev, Frank Dobbin and Erin Kelly (2006) 'Best practices or best guesses? Assessing the efficacy of corporate affirmative action and diversity policies', *American Sociological Review*, vol 71, no 4, p 591.

29 Marianne Calnan (2017) 'Only a third of HR managers "confident they are not prejudiced" when hiring', *People Management*, 3 October.

30 Elizabeth Rantzen, in conversation with Hashi Mohamed (2017) [radio] 'Adventures in social mobility', BBC Radio 4, 16 April.

31 Orian Brook, David O'Brien and Mark Taylor (2018) *Panic! Social class, taste and inequalities in the creative industries*, p 14.

32 Justine Greening (2017) 'Education at the core of social mobility', Speech, 19 January.

33 APPG (All-Party Parliamentary Group) on Social Mobility (2017) *The class ceiling: Increasing access to the leading professions*, London, p 10.

34 Sam McKay, quoted in Tracy Brabin, Gloria De Piero and Sarah Coombes (2017) *Acting up report: The Labour Party's inquiry into access and diversity in the performing arts*, London: Labour Party, p 22.

35 See www.socialmobility.org.uk/index/

36 Helen Avery (2016) 'CSR: Can bank hiring help close the socioeconomic divide?', *Euromoney*, 31 October.

[37] Crispin Rapinet, of Hogan Lovells, quoted in Thomas Connelly (2018) 'Hogan Lovells bumps LPC grant by 43% to £10,000', Legal Cheek, 6 April.

[38] The Bridge Group (2017) Social mobility and university careers services, London, p 19.

[39] Civil Service HR (2016) Fast stream and early talent annual report 2016.

[40] See www.rarerecruitment.co.uk

[41] Nicholas Hellen and Sian Griffiths (2017) 'We can work it out: Exam "failures" beat graduates at top firm', The Sunday Times, 5 March.

[42] Nigel Farndale (2013) 'Is there a private school prejudice?', Daily Telegraph, 28 January.

[43] 'Anti-public school bias' is rife in the legal profession: the privately educated are 34 times more likely than the rest of us to become a top barrister.

[44] Peter Preston (2017) 'Ofcom can police equality by race or sex. But class?', The Observer, 24 September.

[45] Sam Friedman, quoted in Jenny Roper (2017) 'Breaking the class ceiling', HR Magazine, 20 November.

[46] Albert Tucker (1963) 'Army and society in England 1870-1900: A reassessment of the Cardwell reforms', Journal of British Studies, vol 2, no 2, May, pp 110-41.

[47] Steve Siebold, quoted in Kathleen Elkins (2017) '11 things to give up if you want to be a millionaire', CNBC, 11 May.

[48] Steve Siebold, quoted in The Early Hour (2017) 'What it's like to be rich – and how to get there', 9 March.

[49] Richard Murphy (2015) 'The self employed's income – new data shows 77% are in poverty', Tax Research UK, 30 January.

[50] Maggie McGrath (2015) 'Meet the guy who says you're not rich because you don't want to be rich', Forbes, 11 November.

[51] Steve Siebold (2016) 'I'm a self-made millionaire, and here are 8 quotes I think will change your outlook on money', Business Insider UK, 23 June.

[52] Roger Burrows (2017) [radio], speaking on 'Super rich: the 1% of the 1%', Thinking Aloud, BBC Radio Four, 4 January.

[53] Rachel Johnson (2016) 'How a "free" holiday from a rich friend can cost a year's salary', The Spectator, 23 March.

[54] Daily Telegraph (2000) 'When the son doesn't rise', 29 October.

[55] Carys Roberts and Mathew Lawrence (2017) Wealth in the twenty-first century: Inequalities and drivers, London: Institute for Public Policy Research, p 15.

[56] Louise Chalkley (2017) 'How entrepreneurship can bring people off benefits – if they're given a chance', The Conversation, 17 March.

[57] Carys Roberts (2016) Start me up, London: Institute for Public Policy Research.

[58] Frank Field, quoted in Michael Savage (2018) 'Universal credit to slash benefits for the self-employed', The Observer, 25 March.

[59] Elisabeth Jacobs (2016) What do trends in economic inequality imply for innovation and entrepreneurship? A framework for future research and policy, Washington, DC: Washington Center for Equitable Growth, p 6.

[60] L. Richards, E. Garratt, A.F. Heath, L. Anderson and E. Altintaş (2016) The childhood origins of social mobility: Socio-economic inequalities and changing opportunities, London: Social Mobility Commission, p 64.

[61] Wilson actually said, 'we are redefining and we are re-stating our socialism in terms of the scientific revolution…. The Britain that is going to be forged in the white heat of this revolution will be no place for restrictive practices or for outdated methods on either side of industry.' Harold Wilson (1963) 'Labour's plan for science', speech, 1 October.

62 Unemployment figures: ONS (Office for National Statistics) (2018) 'Unemployment': data refer to Sept-Nov 2017, released January 2018. Data on over-qualification rates: Michael Jacobs, Izzy Hatfield, Loren King, Luke Raikes and Alfie Stirling (2017) *Industrial strategy: Steering structural change in the UK economy*, London: IPPR Commission on Economic Justice, p 29.

63 Joseph Rowntree Foundation Analysis Unit (2017) *UK poverty 2017: A comprehensive analysis of poverty trends and figures*, York, p 30.

64 The (relatively newly coined) term 'fourth industrial revolution' refers to technologies that build on the digital advances of the third industrial revolution and merge them with physical and biological technology.

65 CBI (Confederation of British Industry) (2017) *Now is the time to innovate: The road to three percent*, p 9.

66 Michael Jacobs (2017) 'Changing direction: How industrial strategy can help remake the UK economy', IPPR Commission on Economic Justice blog, 17 November.

67 For an explanation of this phenomenon, see Will Hutton (2015) *How good we can be: Ending the mercenary society and building a great community*, London: Little, Brown.

68 Paul Johnson (2017) *Autumn Budget analysis 2017: Opening remarks and summary*, London: Institute for Fiscal Studies.

69 Alberto Nardelli (2018) 'This leaked government Brexit analysis says the UK will be worse off in every scenario', BuzzFeed News, 29 January.

70 The UK in a Changing Europe (2018) *Brexit policy panel: Survey results, October 2018*; Kitty Stewart, Kerris Cooper and Isabel Shutes (2018) *What does Brexit mean for social policy in the UK?*, CASE Social Exclusion Seminar, 21 November.

71 Kitty Stewart et al (2018), ibid.

72 Scott Dickinson and Ed Cox (2016) *Brexit North: Securing a united voice at the negotiating table*, IPPR North.

73 Anna Fazackerley (2018) 'Brexit brain drain: Elite universities say they are losing future research stars', *The Guardian*, 6 March.

Chapter Seven: Career progression

1 Jack Britton, Lorraine Dearden, Neil Shephard and Anna Vignoles (2016) *How English domiciled graduate earnings vary with gender, institution attended, subject and socio-economic background: Executive summary*, London: Institute for Fiscal Studies. 'High income' in this case meaning the top 20%.

2 Britton et al (2016) ibid.

3 S. Friedman and D. Laurison (2015) 'Introducing the class ceiling', LSE blog, 31 March. Research for the Institute for Fiscal Studies, by Anna Vignoles, Professor of Education, and the economist, Claire Crawford, found that pay differences between privately educated and state-educated professionals 'holds even when comparing private and state school educated graduates within the same occupation': Claire Crawford and Anna Vignoles (2014) *Heterogeneity in graduate earnings by socio-economic background*, IFS Working Paper W14/30, London: Institute for Fiscal Studies, p 12.

4 Friedman and Laurison (2015) ibid. Other studies find similar data: Claire Crawford, Paul Gregg, Lindsey Macmillan, Anna Vignoles and Gill Wyness (2016) 'Higher education, career opportunities, and intergenerational inequality', *Oxford Review of Economic Policy*, vol 32, no 4, pp 553-75.

5 Norman Pickavance, quoted in Jenny Roper (2017) 'Breaking the class ceiling', *HR Magazine*, 20 November.

6 Kate Fox (2005) *Watching the English*, London: Hodder & Stoughton, p 173.

7   David Tran (2016) 'The hardest part about growing up poor was knowing I couldn't mess up. Not even once', Vox, 27 September.

8   Peter Belmi, quoted in Caroline Newman (2018) '5 factors that fuel income inequality', UVA Today, 13 February.

9   Eduardo Rodriguez-Montemayor (2017) 'How invisible inequality hurts the poor', INSEAD Economics and Finance, 5 April.

10 Louise Ashley, Holly Birkett, Jo Duberley, Louise Higham, Etlyn Kenny, Joanne Moore and Anna Mountford-Zimdars (2016) Socio-economic diversity in life sciences and investment banking, London: Social Mobility Commission, July, p 86.

11 Jake Anders (2015) Does socioeconomic background affect pay growth among early entrants to high-status jobs?, NIESR Discussion Paper No 453, London: National Institute of Economic and Social Research (NIESR).

12 Ashley et al (2016) op cit, p 88.

13 David Devins, Tim Bickerstaffe, Ben Mitchell and Sallyann Halliday (2014) Improving progression in low-paid, low-skilled retail, catering and care jobs, York: Joseph Rowntree Foundation.

14 Marion Spengler, Martin Brunner, Rodica Damian, Oliver Lüdtke, Romain Martin and Brent Roberts (2015) 'Student characteristics and behaviors at age 12 predict occupational success 40 years later over and above childhood IQ and parental socioeconomic status', Developmental Psychology, vol 51, no 9, pp 1329-40.

15 Boston Consulting Group (2014) Pathways to banking: Improving access for students from non-privileged backgrounds, London: The Sutton Trust, p 16.

16 Tim Jay, Ben Willis, Peter Thomas, Roberta Taylor, Nick Moore, Cathy Burnett, Guy Merchant and Anna Stevens (2017) Dialogic teaching: Evaluation report and executive summary, London: Education Endowment Foundation.

17 Sam Friedman, Dave O'Brien and Daniel Laurison (2016) '"Like skydiving without a parachute": How class origin shapes occupational trajectories in British acting', Sociology, 28 February.

18 Sally Weale (2016) 'Trainee teachers from northern England told to modify their accents', The Guardian, 12 May.

19 Katie Edwards (2014) 'Shut yer face! I'm fed up being ridiculed for my regional accent in academia', The Daily Telegraph, 9 December.

20 Sam Friedman and Daniel Laurison (2019) The class ceiling: Why it pays to be privileged, Bristol: Policy Press, pp 46-8.

21 Sam Friedman, Daniel Laurison and Lindsey Macmillan (2017) Social mobility, the class pay gap and intergenerational worklessness: New insights from the Labour Force Survey, London: Social Mobility Commission.

22 Keir Starmer, in conversation with author, Portcullis House, Westminster, 13 September 2016.

23 Mike Savage (2015) Social class in the 21st century, London: Pelican, p 209.

24 Friedman et al (2017) op cit.

25 John Prescott (2009) Docks to Downing Street: My story, London: Headline.

26 Regus company profile (www.regus.co.uk/investors/company-profile).

27 SME Alliance, quoted by Caroline Binham (2018) 'Banks "reluctant to lend" to small businesses, MPs told', Financial Times, 30 March.

28 Federation of Small Businesses (2018) 'Alternative finance'.

29 L. Noakes (2000) 'Regus gets £1.5b price tag', Citywire, 17 October.

30 Friedman and Laurison (2019) op cit, Chapter 6.

31 Chris Moss (2015) 'A career that progressed from cleaner to board member', Daily Telegraph, 23 September.

32 Social Mobility Commission (2016) *State of the nation 2016: Social mobility in Great Britain*, London: The Stationery Office, p iv.

33 Sarah O'Connor (2017) 'For clues to the productivity puzzle, go shopping', *Financial Times*, 22 February.

34 Lauren Weber (2017) 'The end of employees', *Wall Street Journal*, 2 February.

35 Torsten Bell (2017) 'Britain's labour market has passed peak insecurity', *Financial Times*, 24 June.

36 Lindsay Judge and Daniel Tomlinson (2016) *Secret agents: Agency workers in the new world of work*, London: Resolution Foundation, p 37.

37 Shaun Richards (2017) 'What do the UK self-employed actually earn?', Notayesmanseconomics blog, 9 February.

38 Nida Broughton and Ben Richards (2016) *Tough gig: Tackling low-paid self-employment in London and the UK*, London: Social Market Foundation.

39 Steven Toft (2016) 'Why low paid self-employment is everyone's problem', Flipchart Fairytales, 26 October.

40 Charlotte Allery (2018) 'The gig economy cases just keep on gigging', *Lawyer Monthly*, 11 June.

41 TUC (2018) *Taylor Review: Agency workers recommendations. TUC response to the BEIS consultation*, London.

42 House of Commons Committee of Public Accounts (2018) *The higher education market: Forty-Fifth report of Session 2017-19*, London, p 10.

43 Christine Drabwell (2018) 'OU calls for action after figures show disadvantaged students "let down"', OU News, 1 February.

44 Justine Greening (2016) 'UK social mobility: Lessons learnt from international development: Secretary of State for International Development Justine Greening's speech to the Centre for Social Justice', 16 February.

45 Spencer Thompson, Catherine Colebrook, Izzy Hatfield and Patrick Doyle (2016) *Boosting Britain's low-wage sectors: A strategy for productivity, innovation and growth*, London: Institute for Public Policy Research, p 30.

46 Will Hutton (2015) *How good we can be: Ending the mercenary society and building a great community*, London: Little, Brown, p 7.

47 Anthony Hilton (2017) 'Top bosses need to treat HR with respect', *Evening Standard*, 19 January.

48 Of course, some of the higher-skilled will have attained their current status *because* they underwent some form of learning, but this does not account for most of the gradient. See Hilton (2017) op cit, p 51.

49 Anne Green, Paul Sissons, Kathryn Ray, Ceri Hughes and Jennifer Ferreira (2016) *Improving progression from low-paid jobs at city-region level*, York: Joseph Rowntree Foundation, p 2.

50 Norman Pickavance (2015) *The reconnected leader: An executive's guide to creating responsible, purposeful and valuable organisations*, London: Kogan Page, p 47.

51 Richard Excell (2017) 'Public sector employment under Labour, the Coalition and the current government', *Touchstone*, TUC, 6 January. Excell excludes the effect of organisations that were reclassified into or out of the public sector.

52 Joe Dromey and Clare McNeil (2017) *Skills 2030: Why the adult skills system is failing to build an economy that works for everyone*, London: Institute for Public Policy Research, p 24.

53 Tim Stacey and Lucy Shaddock (2016) *The aspiration tax: How our social security system holds back low-paid workers*, London: The Equality Trust.

54 Anonymous employee, quoted in Sarah O'Connor (2017) 'For clues to the productivity puzzle, go shopping', *Financial Times*, 22 February.

[55] House of Commons Business, Innovation and Skills Committee (2016) *Employment practices at Sports Direct: Third report of Session 2016-17*, London, p 19.

[56] House of Commons Business, Innovation and Skills Committee (2016) ibid, p 27.

[57] Jeremy Baker, speaking on BBC Radio 4 *Today*, 7 June 2016.

[58] Simon Neville (2013) 'Sports Direct: 90% of staff on zero-hour contracts', *The Guardian*, 28 July.

[59] ONS (Office for National Statistics) (2016) *Contracts that do not guarantee a minimum number of hours: September 2016*, Newport.

[60] Citizens' Advice (2016) '4.5 million people in insecure work, reveals Citizens Advice', Press release, 13 June.

[61] Kayte Lawton and Graeme Cooke, (2013) *The condition of Britain, Briefing 5: Finding a decent job and achieving financial security*, London: Institute for Public Policy Research.

[62] Francis Green (2015) 'Health effects of job insecurity', *IZA World of Labor*, vol 212, pp 1, 4.

[63] Brhmie Balaram and Fabian Wallace-Stephens (2018) *Thriving, striving, or just about surviving? Seven portraits of economic security and modern work in the UK*, London: RSA, pp 7, 9.

[64] Matt Padley, Laura Valadez Martinez and Donald Hirsch (2017) *Households below a Minimum Income Standard: 2008/09-2015/16*, York: Joseph Rowntree Foundation.

[65] Barclays (2014) 'Financial well-being: The last taboo of the workplace' (https://wealth.barclays.com/global-stock-and-rewards/en_gb/home/research-centre/financial-wellbeing.html).

[66] Wayne Lewchuk, Michelynn Laflèche, Stephanie Procyk, Charlene Cook, Diane Dyson, Luin Goldring, Karen Lior, Alan Meisner, John Shields, Anthony Tambureno and Peter Viducis (2015) 'The precarity penalty: How insecure employment disadvantages workers and their families', *Alternate Routes: A Journal of Critical Social Research*, vol 27, pp 87-118; Shelly Lundberg, Robert Pollak and Jenna Stearns (2016) 'Family inequality: Diverging patterns in marriage, cohabitation, and childbearing', *Journal of Economic Perspectives*, vol 30, no 2, pp 79-102; Francesca Modena, Concetta Rondinelli and Fabio Sabatini (2011) 'Economic insecurity and fertility intentions: the case of Italy', Paper presented at the IARIW-OECD Conference on Economic Insecurity Paris, France, 22-23 November 2011.

[67] Bob Dylan (1963) 'Masters of war', *The Freewheelin' Bob Dylan*, Warner Bros.

[68] Walter Torres and Raymond Bergner (2010) 'Humiliation: Its nature and consequences', *Journal of the American Academy of Psychiatry and the Law*, vol 38, pp 196, 201.

[69] Tarani Chandola and Nan Zhang (2018) 'Re-employment, job quality, health and allostatic load biomarkers: Prospective evidence from the UK Household Longitudinal Study', *International Journal of Epidemiology*, 1 February, pp 47-57.

[70] Noortje Uphoff (2018) 'Growing up in poverty weakens later health – even if you escape it', *The Conversation*, 20 February.

[71] Michael Marmot, G.D. Smith, S. Stansfeld, C. Patel, F. North, J. Head, I. White, E. Brunner and A. Feeney (1991) 'Health inequalities among British civil servants: The Whitehall II study', *The Lancet*, vol 337, issue 8754, pp 1387-93.

Chapter Eight: For richer or poorer

[1] NatCen Social Research (2016) *British Social Attitudes 33: Social class*, London.

[2] Ministry of Housing, Communities and Local Government (2018) *English Housing Survey headline report, 2016-17*, London.

[3] Hometrack (2017) 'UK Cities House Price Index – 2017' (www.hometrack.com).

Notes

4 BBC News (2016) '"Sky-high" rental hotspots across England revealed', 5 August.

5 Ipsos MORI (2017) *CIH Housing 2017 Survey* (Question 4D).

6 Stephen Clarke (2017) *Get a move on? The decline in regional job-to-job moves and its impact on productivity and pay*, London: Resolution Foundation, p 14.

7 Chris Giles (2013) 'Cranes lift London to towering height over rest of UK', *Financial Times*, 5 May.

8 Kitty Stewart, Kerris Cooper and Isabel Shutes (2018) *What does Brexit mean for social policy in the UK?*, CASE Social Exclusion Seminar, 21 November.

9 James Pickford (2018) 'Brexit effect "limited" on UK house prices', *Financial Times*, 28 November.

10 Savills (2018) 'Market impact on affordable supply', Figure 3.

11 Peter Ganong and Daniel Shoag (2017) 'Why has regional income convergence in the US declined', manuscript, Harvard University.

12 Kate Vershov Downing (2016) 'Letter of resignation from the Palo Alto Planning and Transportation Commission', NewCo Shift, 10 August.

13 Social Mobility Commission (2017) *State of the nation 2017: Social mobility in Great Britain*, London, p viii.

14 Judith Evans and Richard Milne (2016) 'Duke of Westminster dies', *Financial Times*, 10 August; Hunter Davies (1992) 'Happy is the soldier of fortune', *The Independent*, 6 July.

15 Kathryn Cain (2016) 'Loopy loophole: Duke of Westminster's family "will avoid paying billions in inheritance tax because his fortune was placed in series of trusts"', *The Sun*, 11 August.

16 Resolution Foundation (2018) 'Britain has excelled at generating wealth – but lower income families are being left behind', Press release, 1 February.

17 Adam Corlett and Laura Gardiner (2018) *Options for reforming property taxation*, London: Resolution Foundation.

18 Michael Klimes (2018) 'IFS director: Inheritance increasingly determines wealth in UK', *Money Marketing*, 1 February.

19 Kent Reliance (2017) *Buy to Let Britain report, Edition Six* (www.kentrelianceforintermediaries.co.uk), p 16.

20 Adam Corlett and Lindsay Judge (2017) *Home affront: Housing across the generations*, London: Resolution Foundation, p 6.

21 Jack Airey (2017) *Disrupting the housing market: A policy programme to save the home-owning democracy*, London: Localis, p 7.

22 Adam Corlett and Stephen Clarke (2017) *Living standards 2017: The past, present and possible future of UK incomes*, London: Resolution Foundation, p 29.

23 Jo Blanden and Stephen Machin (2017) *Home ownership and social mobility*, Centre for Economic Performance Discussion Paper No 1466, London: Centre for Economic Performance.

24 Santander (2017) 'One in ten first time buyers cash in on the Bank of Gran and Grandad', Press release, March.

25 See www.helptobuy.gov.uk

26 DCLG (Department for Communities and Local Government) (2017) *Help to Buy (Equity Loan scheme) and Help to Buy: NewBuy statistics: Data to 30 June 2017, England*, London.

27 Association of British Insurers (2016) 'ABI pension freedom statistics one year on factsheet' (www.abi.org.uk).

28 Rowena Crawford (2018) 'The use of wealth in retirement', IFS Briefing Note BN237, London: Institute for Fiscal Studies, p 9.

[29] Christine Whitehead (2011) 'Reviving the Right to Buy has garnered criticism, as it did in 1979, but 2 million households benefitted then and many will likely benefit now', LSE Politics and Policy blog, 12 October.

[30] Ministry of Housing, Communities and Local Government (2018) 'Brokenshire confirms social housing investment boost', Press release, 26 June.

[31] London Councils (2013) Right to Buy and Use of Receipts, Briefing Paper.

[32] Ministry of Housing, Communities and Local Government (2017) 'Live tables on house building: New build dwellings; Table 208: permanent dwellings started, by tenure and country.'

[33] Tom Kibasi and John Penrose (2018) 'How to future-proof the economy: Tax all income equally', UnHerd, 5 February.

[34] Ministry of Housing, Communities and Local Government (2018), op cit.

[35] HM Revenue & Customs (2017) Restricting finance cost relief for individual landlords, Policy Paper.

[36] Carys Roberts and Mathew Lawrence (2017) Wealth in the twenty-first century: Inequalities and drivers, London: Institute for Public Policy Research, p 20.

[37] David Finch (2017) 'Automatic success for the people?', Resolution Foundation blog, 3 March.

[38] Matt Singh (2018) 'The UK "youthquake" was all about the rent', Bloomberg View, 5 March.

[39] David Cameron, quoted in Chris Mason (2011) 'Cameron faces questions over home defence pledge', BBC News, 21 June.

[40] See Poppy Terry (2017) 'Conservative Party Conference: Government rallies around renters!', Shelter blog, 3 October.

[41] Chaminda Jayanetti and Michael Savage (2018) 'Tax cuts on empty homes costing cash-strapped councils millions', The Observer, 1 April.

[42] Roberts and Lawrence (2017) op cit, p 29.

[43] Dan Wilson Craw (2017) 'Politics is dominated by the voices of homeowners – Time for renters to make their voices heard too', Huffington Post, 15 May.

[44] Christian Hilber and Wouter Vermeulen (2016) 'The extraordinarily rigid planning system is the main reason homes in England are unaffordable', LSE Politics and Policy blog, 12 March.

[45] Office for Budget Responsibility (2018) 'Inheritance tax' (https://obr.uk/forecasts-in-depth/tax-by-tax-spend-by-spend/inheritance-tax/).

[46] Daisy-Rose Srblin (2015) The tax detox: Winning public consent for radical tax reform, London: Fabian Society, pp 32-3.

[47] Karen Rowlingson and Stephen McKay (2005) Attitudes to inheritance in Britain, Bristol: Policy Press, p 73.

[48] Levying taxes on the estate rather than the beneficiary allow economically illiterate but nonetheless powerful objections to 'being taxed twice'.

[49] James Chapman (2015) 'Tories WILL raise threshold on inheritance tax to £1m: Pledge to be part of manifesto after forecasts suggest number of families hit by death duty could double in five years', Daily Mail, 18 March; Nicole Blackmore (2015) 'Budget 2015: How inheritance tax changes affect you', Telegraph, 8 July.

[50] Nick Clegg (2012) 'Supporting working families', Speech, 26 January.

[51] Matt Whittaker (2016) Changing tax: Pressing reset on the UK's tax policy, London: Resolution Foundation.

[52] Mr Fitzwilliam Darcy, in Jane Austen's Pride and Prejudice, the romantic interest of the novel's heroine, is of considerably higher social status than her.

[53] IPPR (Institute for Public Policy Research) (2012) 'Modern women marrying men of the same or lower social class', Press release, 5 April.

54 Jani Erola and Elina Kilpi-Jakonen (2017) 'How can parental disadvantages be compensated?', Population Europe, 12 April.

55 Fox is specifically writing about the English, but in this case, the test applies just as well to the rest of the UK.

56 Kate Fox (2005) Watching the English, London: Hodder & Stoughton, p 328.

57 The Student Room (2012) 'One fifth of British students meet the love of their life on campus', Blog.

58 Ursula Henz and Colin Mills (2017) 'Social class origin and assortative mating in Britain, 1949-2010', Sociology, July.

59 Niall Cunningham and Mike Savage (2017) 'An intensifying and elite city', City, vol 21, issue 1, pp 25-46; see also Danny Dorling (2014) 'Class segregation', in Christopher D. Lloyd, Ian G. Shuttleworth and David W. Wong (eds) Social–spatial segregation: Concepts, processes and outcomes, Bristol: Policy Press, pp 363-88.

60 Eleanor Muffitt (2017) 'Six reasons you should consider online dating', The Telegraph, 14 August.

61 Gina Potarca (2014) 'Modern love: Comparative insights in online dating preferences and assortative mating', Doctoral thesis, University of Groningen.

62 Stitch (2005) Commenting on Mumsnet discussion 'Did you marry "beneath" you?', 29 May.

63 Ferdinand Mount (2004) Mind the gap: The new class divide in Britain, London: Short Books, p 17.

64 For anyone who does believe in said 'guff', I refer you to XKCD's soul mates comic strip.

65 Karl Marx (1852) The Eighteenth Brumaire of Louis Bonaparte. The actual quotation (from the 1869 English translation) is: 'Men make their own history, but they do not make it as they please; they do not make it under self-selected circumstances, but under circumstances existing already, given and transmitted from the past.'

66 Fabrice Murtin and Marco Mira d'Ercole (2015) Household wealth inequality across OECD countries: New OECD evidence, OECD Statistics Brief, June, Paris: Organisation for Economic Co-operation and Development (OECD), p 7.

Chapter Nine: Does social mobility matter?

1 Barry Lopez (1986) Arctic dreams, London: Picador, p 344. Details of Frobisher's voyage are from Lopez, and also from Anthony Dalton (2007) Alone Against the Arctic, Victoria, Canada: Heritage House; and the National Maritime Museum, Greenwich.

2 Lopez (1986) ibid, p 344.

3 Sheila McNulty (2006) 'Faults at BP led to one of worst US industrial disasters', Financial Times, 18 December.

4 Norman Pickavance (2015) The reconnected leader, London: Kogan Page.

5 Simon Collins (2017) 'Inclusion is the key to an extraordinary workforce', KPMG Insights, 17 March. Collins is UK Chair of KPMG, one of the 'Big Four' accountancy firms.

6 David Rock and Heidi Grant (2016) 'Why diverse teams are smarter', Harvard Business Review, 4 November.

7 Oleg Chuprinin and Denis Sosyura (2016) Family descent as a signal of managerial quality: Evidence from Mutual Funds, Melbourne, VIC: Melbourne Business School, p 1.

8 World Economic Forum (2015) The global competitiveness report 2015-2016, Cologny, Switzerland.

9   Quoted in Elizabeth Gibney (2016) 'United Kingdom: The paths not taken' (In 'Is science only for the rich?', *Nature*, vol 537, pp 466-70, 22 September 2016).

10 David Leonhardt (2017) 'Lost Einsteins: The innovations we're missing', *The New York Times*, 3 December.

11 Alex Bell, Raj Chetty, Xavier Jaravel, Neviana Petkova and John van Reenen (2017) *Who becomes an inventor in America? The importance of exposure to innovation: Executive summary*, Equality of Opportunity Project, p 5.

12 The Sutton Trust (2015) *Improving social mobility through education 2014/15*, London, p 7.

13 City of London Corporation (2017) 'City of London Corporation: Firms need to be more "ambitious" on social mobility', Press release.

14 Giles Fraser (2016) 'Brexit brought democracy back – now we need to start listening to each other', *The Guardian*, 24 June; Sally Newall (2016) 'How to heal a country divided by Brexit', *The Independent*, 30 June; Camilla Tominey (2016) 'Politicians should listen to real people, says Camilla Tominey', *Sunday Express*, 3 July.

15 Deborah Mattinson (2017) 'Bregrets? I've found very few. Polls show remainers are getting over it', *The Guardian*, 18 January.

16 *The Spectator* 'Advertising and Media Pack' (www.spectator.co.uk/advertising/).

17 Brendan O'Neill (2016) 'Brexit voters are not thick, not racist: just poor', *The Spectator*, 2 July.

18 Lorenza Antonucci, Laszlo Horvath and André Krouwel (2017) 'Brexit was not the voice of the working class nor of the uneducated – it was of the squeezed middle', LSE Politics and Policy blog, 13 October.

19 *The Others* is the title of a 2001 film by Alejandro Amenábar, in which a family initially thinks their house is haunted but slowly realises that they themselves are the ones who have died, and the 'ghosts' are the new owners of the house.

20 Bruce Anderson (2016) 'Meet Stephen Crabb, the next Tory leader', CapX, 17 March.

21 ONS (Office for National Statistics) (2013) *A century of home ownership and renting in England and Wales*, Newport.

22 Lee Elliot Major (2017) 'Stuck: Britain's social mobility problem', Presentation, Warwick University, November.

23 Sam Freedman, Tweet, 19 August 2017.

24 Alan Milburn, in conversation with the author, London, W1, 21 July 2016.

25 Antonucci et al (2017) op cit.

26 Social Mobility Commission (2017) *Social mobility barometer: Public attitudes to social mobility in the UK*, London, p 12.

27 John Harris (2017) [radio] 'Us versus them', *The New World*, BBC Radio 4, 4 January.

28 Sam Freedman (2017) 'Why the educational divide in voting presents a real danger', *TES*, 15 September.

29 John Denham (2016) 'Progressive patriotism', Speech to Scottish Fabians Conference.

30 J.P. Floru (2018) 'Let's be Singapore – and prosperous, post-Brexit, beyond our wildest dreams', *Conservative Home*, 29 January.

31 IPPR (Institute for Public Policy Research) (2018) 'No public appetite for deregulation post-Brexit according to new polling for IPPR', Press release, 19 February.

32 Jon Snow (2017) 'Grenfell proved it: The British media are part of a disconnected elite', *The Guardian*, 23 August.

33 Ed Balls (2016) *Speaking out: Lessons in life and politics*, Cornerstone Digital.

34 Jennifer Whitson and Adam Galinsky (2008) 'Lacking control increases illusory pattern perception', *Science*, vol 322, issue 5898, pp 115-17.

Notes

35 Department for Transport (2018) *National Travel Survey: England 2017*, London, p 17.

36 Laurie Heykoop (2018) 'The rising cost of living will hit low-income households hard in 2018', JRF blog, 11 January.

37 Labour Party (2017) 'Rail passengers £1,000 better off under Labour', Press release, 1 June.

38 Labour Party (2017) *For the many not the few: The Labour Party manifesto 2017*.

39 Matthew Elliott and James Kanagasooriam (2017) *Public opinion in the post-Brexit era: Economic attitudes in modern Britain*, London: Legatum Institute, p 15.

40 Paul Hunter and Dan Holden (2015) *Who governs Britain – A profile of MPs in the 2015 parliament*, Smith Institute.

41 Roger Eatwell and Matthew Goodwin (2018) *National populism: The revolt against liberal democracy*, London: Pelican, p 239.

42 Rebecca Montacute and Tim Carr (2017) 'Parliamentary privilege – The MPs in 2017', Sutton Trust Research Brief, June.

43 Tim Bale, Paul Webb and Monica Poletti (2018) *Grassroots. Britain's party members: Who they are, what they think, and what they do*, London: Mile End Institute, Queen Mary University of London, p 7.

44 ESRC (Economic and Social Research) Party Members Project 2017, sent to author in correspondence.

45 Matt Henn, Mark Weinstein and Sarah Forrest (2005) 'Uninterested youth? Young people's attitudes towards party politics in Britain', *Political Studies*, vol 53, no 3, pp 556-78.

46 Nicole Vosper (2016) 'Overcoming burnout, Part 9 – When class is a struggle', Empty Cages Design blog, 13 May.

47 Roger Harding (2017) 'Why is speaking up for working class people a middle class job?', *Huffington Post*, 26 September.

48 Jameel Hampton (2017) 'Book review: *Diploma democracy: The rise of political meritocracy* by Mark Bovens and Anchrit Wille', *LSE Review of Books*, 29 November.

49 Quoted in Kiran Nihalani (2019) 'Moving beyond mainstream ways of thinking about "dependency", "responsibility" and "help": An exploration of collaborative/ horizontal forms of "welfare"', Doctorate in Social Sciences thesis, Open University.

50 Polly Billington (2017) 'Climate change is a class issue', *Renewal*, vol 25, no 2.

51 Kristian Niemitz (2013) 'Freeing the poor from the cost of environmentalism', Institute for Economic blog, 4 February.

52 Ipsos MORI (2000-17) 'Issues index archive.'

53 Ruth Davis (2016) 'Home is where the heart is', *Fabian Essays*, 22 July.

54 Foyez Syed (2018) 'Campaigning organizations need to do a better job at reaching diverse communities', Oxfam blog, 2 February.

55 Thomas Hardy (1979 [1896]) *Jude the obscure*, London: Penguin.

56 *Evening Standard* (2011) 'Tulisa is branded a "scumbag" at X Factor audition', 8 July.

57 Kate Fox (2005) *Watching the English*, London: Hodder & Stoughton, p 164.

58 David Azerrad (2016) 'How equal should opportunities be?', *National Affairs*, no 28, Summer, Washington, DC.

59 Jessica Shepherd and Polly Curtis (2009) 'Middle-class pupils have better genes, says Chris Woodhead', *The Guardian*, 11 May.

60 Sam Kean (2017) 'The Soviet era's deadliest scientist is regaining popularity in Russia', *The Atlantic*, 19 December.

61 Nicholas Shakeshaft, Maciej Trzaskowski, Andrew McMillan, Kaili Rimfeld, Eva Krapohl, Claire Haworth, Philip Dale and Robert Plomin (2013) 'Strong genetic

influence on a UK nationwide test of educational achievement at the end of compulsory education at age 16', *PLoS One*, vol 8, no 12, e80341.

62 Alexander Young, Michael Frigge, Daniel Gudbjartsson, Gudmar Thorleifsson, Gyda Bjornsdottir, Patrick Sulem, Gisli Masson, Unnur Thorsteinsdottir, Kari Stefansson and Augustine Kong (2018) 'Relatedness disequilibrium regression estimates heritability without environmental bias', *Nature*, 13 August.

63 Donald Trump, interviewed by Barbara Walters, *Meet the Trumps*, ABC TV, 20 November 2015.

64 Justin Brienza and Igor Grossmann (2017) 'Social class and wise reasoning about interpersonal conflicts across regions, persons and situations', *Proceedings of the Royal Society*, vol 284, issue 1869, 20 December.

65 BBC Radio 4 (2015) *The Life Scientific*, 20 October.

66 Helen Amass (2017) 'TES talks to ... Sarah-Jayne Blakemore', *TES*, 17 March. See also Sarah-Jayne Blakemore (2012) 'The mysterious workings of the adolescent brain', TEDGlobal.

67 Richard E. Nisbett, Joshua Aronson, Clancy Blair, William Dickens, James Flynn, Diane F. Halpern and Eric Turkheimer (2012) 'Intelligence: New findings and theoretical developments', *American Psychologist*, February-March.

68 Anna Cristina d'Addio (2007) *Intergenerational transmission of disadvantage: Mobility or immobility across generations? A review of the evidence for OECD countries*', OECD Social, Employment and Migration Working Paper 52, Paris: Organisation for Economic Co-operation and Development (OECD), p 25. (d'Addio is citing E. Turkheimer, M. Haley, M. Waldron, B. D'Onofrio and I. Gottesman [2003] 'Socioeconomic status modifies heritability of IQ in young children', *Psychological Science*, vol 14, no 6, pp 623-6.)

69 Almost certainly a reference to Tim Nice-But-Dim, the posh, stupid character from *Harry Enfield's Television Programme*.

70 Jo Blanden and Lindsey Macmillan (2011) 'Recent developments in intergenerational mobility', in Paul Gregg and Jonathan Wadsworth (eds) *The labour market in winter: The state of working Britain*, Oxford: Oxford University Press, p 201.

71 Danny Dorling (2016) 'What happens in societies where social mobility ends?', The Question, Blog.

72 John Hayes (2011) 'Changing lives by changing life chances', in Respublica, *Changing the debate: The ideas redefining Britain*.

73 David Brooks (2016) *The road to character*, London: Random House, p 253.

74 Quoted in Jenny Roper (2017) 'Breaking the class ceiling', *HR Magazine*, 20 November.

75 Quoted in Maggie McGrath (2015) 'Meet the guy who says you're not rich because you don't want to be rich', *Forbes*, 11 November.

76 Geoff Dench (2012) 'Meritocracy and the fair society', Policy Network blog, 4 October.

77 Jon Cruddas, quoted in CLASS (Centre for Labour and Social Studies) (2015) *What is aspiration? How progressives should respond*, London, p 2.

78 Nick Clegg, quoted in Randeep Ramesh (2012) 'Nick Clegg's social mobility speech condemned by inequality experts', *The Guardian*, 24 May.

79 Ramesh (2012) op cit.

80 HM Government (2011) *Opening doors, breaking barriers: A strategy for social mobility*, London, p 15.

81 Christine Blower (2015) 'Teaching aspiration', in CLASS (Centre for Labour and Social Studies), *What is aspiration? How progressives should respond*, London, p 9.

82 Owen Jones (2012) *Chavs*, London: Verso, p 258.

83   Graeme Atherton (2016) 'Success isn't just about money: Rethinking social mobility', LSE Politics and Policy blog, 11 April.

84   Neil O'Brien (2011) *Just deserts? Attitudes to fairness, poverty and welfare reform*, London: Policy Exchange, p 10.

85   See the contrast between 'traditional' working-class culture in Young and Willmott's studies of Bethnal Green and the findings of Cottrell in his study of Essex new towns in David Kynaston (2015) *Modernity Britain*, London: Bloomsbury, pp 22-3.

86   Donna Loftus (2011) 'The rise of the Victorian middle class', BBC British History website, 17 February.

87   William Stewart (2018 [1921]) *J. Keir Hardie, A biography*, Sagwan Press.

88   Clegg (2012) op cit.

89   Selina Todd (2017) 'Labour is right: Social mobility is not a good goal for education', *The Guardian*, 1 August.

90   Fox (2005) op cit, p 11.

Chapter Ten: Conclusion: Barriers and opportunities

1   Tom Gilovich, quoted in Robert Frank (2016) *Success and luck: Good fortune and the myth of meritocracy*, Princeton, NJ: Princeton University Press, p 80.

2   Timothy Halliday, Bhashkar Mazumder and Ashley Wong (2018) *Intergenerational health mobility in the US*, IZA Institute of Labor Economics Discussion Paper No 11304, p 2.

3   David Buck (2017) 'Reducing inequalities in health: Towards a brave old world?', Blog, The King's Fund, 13 August.

4   BMA (British Medical Association) (2018) 'New BMA research unveils blindspot in mental healthcare', Press release, 26 February.

5   Sarah O'Connor (2018) 'Millennial insecurity is reshaping the UK economy', *Financial Times*, 20 February.

6   Diane Reay (2017) *Miseducation: Inequality, education and the working classes*, Bristol: Policy Press, p 41.

7   Tim Pat Coogan (2013) *The famine plot: England's role in Ireland's greatest tragedy*, London: Macmillan.

8   Kevin Cullen (2013) 'Famine to feast – living the dream', *Irish Times*, 19 June.

9   Jonathan Moules (2018) 'The parents who pay for their child's MBA', *Financial Times*, 12 February.

10   Joan Wilson (2011) 'By scrapping the Education Maintenance Allowance the Coalition government risks losing their opportunity to target entrenched problems of social mobility and educational disadvantage among pupils from deprived backgrounds in England', LSE Politics and Policy, 21 February.

11   W.H. Auden (1973) 'Unpredictable but providential', *The New Yorker*, 14 April (via Rob Newman).

12   Jon Andrews, Jo Hutchinson and David Robinson (2017) *Closing the gap? Trends in educational attainment and disadvantage*, Education Policy Institute.

13   UCAS (2017) *2017 End of cycle report*.

14   See Hannah Gousy (2014) *Safe and decent homes: Solutions for a better private rented sector*, Shelter.

15   See The Children's Society (2018) 'Breathing space: The impact of money worries on children's mental health' (website).

16   Joan Williams, Saravanan Kesavan and Lisa McCorkell (2018) 'Research: When retail workers have stable schedules, sales and productivity go up', *Harvard Business Review*, 29 March.

[17] Matt Scott (2017) 'How accidental managers are draining productivity', Chartered Management Institute, *Insights*, 20 September.

[18] Steve Ballinger (2018) *Many rivers crossed: Britain's attitudes to race and integration 50 years since 'Rivers of Blood'*, British Future, p 30.

[19] For a summary of such payments, see Julie Henry (2018) 'Private schools "abuse charity status" by giving discounts to richer families', *The Guardian*, 3 June.

[20] EEF (Education Endowment Foundation) (2018) 'Setting or streaming' (website). (The EEF is part of the government-designated What Works Centre for Education.) For evidence on the impact of selective education on social mobility, see 'Selection by ability' in Chapter 3.

[21] David Barboza (2015) 'How a Chinese billionaire built her fortune', *The New York Times*, 30 July.

[22] National Citizen Service (no date) 'About Us' (website).

[23] Lucy Hunter-Blackburn (2017) 'Widening access: A modest proposal', Adventures in Evidence blog, 5 August.

[24] David Willetts (2016) 'Our education system is tilted against social mobility', Resolution Foundation blog, 12 September.

[25] David Willetts (2016) ibid.

[26] Sarah O'Connor (2018) op cit.

[27] John Bynner and Sofia Despotidou (2011) *Case study on the impact of IOE research that underpinned the Child Trust Fund scheme*, Institute of Education.

[28] Resolution Foundation (2018) *A new generational contract: The final report of the Intergenerational Commission*; Carys Roberts and Mathew Lawrence (2018) *Our common wealth: A citizens' wealth fund for the UK*, London: Institute for Public Policy Research.

[29] Mariana Mazzucato (2013) *The entrepreneurial state*, Anthem.

[30] Mazzucato (2013) ibid.

[31] For a more thorough account of why and how this should be done, see Will Hutton (2015) *How good we can be*, London: Abacus.

[32] See Phil Tomlinson, Christos Pitelis and David Bailey (2018) 'How to make a "place-based" industrial strategy work', *The Conversation*, 1 July.

[33] Madeleine Power and Tim Stacey (2014) *Unfair and unclear: The effects and perceptions of the UK tax system*, The Equality Trust.

[34] Matt Singh (2018) 'The UK "Youthquake" was all about the rent', *Bloomberg View*, 5 March.

[35] Ministry of Housing, Communities and Local Government (2018) *Public attitudes to house building: Findings from the 2017 British Social Attitudes survey*, p 8.

[36] Julia Irvine (2018) 'Incoming ICAEW president hits the ground running', *Economia*, 7 June.

[37] Neil O'Brien (2011) op cit; Alison Park, John Curtice, Elizabeth Clery and Caroline Bryson (2011) *British Social Attitudes: The 27th report*; Abigail Davis, Donald Hirsch, Matt Padley and Claire Shepherd (2018) *A Minimum Income Standard for the UK 2008-2018: Continuity and change*, York: Joseph Rowntree Foundation.

Index

Page references for notes are followed by the note number